Duane

May you find this Book
helpful in your understanding
appreciation and use of
God's great Creation.

Till He Comes

Dominion over Wildlife?

Dominion over Wildlife?

*An Environmental Theology
of Human-Wildlife Relations*

STEPHEN M. VANTASSEL

RESOURCE *Publications* · Eugene, Oregon

DOMINION OVER WILDLIFE?
An Environmental Theology of Human-Wildlife Relations

Resource Publications
A Division of Wipf and Stock Publishers
199 W. 8th Ave., Suite 3
Eugene, OR 97401
www.wipfandstock.com

ISBN 13: 978-1-60608-343-7

Manufactured in the U.S.A.

This book is dedicated to the thousands of sports-people who continue to be connected to the earth in an environmentally responsible way. In particular, this book is dedicated to fur trappers who, every winter, brave the harsh weather in continuance of America's oldest industry. Regrettably, they must also endure the ravages of urban sprawl and the derision of an ungrateful and ignorant public. It is my ardent hope that this book will help Christians and non-Christians alike appreciate the vital role that trappers play in the responsible management of our natural resources. May the traps of these great sports-people be always full.

To my parents, for leading me to Christ, and for their years of faithful prayer and encouragement. May they be honored by this publication.

To my wife, who for too many years has untiringly and joyfully endured the life of an academic widow. She has my unfailing appreciation, and the prayer that Christ credits to her any rewards this book brings to the Kingdom of God.

Contents

Acknowledgments

SEVERAL PEOPLE PLAYED KEY roles in helping me with this book. First, I would like to thank two doctoral committee members, Daniel T. Lioy and James L. Codling for their shepherding role in the completion of my degree. Second, I am grateful for the help provided to me by Mark D. Mathewson and Calvin L. Smith. Their insightful and thoughtful critiques helped strengthen the book's rigor and clarity. They have confirmed the truth that in the counsel of many there is wisdom. Of course, any errors contained in this book are my own.

Terminology

Animal protectionist.[1] A broad term identifying individuals and groups who seek to minimize or mitigate human interactions with animals deemed to have a negative impact on animals. The term includes both those who support the enactment of animal rights and those who do not. Ultimately, the representatives of these disparate ideologies unite around the practical action of reducing what they perceive to be unwarranted animal suffering at the hands of humans. Animal protectionism has many similarities to what was known as the "Humanitarian View" in the 1970s. The humanitarian view stands in opposition to the wildlife management view, in that humanitarians believe life is sacred and any type of killing, no matter how it is performed, is deemed immoral.[2]

Animal rights.[3] The philosophy that holds animals to be individuals with intrinsic rights, who therefore have the same rights, or at least similar rights, as those believed to belong to humans. These rights include the right to life, liberty, and the freedom to live their lives undisturbed by humans.

Animal welfare.[4] The philosophy that holds animals may be eaten, hunted, trapped, fished, and owned provided the animals are treated in a humane way and avoids "unnecessary suffering."[5]

---

1. More insight on the parameters of the term can be gleaned from Paul G. Irwin, "A Strategic Review of International Animal Protection," 1ff.

2. Boddicker, "The Issue of Trapping: A Review and Perspective of Contemporary Analysis of Traps and Trapping by Martha Scott-Garrett and the Humane Society of the United States," 6.

3. Regan, *The Case for Animal Rights,* Chapter 8. For insight on the complexity of animal rights movement see Varner, "The Prospects for Consensus and Convergence in the Animal Rights Debate," 24-28.

4. Adapted from Regan, *The Case for Animal Rights,* 99.

5. Joy, "Humanistic Psychology and Animal Rights: Reconsidering the Boundaries of the Humanistic Ethic," 110.; Guither, *Animal Rights: History and Scope of a Radical Social Movement.*

Anthropocentrism. The belief that human interests and needs are primary to the interests of non-human creatures.

Body-grip trap. A device used to capture and kill the animal by crushing a vital section of its body.

Christian Animal Rights. A philosophy that uses Scripture and Christ's redemptive work as the basis for its support for animal rights.

Consumptive use of wildlife. Those activities which are purposefully performed that involve the killing of free-ranging animals for the purpose of harvesting a product from them. Typically, these activities are known as hunting, trapping, and fishing.

Dominionism.[6] This term should not be confused with the theology of the Theonomist movement. In this paper, the term will simply refer to the traditional view that humans were divinely placed in a position superior to animals in power and/or ontology and bestowed the privilege to utilize animals to fulfill human needs and desires. See *Shepherdism.*

Euthanasia. Literally, "good death." It is a technical term meaning the animal is unconscious—therefore unable to experience pain—before death.

Foothold trap. A metal device designed to hold an animal's foot between two spring-powered, semi-circular jaws when triggered.

Homocentrism. See anthropocentrism.

Human-wildlife relations. A field of study that investigates the values and socio-political aspects of how humans view and treat wildlife.[7] This field of study is also known as human dimensions and human-wildlife interactions.

Hunting. Refers to any activity where an individual seeks to kill a wild animal and would include activities known as hunting and trapping.

Hunting$_2$. Refers to any activity where an individual seeks to take a wild animal by means of a projectile, such as a firearm, arrow, or other high-velocity object. Hunting$_2$ is meant to be distinguished from

6. Mason, *An Unnatural Order*, 25. Mason employed this term to describe the traditional view.

7. Bath, "Ursus: The Role of Human Dimensions in Wildlife Resource Research in Wildlife Management," 349–55. Bath's discussion of bear management provides a helpful example of the issues involved in bear management from a human dimensions perspective.

trapping. The term hunting without the subscript shall be understood as including the taking of wildlife by any means.[8]

Live trap. A broad category of devices that capture animals alive, including box traps, cage traps, footholds, snares, and other species-specific traps.

Shepherdism. Term coined by the author, Stephen M. Vantassel, to express the principles of Dominionism without having to respond to the negative connotations of Dominionism.

Speciesism.[9] The belief that one shows moral preference to members of one's own genetically related group over individuals that are non-members.

Traditional View. See "Dominionism."

Veganism.[10] A more extreme behavioral philosophy than vegetarianism in that adherents will not eat or wear anything derived from animals.

Vegetarianism.[11] The philosophy whereby the adherents only eat plant material and animal products that do not require the animal to be killed or harmed, such as milk. Sometimes adherents are called lacto-vegetarians.[12]

Wildlife Damage Control. Activities employed by humans to mitigate free-roaming animal behavior deemed detrimental to human goals. Wildlife damage control is also known as "wildlife damage management."[13]

Wildlife Management View. An approach that sees natural areas as living resources to be utilized while being protected. State agencies, such as Game and Parks, are living examples of this view.

8. Cf. Boddicker, "The Issue of Trapping," 75. He says that the term "trapper" (as distinguishable from hunter) is of recent origin.

9. Wise, "Animal Rights One Step at a Time," 26. Wise says that Richard Ryder first coined the term speciesism, which is defined by the Oxford English Dictionary as discrimination against animal species by human beings, based on an assumption of man's superiority.

10. Young, *Is God a Vegetarian?* xvi.

11. Young, *Is God a Vegetarian?* xiv. Young presents a more complex and detailed version, e.g. ovo-vegetarians will eat eggs, lacto-vegetarians will eat dairy products, total vegetarians will eat nothing derived from animals but will wear animal products.

12. Pollan, *Omnivore's Dilemma*, 5; Kaufman and Braun, *Vegetarianism as Christian Stewardship*, ix.

13. Hygnstrom et al., *Prevention and Control of Wildlife Damage*. The text is considered the "Bible" of wildlife damage control.

Permissions

S EVERAL OF MY ARTICLES have been adapted for inclusion into this text. I gratefully acknowledge the editors for granting reprint permission.

Chapters 2–3, "A Biblical View of Animals: A Critical Response to the Theology of Andrew Linzey." *Emmaus Journal* 12 (2003): 177–195.

Chapter 6, "Should Wildlife Trapping Have a Place in a Christian Environmental Ethic?" *Evangelical Review of Society and Politics* 1, no. 2 (2007): 20–41.

Chapter 8, "The Ethics of Wildlife Control in Humanized Landscapes— a Response." In *Proceedings of the Twenty-Third Vertebrate Pest Conference*, ed. R. M. Timm and M. B. Madon, 23, 294–300. San Diego, CA: University of California, Davis, 2008.

Unless otherwise noted, all biblical citations will be from the *New American Standard Bible.* updated ed. La Habra, CA: Lockman Foundation, 1977, 1995.

Abbreviations

AR—Animal Rights
BMP—Best Management Practices
CAR—Christian Animal Rights
COTW—(Cull of the Wild), publication by the Animal
    Protection Institute
DDT—Dichloro-Diphenyl-Trichloroethane (a synthetic pesticide)
FAF—(Facts about Furs), publication by the Animal Welfare
    Institute
ICWDM—The Internet Center for Wildlife Damage Management
IPM—Integrated Pest Management
KJV—King James Version (of the Bible)
LXX—The Septuagint (Greek translation of the Old Testament)
NASB—New American Standard Bible
N.T.—New Testament
O.T.—Old Testament
NWCO—Nuisance Wildlife Control Operator
PCO—Pest Control Operator
WCO—Wildlife Control Operator
WS—Wildlife Services (Agency of the U.S. Federal Government)

List of Figures

Foreword

I FIRST BECAME FAMILIAR with the exceptional writings of Stephen M. Vantassel close to a decade ago. He is a rare and valuable gem. Indeed, his unique background with various kinds of wildlife, along with his biblically sound theology and careful reasoning, makes him and this book vital "for such a time as this." I can say without hesitation that Dr. Vantassel is an expert among experts. Even if you do not fully agree with his conclusions, I can guarantee that by reading this book your views will be challenged, sharpened, or tempered.

Although I have spent decades either studying, writing, or grappling with many of the issues contained in this work, I am convinced that only Stephen, with his deep understanding of these opposing arguments, could have adequately composed this much needed and valuable resource. While it is true that my own works (*Hunting and the Bible: A Scripture Safari* and *Hunting Arguments: Biblical Responses to a Loaded Issue*) address some of the issues covered here, Stephen deals far more directly and extensively with the actual arguments set forth by various segments of the animal rights movement. The fact that he chose to address the more volatile issue of wildlife trapping is significant in and of itself. As the reader will discover, Dr. Vantassel doesn't simply choose to select and challenge some of the shakiest arguments. On the contrary, he confronts the more powerful and problematic reasoning frequently touted by members of the Christian animal rights movement.

As a pastor, hunter, and Executive President of the Christian Deer Hunters Association* (a national volunteer ministry to the hunting world), I am convinced that these issues regarding our relationship to the nonhuman members of creation are not going to disappear anytime soon. It is for this reason (and others) that this book should be viewed as an absolute must for anyone who wants to have a truly biblical view of creation and its human and nonhuman inhabitants. Indeed, this is a theologically sound, scholarly work with profound implications, and positive practical applications for our planet.

It should be noted that this highly technical and well-documented work will probably lack appeal for the merely curious and for those who seek only a cursory understanding of the issues. However, the contents of this book will certainly guide the serious student through the ever-growing maze of contemporary arguments and objections presented by both the secular and the Christian animal rights movements. Not only are broad categories addressed, but so are specific questions which are raised with regards to the basic assumptions and principles of interpretation as it pertains to Holy Scripture. I believe readers will especially find Dr. Stephen M. Vantassel's examination and thoughtful insight into pertinent biblical passages to be of tremendous help.

I have no doubt that with the passing of time this book will prove to be a powerful polemic in addressing views which either distort or dilute the true meaning of relevant and crucial Bible passages that pertain to issues regarding the animal rights movement. With the abundance of sources cited this should also serve as an invaluable reference tool for those who seek to do further research. Again, this is a work that is greatly needed "for such a time as this."

Dr. Tom C. Rakow
Silver Lake, MN USA

Introduction

Human-wildlife relations (also known as human-wildlife inter-actions) is a field of study that investigates the legal, ethical, behavioral, and environmental intercourse between wildlife and people. This academic discipline developed because wildlife biologists realized that management of wildlife could not be accomplished simply by looking at biological survey data and charts. Management choices, such as to hunt or not to hunt, had to account for the variety of ways people understand and appreciate animals. Management choices are ultimately about values, i.e. human values. Our values tell us what goals our management choices should seek to fulfill. For example, in the United States we believe that species in danger of becoming extinct should be protected. Therefore, we will implement predator control programs (i.e. trapping of mesopredators [medium-sized predators] such as raccoons, skunks, coyotes, etc.) to protect sea turtle nests.

To most readers, the thought of a theologian addressing the topic of human-wildlife relations seems strange indeed. The topic simply does not fit within traditional theological categories, such as soteriology, ecclesiology, and the like. A discussion concerning our treatment of wildlife (e.g. to trap or not to trap) is just too mundane or too tangential for theologians to consider, particularly when compared to larger ethical issues, such as global warming or poverty reduction.

These opinions are understandable. Human-wildlife relations in general and trapping in particular are rather parochial concerns. They lack the global scope typical of theological issues in that the questions are really centered in resource-rich societies found in Europe, the U.S., and Canada. I contend, however, that the recent resurgence of environmental concern in the Western world makes this topic particularly relevant for the Christian. For if the earth is the Lord's and the fullness thereof (Psa 24:1), Christians must behave in a manner that respects God's ownership. This book seeks to present a perspective on how Christians ought to respect that ownership. However, this text approaches the topic in a different manner. Unlike other books and articles, I want to move beyond the glittering platitudes which say, "Christians ought to care for the earth," and actually provide concrete guidelines that will help them make moral decisions. At minimum, this book will answer the question of whether it is morally proper for Christians to hunt, fish, and trap wildlife.

Yet I have another, much broader goal in mind, namely to have Christians think more deeply about our role in the environment. I believe that what Scripture (book of the Word) and Science (book of Nature) have to say about wildlife is instructive, and that the principles gleaned from that study should shape our environmental philosophy. I contend that understanding our role as shepherds will prevent us from over- and under-exploiting the environment that God has so graciously granted to our care.

I strongly encourage readers to consult the terminology section in order to familiarize themselves with the terms and abbreviations used in this book. The field of human-wildlife relations employs its own vocabulary, and although not exceedingly arcane, it is exceptional enough to cause some confusion if one is not familiar with the terms.

Dominionism Under Fire

INTRODUCTION

FOR ALMOST 2,000 YEARS, Western Christians held that humans had the moral right to utilize creation, including animals, for their own purposes.[1] They could have summarized their understanding of humanity's place in creation in a manner generally consistent with that found in chapter 2, article 7 of the 1995 edition of the Catechism of the Roman Catholic Church.[2] The section entitled, "Respect for the integrity of creation" says,

> "2415 The seventh commandment enjoins respect for the integrity of creation. Animals, like plants and inanimate beings, are by nature destined for the common good of past, present, and future humanity.[194] Use of the mineral, vegetable, and animal resources of the universe cannot be divorced from respect for moral imperatives. Man's dominion over inanimate and other living beings granted by the Creator is not absolute; it is limited by concern for the quality

1. It must be mentioned that Dominionism was not universally or uniformly held either within the church or without. Some denied that mankind's position over the animal kingdom was absolute. The Greek philosopher Plutarch strenuously argued for the adoption of vegetarianism for ethical reasons. Newmyer, *Animals, Rights and Reason in Plutarch and Modern Ethics*. St. Francis of Assisi, frequently heralded as a Saint for Animals, believed that the gospel should be proclaimed not only to humans but also to the animals, arguing that Christ came to save the cosmos, not just humans. Others believed that while humans were superior, they should avoid consuming animal flesh in order to maintain or achieve a higher spiritual plane. Yet, aside from these few examples, Christianity maintained a remarkable unanimity on the doctrine of man's dominion in regard to the animal creation throughout its long history. Robinson, "St. Francis of Assisi." It should be observed, however, that Assisi did wear fox fur.

2. Linzey, *Animal Gospel*, 57–58.

of life of his neighbor, including generations to come; it requires a religious respect for the integrity of creation.[195]

2416 Animals are God's creatures. He surrounds them with his providential care. By their mere existence they bless him and give him glory.[196] Thus men owe them kindness. We should recall the gentleness with which saints like St. Francis of Assisi or St. Philip Neri treated animals.

2417 God entrusted animals to the stewardship of those whom he created in his own image.[197] Hence it is legitimate to use animals for food and clothing. They may be domesticated to help man in his work and leisure. Medical and scientific experimentation on animals is a morally acceptable practice, if it remains within reasonable limits and contributes to caring for or saving human lives.

2418 It is contrary to human dignity to cause animals to suffer or die needlessly. It is likewise unworthy to spend money on them that should as a priority go to the relief of human misery. One can love animals; one should not direct to them the affection due only to persons."[3]

The essential elements of this doctrine, called Dominionism,[4] holds that humanity has a superior status in creation, and that this status provides a moral basis for humans to wield power over nature, and to compel it to serve human needs and interests. In other words, Dominionism [5] views the cosmos in a hierarchical way, in that humanity's distinctiveness morally justifies human treatment of non-human creation in a manner categorically different than would be done within the human family.

The belief by Dominionists (those who adhere to Dominionism) that the non-human world should serve human interests has been ridiculed as anthropocentric/homocentric. With the non-human world in effect humanity's workshop, Dominionism was also characterized as having

3. The Magisterium, "Catechism of the Catholic Church." In Linzey's quotation, he removed the section numbers and italicized the first use of animals in line 2416. His source was The Catholic Catechism (London: Geoffrey Chapman, 1994), paras. 2415–418, 516–17.

4. Mason, *An Unnatural Order*, 25. Mason uses the word "Dominionism" to describe this view. Although "dominion" can be mistaken for the theology held by the Theonomist movement, use of the term here should not be understood in an eschatological or political sense. Dominion, in this book, simply refers to the relationship between humans and animals as one not between equals in power or ontology.

5. This explanation of Dominionism was synthesized with the help of Martin, "New Ways of Knowing and Being Known," 27–35.

an instrumentalist, if not a mechanistic, view of creation. Following the example of Bacon and Newton, Dominionists were accused of believing: 1. that the non-human world was to be studied, dissected, and controlled; 2. that animals were morally equivalent to trees and rocks in that all were subject to natural laws; and 3. creation was valuable not in and of itself, but only in relationship to its usefulness to human interests.[6]

Although non-Christians certainly held a similar view in practice,[7] if not in theory, the Western Church, influenced by Aquinas,[8] adopted Dominionism as dogma for several reasons. First, Genesis 1:26–8 led her to conclude that God granted mankind authority over the animals, and, by implication, over the rest of creation. In a time and culture familiar with notions of kingship and monarchy, she would readily understand the passage's use of kingly language as including humanity's authority over an animal's life and death, building cities, mining minerals, and other activities that extracted resources from the earth. Second, history, mediated through cultural tradition and textual sources, revealed that humans have extracted the earth's resources for millennia. More importantly, Holy Scripture was replete with examples of people, later called Saints, who ate and killed animals, cut down forests, and built cities, for centuries. Scripture even records that Jesus Christ Himself, cooked a fish breakfast for His disciples on the shores of Galilee after His resurrection (Jn 21:9ff). Finally, Christians believed, along with non-Christians,[9] that Nature herself taught the superiority of humanity. Humans were of a higher order than beasts, plants, and inanimate objects (cf. Gen 1:26ff).[10] Humans, either by design or by

6. The point being made here is not whether Dominionism properly understands Scriptural teaching on humanity's rule over the earth, only that this was how CAR activists have defined the opposing view.

7. Wright, "Responsibility for the Ecological Crisis," 851–53.

8. Aquinas, *Summa Theologica,* 96:2. As if anticipating the claims of the modern Animal Rights movement, Aquinas even believed that predation existed prior to the Fall. He did not believe that human sin affected animal natures (*Summa* 96:1 reply to objection 2). See also Schafran, "Is Mankind the Measure? Old Testament Perspectives on Mankind's Place in the Natural World," 92–102.

9. Adler, *Aristotle for Everybody*, 6–7. Even Pythagoras, who opposed meat eating partly because humans and animals shared a soul, was reputed by later Greek sources to have held that the human soul had rationality whereas animal souls did not. See Wheelwright, *The Presocratics*, 222, 225.

10. Calvin, *Commentaries on the First Book of Moses Called Genesis*, vol. 1. Comments on Genesis 1:26. Calvin explained how Scripture identified humanity's special place as lord of creation. First, God deliberated over the creation of Adam and Eve rather than

accident, were the masters of the world. This traditional view became so entrenched that Church leaders spanning the centuries could assert it with little fear of being contradicted or stirring controversy.[11]

Today, however, Dominionism is under siege. Ginger Louder, adjunct biology professor at Purdue University and Sierra Club member said, in a recent newswire article on religion and the environment that a religious view that supports domination over the environment caters to the egoism of humans. She made the connection to Scripture more explicit by saying, "Genesis 1:27–28 is a comforting thought for many people because we're given a mandate to dominate. We feel that we have the right to do whatever we want to. We feel that we're in control."[12]

Louder was not alone in her criticism. For in the same article, Rev. Dennis McCarty of the Unitarian Universalist Congregation of Columbus also rejected the notion of humanity's right to dominate the environment. He condemned the belief that humans "…are the monarchs of the ecosystem in which we live; we have been given dominion over it by a greater power." He believed that, "This adversarial relationship with nature has governed our attitude toward it right up to the present day, hardening our sense of entitlement in the process." McCarty preferred

---

simply speaking them into existence. Second, they were given explicit power over the animal kingdom. Finally, they were created in God's image, which for Calvin included rational and moral excellence.

11. A brief survey of commentators should suffice to underscore the notion that the belief of humanity's dominion over animals was divinely ordained. Augustine observed that although humanity shares qualities with animals, it exhibits God's providence by human form, speech, and power over nature, including hunting and domestication of wild animals. Augustine, *Concerning the City of God against the Pagans*, 1072–3 Book XXII:24.; He also explicitly defended the right of humans to kill animals, by appealing to human reason against animal lack thereof, against those who sought to use the command against killing to include the animal kingdom. I:20. ; Aquinas. *Summa* 96:1; 66:1 Aquinas cites Aristotle's support of humanity's right to hunt animals. Aquinas also said that humanity's dominion was subsidiary to God's ownership. See also Aquinas' clear comment regarding humanity's rule over animals in *Summa* 102:6 reply to objection 8. Aquinas also appealed to natural reason for support of humanity's dominion over the animals. A key element of his argument lay with his notion of the hierarchy of being based on the idea that different creatures obtained different levels of perfection. God, of course, exhibited ultimate perfection (*Summa* 4:1). He said it was natural for greater creatures to utilize the lesser (*Summa* 96:1). Plants use the earth, animals use plants, and therefore humans, who are greater than them all, use both. Aquinas reasserts this notion of human superiority over creatures in *Summa* 96:2.

12. Bouthier, "Religious Leaders Weigh in on Responsibility toward Environment." See also Fox, *Toward a Transpersonal Ecology*, 5f.

the Asian understanding of human-nature relations, which exhibits a reduced sense of ownership saying, "Eastern religious traditions have a strong feeling of kinship with the land . . . The earth itself is seen as a source of strength and power."

It would be wrong to think that the criticism of Dominionism simply hails from non-Christians. In 1976, Anglican priest and theologian Andrew Linzey published *Animal Rights: A Christian Assessment of Man's Treatment of Animals* [13] where he decried Christianity's lack of concern for animals and called for a realignment of its view concerning animals. Linzey claimed that Christianity justified humanity's continued use, consumption, and exploitation of animals on the hierarchal and anthropocentric bias handed down by Aristotle, Aquinas, and Descartes. Linzey argued that if Christians would only read the Bible with a critical awareness of our past anthropocentric bias, we would recognize how misguided was Aquinas' belief that humans had no direct duties to animals, as Scripture portrays humanity as creation's partner, not its master.

Linzey's reading of Scriptural narrative, which is echoed by many other Christian Animal Rights (CAR) activists, [14] can be summarized as follows: In the beginning, God established non-violent harmony between animals and humans. Both were vegetarian and sustained themselves without killing each other. Human sinfulness broke that harmony and spawned violence, which flourished until God brought it to an end by sending a great flood. The Noahic Covenant's allowance to eat meat was in fact a concession made by God to slow the inevitable growth of violence (particularly human versus human). The idea being that if humans could express their violence against animals (i.e. eating meat), they would be less inclined to exhibit violence against each other. Meat eating was to be a sort of emotional pressure release valve to channel our violent tendencies away from murder and war. [15] However, God still showed His true desire to protect animals by instituting rules to limit humanity's violence of animals. These rules, such as the prohibition against eating blood, Kosher laws, Sabbath regulations, and others, were instituted to direct humanity's

13. Linzey, *Animal Rights*.

14. Dear S. J., "Christianity and Vegetarianism: Pursuing the Nonviolence of Jesus"; Hyland, *The Slaughter of the Terrified Beasts*,.; Kaufman and Braun, *Vegetarianism as Christian Stewardship*.

15. For a detailed discussion of the theory connecting humanity's adoption of hunting and other violent actions, read Cartmill, *A View to a Death in the Morning*.

vision to the coming harmony in the Messianic age as foreseen by Isaiah (Isa 11:1–17).

Since Christ died to reconcile all creation (including animals), disciples of Christ should embrace vegetarianism as part of a broader ministry of reconciliation. God wants peace on earth, which cannot include the human exploitation and consumption of God's animal creation. Linzey asserted that humanity's violence against animals is representative of its violence against the earth. Hunting, trapping, cattle production, and other consumptive uses of animals violate God's law, cause animal suffering, and damage the environment. In contrast, vegetarianism/veganism is "violence free" and better for the environment. It is just one small step that people can take toward establishing the harmony God wants us to have. Linzey argued that it is patently inconsistent for the Church to continue to offer tacit or explicit approval to bull fighting, trapping, and eating animals, while claiming that animals were created by God and consequently have value independent of human needs and wants[16] Therefore, the Church, in a spirit of "penitence" should correct this failure.[17] In brief, Linzey believed that this animal-friendly interpretation made better sense of Scripture, the ethics exhibited by Christ, and the findings of environmental science.

HISTORICAL AND IDEOLOGICAL ROOTS FOR THE REJECTION OF THE DOMINION VIEW

To better understand the rationale for the aforementioned criticism of Dominionism, it will be necessary for us to review the ideas and events that prompted many to question its warrant.[18] The foundational dogmas underpinning Domininionism were shaken by three pivotal ideological shifts, which destabilized the foundation of the West's worldview. The first tectonic shift occurred with the publication of Darwin's *Origin of the Species*. Darwin's evolutionary theory destroyed the fundamental assumption of humanity's uniqueness. Previously, humans 'knew' they were different from, and superior to, the animals. Humans were special because they were created in God's image (Gen 1:26, 28). Evolution knocked hu-

---

16. Linzey, *Animal Gospel*, 61–62.

17. Linzey and Cohn-Sherbok, *After Noah*, xviii.

18. Booth, et al., *The Craft of Research*, 85–148.

mans off their pedestal by arguing that humans were just animals who arose on a different branch of the tree of life.[19]

Undoubtedly, the significance of that challenge was not completely understood at the time.[20] Most simply saw evolution in teleological terms, so that humans were evolution's ultimate goal and crowning achievement. Enlightenment's Humanism stunted the impact of Darwin's theory by reinforcing human dominion over the earth, by positing that humanity was the ultimate measure of all things.[21] In fact, Enlightenment's belief in humanity's superiority actually justified an expansive understanding of human authority over creation, as creation's value was correlated to its utility in serving humanity's needs, whether real or perceived.[22] Nevertheless, the notion that unguided random chance culminated in humans undercut the teleological view of humanity's importance. The intellectual impact of this new perspective on the significance of "being human" had far reaching effects. Humans were now just another animal that happened to be powerful, complex, and successful survivors in the lottery of selective adaptation.[23]

19. Dennett, *Darwin's Dangerous Idea*, 62, 118, 121. On page 121, Dennett's argument can be summarized as follows: "Either we, meaning all living things, are related or we are not." See also 135.

20. Preece, "Darwinism, Christianity, and the Great Vivisection Debate," 419. Preece asserts that any claim that blames the rise of animal rights, at least as understood in terms of vivisection, is simplistic, as opposition to vivisection existed prior to Darwinism, and Darwinists actually supported vivisection. There is no need to dispute Preece's point other than to say that animal rights activists appear to have found greater solace in employing Darwinian arguments than in utilizing Biblical ones.

21. Mason, *An Unnatural Order*, 33–37; Linzey and Regan, *Animals and Christianity*, x–xi.

22. Linzey and Regan, *Animals and Christianity*, xi–xii.; Descartes, "Discourse on the Method of Rightly Conducting the Reason and Seeking Truth in the Sciences," 82. Catholic philosopher Descartes contended that animals were nothing more than machines, in order to distinguish humans from animals and defend the existence of God, and that their cries during vivisection procedures were nothing more than audible twitches. Unlike Descartes, Kant believed animals could suffer, but this fact was not sufficient for him to include animals under the umbrella of his categorical imperative. He argued that mankind owed no direct duties to animals, saying that we do not torture animals because it would bother our human neighbor, make it easier for us to be cruel to fellow humans, or because the animal is the property of our neighbor. Francione, "Animals—Property or Persons?" 111–12.

23. Dennett. *Darwin's Dangerous Idea*, 370–71. Dennett says humans differ from animals in three ways: 1. features lacking in other animals, 2. our ability to transmit culture, and 3. our intelligence and language.

The second tectonic shift was the Enlightenment's growing disen-
chantment with ruling institutions, both religious and aristocratic.[24] As
democratic ideals of equality among "men" undercut aristocratic notions
of "divine right," people began to reason that if humans were just another
animal, "What gave humans the right to decide the fate of this or that
animal?" The belief that human animals were somehow special or more
valuable than other animals was simply undemocratic, and exhibited the
snobbish arrogance of aristocrats. Such elitist opinions, therefore, needed
to be opposed. For just as distinguishing people based on race exhibited
racial prejudice, so distinguishing between humans and animals exemplified the prejudice that came to be called "speciesism."[25]

The third tectonic shift began during the 1960s, when scholars started to doubt whether humanity had the wisdom needed to rule creation
in a responsible way. With the publication of Silent Spring,[26] this doubt
penetrated the American and Western European culture, whose citizens
became increasingly concerned about protecting the environment. The
environmental damage resulting from the West's so-called scientific advances raised serious questions about the ethics surrounding humanity's
use of nature. Carson succinctly explained the new perspective by writing, "The 'control of nature' is a phrase conceived in arrogance, born of
the Neanderthal age of biology and philosophy, when it was supposed
that nature exists for the convenience of man."[27] Due to man's desire for
domination, many now blamed human activity[28] for the damage to the
environment. After all, if Homo sapiens were so intelligent,[29] how could

24. Cartmill. A View to a Death in the Morning, 84–88. Cartmill explains that the rise
of anti-hunting attitudes in the 1500s stemmed from the decline of aristocratic power,
adoption of a Classical attitude that hunting is done by slaves, and growing intellectual
security with religion and reason.

25. Wise, "Animal Rights One Step at a Time," 26. Wise says that Richard Ryder
first coined the term speciesism (which is defined by the Oxford English Dictionary
as discrimination against animal species by human beings) based on an assumption of
humanity's superiority.

26. Carson, Silent Spring. It is difficult to underestimate the extent of this book's
impact.

27. Ibid., 261.

28. The view that humans are "principally consumers and polluters" is common
among "environmentalists." Beisner, Where Garden Meets Wilderness, 111.

29. Homo sapien, the scientific name for humans, can be translated as "intelligent
man."

we have been so irresponsible as to cause so many environmental catastrophes, ranging from the extinction of species to toxic pollution and environmental degradation?[30] If we were so superior, how could we cause so many environmental problems?

During the ideological turmoil of the 1960s, scholars searched for an intellectual framework that would correctly guide us away from an ecological catastrophe.[31] Some suggested more studies so that we could foresee and prevent catastrophes. Others wanted greater regulatory oversight to restrain negative human behavior. Many searched for a deeper solution; one tied to our values. In their mind, Christianity, and its belief in the dominion of mankind, caused our environmental crisis. Lynn White, Jr. emerged as the key spokesperson for this view. He wrote that Christianity, particularly Western or Latin Christianity,[32] bore a central responsibility for environmental degradation.[33] White asserted that Christianity's belief that God created the world for humanity's benefit led to the idea that humanity should exploit nature. The result of this attitude, dubbed "anthropocentrism,"[34] encouraged human arrogance and justified a "mood of indifference to the feelings of natural objects."[35] If human needs were primary, then the needs of other creatures were by definition secondary and in practical terms irrelevant. Any cursory review of the literature, whether popular or scholarly, shows that White's conclusions were, and frequently remain, accepted as gospel.[36]

---

30. Diamond, *Collapse*. Diamond, in chapter 16, outlines the major environmental issues facing the planet.

31. One cannot overemphasize the apocalyptic predictions of environmental futurists. Gordon and Suzuki, *It's a Matter of Survival*, 7. provides an excellent example as it predicts catastrophe in 2040, a year called "Despair." As expected, the authors cited Biblical values as a key reason for the coming catastrophe, 53, 235–36.

32. Fox, *Toward a Transpersonal Ecology*, 5.

33. White, Jr., "The Historical Roots of Our Ecologic Crisis," 1203–7.

34. Stanton and Guernsey, "Christians Ecological Responsibility: A Theological Introduction and Challenge." They use the term "Cartesian/Newtonian world view" to denote the philosophy that promotes a human/nature dualism to justify humanity's right to exploit nature for its own goals.

35. White Jr., "The Historical Roots of Our Ecologic Crisis," 1205.

36. For example, see echoes of White Jr.'s notions in Powell, "An Ecologist Struggles with the Problem of Evil," 101. Note, however, that White's claims were thoroughly rebutted in Wright, "Responsibility for the Ecological Crisis," 851–53.

Some environmentalists took White's view to heart and sought a "deeper ecology." Where mainstream environmentalists sought to mitigate the negative aspects of human-originated environmental impacts, Deep Ecologists[37] rejected the mainstream's instrumentalist stance toward the human-nature relations that spawned the environmental crisis in the first place.[38] These "Deep Ecologists," argued that environmentalism should be based on more than enlightened self-interest for humans. Humans should recognize that their interests are no more important than the interests of other organisms. Therefore, proper environmental policy must reject the idea that humans should control any part of the natural world.[39] Just as humans progressed to recognize inalienable rights for humans different than themselves, so should those rights be extended to non-human members of the animal kingdom. Deep Ecologists believed that the only way to protect the planet was through a fundamental transformation of our view of humanity's place in the world. Humans had to grant animals the same sorts of rights as would be granted to other humans.[40]

One way that the principles of Deep Ecology developed can be observed in Peter Singer's landmark work, *Animal Liberation*. Drawing from Deep Ecology's rejection of humanity's instrumental view of nature, Singer rejected the notion that humans had the right to treat animals as just another resource comparable to coal or trees. He said that animals, as sentient beings, had a *prima facie* right to life and liberty, free of human interference, not just collectively but as individual creatures. In short, humans should have no more right over animals than they have over members of their own species. In Singer's mind, dominion, as Christians had traditionally understood it, was patently immoral.[41] He believed that our actions should be governed not by ontological speculation or divine

37. Wells and Schwartz, "Deep Ecology," 61.

38. Bishop, "Green Theology and Deep Ecology: New Age or New Creation?" 8–14. Bishop provides a worthy review of some of the various issues at stake.

39. Wright, "Tearing Down the Green: Environmental Backlash in the Evangelical Sub-Culture."

40. The environmental aspect of the animal rights movement will be clearly apparent to anyone surfing environmental websites. Many will dedicate an area of their site to animal rights. However, it must be known that for some, animal rights is not strictly an environmental issue. Some would put more emphasis on an ethical view of how fellow beings should be treated, whether or not there was an environmental benefit to such treatment.

41. Singer, *Animal Liberation*, 192–222. Singer outlines his understanding of the history and impact of dominion thinking.

revelation, but by whether science tells us if a creature can suffer. For example, if a creature can suffer, it does not matter whether the creature is weaker than the human. The human must respect its right to life and liberty because evolution teaches us that all sentient creatures are related. Singer's work energized the animal rights movement by his straightforward presentation of the animal rights philosophy; a presentation that resonated with the culture's acceptance of science and love of equality. With the resultant respectability provided by Singer's book the topic of animal rights could no longer be ignored, either in the academy or in politics. Recently, animal activists have achieved political success by enacting legislation[42] restricting various human uses of animals, including consumptive use of wildlife.[43]

THE IMPORTANCE OF THE TOPIC

There are several reasons why a study of CAR (Christian animal rights) is needed. First, the question, "How should humans understand their role in the environment?"[44] has been generally ignored by Evangelicals.[45] However, that lack of attention is beginning to change as exemplified by Moo's citation of Ray van Leeuwen, "All of reality is Christ's good creation, all of reality is redeemed by him; therefore all of reality is the responsibility of God's people."[46] Nevertheless, if the wider topic has been inadequately

42. For a brief overview of animal protectionist legislation in the United States and around the world see Rowan and Rosen, "Progress in Animal Legislation: Measurement and Assessment"; Irwin, "A Strategic Review of International Animal Protection."

43. Animal protectionists are not always clear about their ultimate goals. They frequently decry animal cruelty but are unable or unwilling to establish a point where human use of animals remains valid. In other words, their view of what constitutes cruelty expands from generation to generation, suggesting to some that animal protectionists will not stop their political activism until all human use of animals is banned.

44. Ball, "The Use of Ecology in the Evangelical Protestant Response to the Ecological Crisis," Np. Ball notes ". . . one of the key theological questions underlying the ecological crisis: "What is humanity's relationship to the rest of creation?""

45. See Sheldon, "Twenty-One Years After 'Historical Roots of Our Ecologic Crisis' How Has the Church Responded?" 152. Sheldon says, "On the theological side, the Church has struggled to determine humanity's intended relationship with Creation." Davis, "Ecological 'Blind Spots' In the Structure and Content of Recent Evangelical Systematic Theologies," 273–86. This neglect is changing but remains true to this day, with Schaeffer, *Book One: Pollution and the Death of Man*, 3–82, and Beisner among the exceptions.

46. Moo, "Nature in the New Creation: New Testament Eschatology and the Environment," 470.

investigated, it should not surprise us that narrower environmental questions raised by a small community of animal rights activists have not been
sufficiently engaged either.[47] This book seeks to help address this gap in
Evangelical theology.

Second, while Linzey's ideas regarding animal rights remain in the
theological eddies of Christendom, there are signs that this is beginning
to change.[48] Christians are adopting animal rights views as part of their
overall desire to "care for the earth." One need only look at Matthew
Scully's *Dominion: The Power of Man, the Suffering of Animals, and the
Call to Mercy* and the positive reviews it received in *Christianity Today*[49]
and by Rev. Richard John Neuhaus,[50] to recognize that the topic of our
treatment of the animal kingdom (and its more radical relative, animal
rights) is gaining in importance. Since theologians investigate influential
ideas, it is certainly worthwhile to review this one.

Third, CAR theology challenges Christendom's understanding of the
role of humanity in creation, specifically in regards to animals. The implications of CAR theology extend beyond just Christian dietary choices. For
example, if killing animals, except for self-defense, is morally wrong, then
how should Christians understand Jesus Christ's moral standing when
Scripture suggests He tolerated social customs involving the killing and
eating of animals? (Lk 5:5; 8:32ff; Jn 21:9ff). Furthermore, does Christ's
reconciling work on the cross redeeming all of creation (cf. *cosmos* Col
1:18f.) mean that we should expect to see animals in heaven as the CAR
activists suggest?[51] It is appropriate, therefore, to use this opportunity to

---

47. Several reasons can be postulated, including its relative newness, its relative small
but vocal number of adherents, and the distance theologians have from their ties to the
earth. Animal rights activists see themselves as part of the larger Environmental movement. Williams, "Rights, Animals," 592. "Sadly, little effort has been made on the part of
evangelicals to look at the Biblical basis for an understanding of our dealings with the
animal world."

48.   Evidence of growing interest can also be seen in the growth of web pages.
Search done on Google.com using the key words/phrase: *Christianity+"Animal Rights"*
on 11/23/02 yielded 13,600 hits. But the same search performed on 04/16/07 yielded
417,000 hits. "Google Search Engine," (Google Inc., 2007).

49. Scully, *Dominion*. The book also received some positive attention by the book
reviewer at *Christianity Today*.

50. Neuhaus, *The Best of the Public Square*, 6–17.

51. For an anthology of excerpts from theologians regarding the destiny of animals
see Linzey and Regan, *Animals and Christianity*, 87–109.

reflect on Scriptural teaching in order to determine if the Church's traditional understanding should remain unmodified.

Fourth, Evangelicals need moral guidance on specific human behaviors. The CAR position has challenged the morality of a number of ways that humans interact with animals, such as eating meat, raising animals for food, pet ownership, consumptive use of wildlife (e.g. hunting and trapping), vivisection, and other forms of animal experimentation. Are Evangelical Churches wrong in their support or tacit approval of these behaviors on behalf of their members?

Finally, the challenge of CAR theology has an important side benefit; namely, it provides specific and concrete problems around which larger environmental practices can be discussed. The trouble with many theological discussions on the environment is their failure to move beyond theory and address concrete particulars.[52] Consider the following platitude: "Christians need to care about the environment." While an important belief and attitude for Christians to hold, it lacks the specificity essential for guiding Christian behavior. In politics, people rarely fight over principles; they fight over particulars.[53] Evangelical Christians need at least as much specificity to guide behavior as Jesus gave when he answered the question "Who is my neighbor?" by telling the story of the Good Samaritan (Lk 10:29–37).

FOCUS OF THIS BOOK

The animal rights debate, both in its Christian and secular forms, centers on two key questions, one foundational (i.e. What is the moral status of animals vis-à-vis humans and other aspects of creation?), and the other practical (i.e. How should humans treat animals, and is it ethical to consume animal flesh and wear fur?).

52. A classic example of this over-attention to theory can be seen in the unending discussion of the meaning of dominion in Genesis 1—2 as demonstrated by the worthy article by Caruthers, Farming in crisis and the voice of silence—a response to David Atkinson, 59–64. While Caruthers' work is important to provide a theoretical framework for our actions, they ultimately fail to provide precise help in determining whether a particular action is moral or not. I avoid this problem by speaking directly to the issue of practice.

53. One need only look at the bitter debates over the North American fur trade. One side thinks fur trapping represents responsible stewardship; an example of humanity's ability to extract a renewable resource in a sustainable way. Yet another, with equal passion, views fur trapping as a form of ecological rape that exhibits the ugly and cruel side of human domination of our fellow sentient creatures.

The scope of this inquiry will be limited to the arguments proffered by self-declared Christians, who assert that animal rights is compatible with, and even prescribed by, anyone claiming to follow Jesus Christ. The impact of animal rights thinking on the doctrines of Soteriology, Christology, Anthropology, and Eschatology will be addressed only as needed to help us determine the more fundamental question of whether humans have been given the moral authority to kill and utilize animals. The critical question that will be addressed is whether CAR activists are correct in their belief that Scripture exhorts us to adopt a vegetarian and non-violent stance toward animals as humanly possible.

Since humanity's lethal use of animals is so diverse (e.g. vivisection, hunting, trapping, and livestock), I have focused on the issue of humanity's treatment of wildlife, with particular attention to trapping.[54] Narrowing the topic in this way provides a number of heuristic advantages. First, all of those activities, fishing, hunting, and trapping, have an ancient history that continues to the present. It is more likely that Scripture could have something to say about less technologically advanced uses of animals, such as trapping,[55] hunting, and traditional farming. Vivisection is certainly an important topic, however, it is difficult to imagine how the Biblical writers could have envisioned a time where our power over creation would allow us to inflict incredible suffering on animals while keeping them alive, as is done in animal experimentation and industrial farming (a.k.a. factory farming). Second, CAR activists consider trapping to be an important topic for both moral (trapping as an activity is especially hated) and environmental reasons.[56] By discussing trapping as a case study, I directly address the challenge of CAR theology. Third, investigating the morality of trapping allows us to avoid discussing an issue that could become obsolete with the next technological advance. Just as technology creates ethical problems, it can also solve them.[57] Fourth, traditional and historic animal use still provides concrete examples with

---

54. Hunting and trapping are both forms of "the consumptive use of wildlife."

55. Europeans typically use the term "snaring." The reader should be aware that for purposes of this book, the word trapping encompasses snaring as well.

56. Young, *Is God a Vegetarian?* 33, 35–36.

57. It is doubtful that any advances in trapping or other technology will ever result in our ability to take an animal's pelt without killing it. In contrast, debates over the use of embryonic stem cells may be resolved by the use of non-injurious extraction of embryonic stem cells. See Fields, "What Comes Next?" 56–58.

which to discuss humanity's relationship to the environment. Thus this book can remain theologically relevant to human behavior. Most contemporary environmental controversies center around humanity's impact on the environment, and deciding whether humans need to change their behavior. Since trapping involves either the capture of wild animals, (animals essentially owned by no one except God), we are forced to engage how humanity, and its human-impacted environments,[58] should interface with the wild/natural environment.[59]

It is fair to ask why CAR activists' opposition to eating meat and trapping should be investigated, given that Evangelicals can easily dismiss CAR claims by appealing to Christ's apparent support of fishing (Lk 5:4) and Paul's comments in 1 Timothy 4:1–3. While 1Timothy 4:1–3 devastates CAR's broader view on veganism (it is also a passage CAR activists generally fail to address), their use of Scripture in support of their position is so nuanced that a simplistic proof-text response, although valid, is not appropriate. There are three important reasons why a flippant treatment of CAR activists' understanding of Scripture should be avoided. First, a cavalier approach will not help Evangelicals develop their own Biblical understanding of the human-animal relationship. Evangelicals cannot afford to ignore this question, as we have already waited too long to get involved in environmental issues. Second, love for others, particularly those who claim to be followers of Christ, includes engaging ideas at their strongest points. Finally, employing an argument from concession will enable the conversation between CAR activists and the broader Evangelical community to continue. Thus this book will attempt to present a Biblical theology of humanity's relationship to the animal kingdom as it relates to wildlife trapping, that appeals to the three authorities that CAR activists and the Evangelical community recognize: Scripture, moral reasoning, and science. In this way, the conversation with CAR activists can continue.

58. The writer recognizes that the distinction between natural and human-impacted environments is artificial and arbitrary. However, despite its weaknesses, the distinction remains a valuable one. For detailed discussion of the topic see Cronon, "Beginnings Introduction: In Search of Nature," 23–56.

59. Animals can provide clues to the relative health of an ecosystem, a fact easily recognized by non-biologists. Wildlife is impacted by a wide range of human activities. See Manning, "The Threat to Montana," 50. Manning explains a Montana mine will have deleterious effects on the superb habitat that is home to grizzly bears, wolves, wolverines, lynx, and the spawning grounds of cutthroat and bull trout.

2

The CAR Movement's Argument
from Old Testament Scripture
Part 1

CAR ACTIVISTS' HERMENEUTICS

BEFORE DETAILING THE CAR activists' interpretation of Scripture, it is appropriate to survey their hermeneutical vantage point. CAR activists' lack of direct attention to explaining or justifying their hermeneutical approach hinders any summarization of their views. It would appear that praxis guides their hermeneutics more than an overarching abstract theory. Nevertheless, by looking at various ways they handle Scripture, one discovers that their view of Scripture is complex and nuanced.[1] It is fair to say that CAR activists have a decidedly modernistic approach to Scripture, as exemplified by the following comment by Young,

> The Bible is primarily narrative; that is, it tells a story about a people struggling with their identity and with how to relate to God and to others. It tells of a journey over some rather rough terrain, with some pilgrims bogging down along the way, others taking detours with killing, wars and the like.[2]

CAR activists' hermeneutics, like Neoorthodox and liberal interpreters, believe the Bible *contains* the Word of God rather than *is* the Word of God.[3] The Bible cannot be said to be pure revelation because God's

1. Contra Patton, "He Who Sits in the Heavens Laughs," 408. She was also wrong to call Linzey "a radical scriptural literalist."

2. Young, *Is God a Vegetarian?* xviii. He makes a number of other comments that give insight to his hermeneutical views on 54–56.

3. Packer, "The Adequacy of Human Language," 204–5; McCartney and Clayton, *Let the Reader Understand*, 39. The authors call this hermeneutical approach "View 3."

message has been contaminated by fallible humans. The trouble lay not with God's revelation but with the imperfect vessel that tried to understand, explain, and transmit God's truth in human words. The interpreter, therefore, must carefully separate God's Word from the human and fallible noise that entered the Scriptural tradition. Since the human portion of Scripture is in question, CAR activists are uncomfortable with historical reconstructions that attempt to explain Scripture's true meaning by getting at authorial intent. They believe that God speaks through the text, not by historical reconstructions which reflect the paucity of evidence and the bias of the observer.[4] Their inattention to historical context makes CAR interpretation follow a sort of "Reader-Response theory"[5] with one critical difference. CAR activists use their understanding of proper human-animal relations to separate the divine Word from the human voice.[6] This hermeneutical divining rod is then coupled with their belief that humanity is progressing to greater moral understanding. Therefore, just as humans grasped the notion that human sacrifice was wrong, so we are learning that the killing of animals is likewise wrong.[7]

CAR activists' acceptance of the modern notion that Scripture represents a broad tapestry of diverse and at times conflicting views,[8] has a significant impact on their hermeneutics. On the one hand, CAR activists do not feel obliged to harmonize conflicting texts. Since Scripture contains a mixture of dross and ore, it is to be expected that conflicting opinions of humanity's encounter with the divine would have emerged. What is interesting, from the Evangelical perspective, is how CAR activists simply ignore passages that directly counter their understanding of

---

4. Young, *Is God a Vegetarian?* 91. Note his statement that the reason why Christ ate meat is a mystery on par with the problem of evil. 12. See also his comments on understanding Isaiah's Edenic vision, 142.

5. Similarly, CAR activists suggest that Scripture is a mixed bag of human (i.e. fallible) reflection on divine revelation, or God's condescension to human behavior. See Young, *Is God a Vegetarian?* 10.

6. Although lacking his exegetical skills, CAR hermeneutics does have many similarities with Barth's method. See McGlasson, *Jesus and Judas*, 11–17. Nor should we be surprised given that Andrew Linzey, the father of the CAR movement, wrote his dissertation on Karl Barth's theology of non-human creation. Linzey, *Animal Theology*, 188.

7. CAR activists' hermeneutics is remarkably similar to those of liberation theologians. Cf. Hyland, *The Slaughter of the Terrified Beasts*, 1; Hyland, *God's Covenant with Animals*, 1.

8. Phelps, *The Dominion of Love*, 77–78; Webb, *On God and Dogs*, 35.

human-animal relations. On the other hand, CAR activists spend a great deal of time outlining and explaining how they understand the Bible's meta-narrative. Santmire, though not directly addressing the issue of animal rights, offers a useful model that can illustrate this point. He says that Western Christianity struggled with two opposing motifs concerning human-nature relations. These motifs are grounded in a foundational view or metaphor that provides an explanatory backdrop for our approach to Scripture and reality.[9] He explains that these two motifs, called the Spiritual Motif and the Ecological Motif, stand in opposition to each other. The Spiritual Motif is characterized by metaphors of ascent, where humanity's greatest goal is to contemplate and experience God, to leave the lower and mundane world and ascend into heaven or the spiritual realm. The Ecological Motif is funded by the metaphors of fecundity and migration. This motif focuses on the interrelatedness of God, nature, and humanity, with the additional insight of moving towards paradise.[10] For our purposes, these two motifs easily match the conflicting motifs of Dominionism (humanity over creation) and the CAR's motif (humanity in fellowship with creation). Just as the Spiritual Motif devalued the natural world, so Dominionism, it is alleged, devalues the natural world, including animal life. In contrast, the Ecological Motif values the natural world and seeks to bring about closer harmony and interrelatedness, so the CAR's view desires to rekindle the harmony between animals and humans that existed in Eden.

The unspoken question is how one rightly determines which of the competing motifs best exemplifies God's will for humanity. On this question, CAR activists seem to follow a hermeneutical approach that is remarkably similar to that taken by Feminist theologians. Feminist theologians take their notion of equality and oppression, and then evaluate Scripture with an eye toward finding what they believe a kind and loving God would want them to find. Passages found to contradict that perspective were either the result of biased editors or biased interpreters. For example, while recognizing that Scripture shows animals being used, eaten, and even sacrificed for human needs,[11] CAR activists believe that a deeper or more comprehensive reading reveals substantial support for animal rights. CAR activists further

9. Santmire, *The Travail of Nature*, 14–15.

10. Ibid., 9.

11. Linzey and Cohn-Sherbok, *After Noah*, 2–6.

suggest that our inadequate understanding of Scripture stems from our being tainted or biased by Aristotelean-Thomistic theology,[12] which held that the lesser was created for the greater.[13] Thus, they contend that it is those later theological readings biased by hierarchal thinking, not Scripture itself, which justified our exploitive treatment of animals.

EVALUATION OF CAR HERMENEUTICS

Evangelicals will find much that is troubling with the CAR approach to Scripture. Their denial of the analogy of Scripture presents a foundational problem, namely "How can CAR activists accurately distinguish between the teaching that resulted from human fallibility and the teaching that accurately expresses God's will?" In the CAR view, it would seem the ultimate arbiter of what is from God and what is from humanity would be the fallible human interpreter.[14] Certainly one could assert that the CAR position is decidedly arbitrary, in that it ignores or denigrates content that does not fit into its model. It is true that we all read Scripture from our own social context,[15] but that is different than simply ignoring evidence one finds troublesome. Evangelicals, in spite of their differences, at least endeavor to wrestle with all the Scriptural data because its adherents believe that Scripture comes from God.[16] Another critical weakness[17] in the CAR approach to Scripture is its avoidance of historical context and reconstruction. For without historical context, how can CAR activists ground the moral imperatives they find in Scripture? As Carson so

12. Ibid., 3, 6, 18. This is not to say that Linzey thinks the Bible, as we have it today, plainly supports an animal rights agenda. Linzey clearly accepts the need for a critical review of scriptural testimony to find the evidence he wants. See p. 3, 18. He suggests that we adopt a pro-animal viewpoint when approaching the texts, in a manner similar to that done by feminists who want to discover overlooked pro-women passages p.18. See also Young, *Is God a Vegetarian?* 82.

13. Webb, *On God and Dogs*, 57.

14. McCartney and Clayton, *Let the Reader Understand*, 39–40.

15. Anderson, *From Creation to New Creation*, 133.

16. In this way, Evangelicals endeavor to develop a coherent theology based on all the evidence.

17. One could also raise the historical problem of how the apostles could have missed the animal rights witness of Christ when He was walking on the earth with them. Despite claims to the contrary, the N.T. was recorded too early in the life of the Church to have been sufficiently buried. For discussion of the issues see Guthrie, *New Testament Introduction*, 13–335.

poignantly observed, drawing conclusions without an ontological or historical basis results in a form of idolatry.[18] Language, lacking any external referent, becomes its own deity. Words also lose their semantic range and become victim to whatever meaning the reader wants to find.

It is axiomatic to assert that everyone reads Scripture with the advantages or disadvantages of their point of view. The unasked question is, "How do CAR activists know that the bias (assuming it was a bias) of Aristotle and Aquinas was the wrong one to have?"[19] Second, given that CAR activists downplay the principle of the analogy of Scripture, how do they know that their selection of Scripture is not a simple case of special pleading? Clearly Evangelicals and CAR activists differ at a foundational level in terms of their approach to Scripture. The question is, "Given these foundational differences, can any meaningful communication or dialogue occur?" Are the paradigms so distinct that communication could only result with a paradigm shift?[20] It is too early to know. Nevertheless, Evangelicals should not become too dismissive of their claims. At the very least, Evangelicals can profit from an analysis of the CAR argument in order to see if our understanding of the meta-narrative and the individual passages needs adjustment.

CAR ACTIVISTS' APPEAL TO O.T. SCRIPTURE

CAR theology is decidedly oppositional in its tone and content. To understand their scriptural arguments, we have to briefly review why they think the Church's historical understanding of human-animal relations became so misguided. CAR activists believe that the Church's understanding of humanity's dominion was improperly grounded by three mistaken arguments. The first two arguments, based upon the hierarchical premise of an Aristotelian-Thomistic worldview,[21] claimed that humans were superior

18. Carson, *The Gagging of God*, 169–73. Carson does an excellent job explaining the elusive topic of contemporary mainline denominational hermeneutics.

19. Gadamer, *Philosophical Hermeneutics*, 9. The author remains open, however, to Vander Goot's notion that the Bible pulls the reader into its world view. See Vantassel, "An Overview of the Hermeneutics of Vander Goot," 58–67.

20. Cf. Kuhn, *The Structure of Scientific Revolutions*.

21. See Russell, *A History of Western Philosophy*, 170ff. for an explanation of how of Aristotle explained the metaphysical differences and similarities between humans and animals. See also Webb's comments about the need to "democratize social organizations." Webb, *On God and Dogs*, 51.

and unique vis a' vis the animals. These two arguments can be known as the ontological argument, and the rationality argument. The ontological argument asserted that humans were of a higher natural order than animals, and therefore humans could treat animals in a manner that was ethically different than the way appropriate for fellow humans. The rationality argument had stated that humans were intellectually superior to animals.[22] The third argument stated that humans were granted dominion, which was understood from a mechanistic view promulgated by Descartes-Newton.[23]

Linzey and other animal rights activists believe that recent findings make these arguments highly questionable. First, they contend that the findings of modern psychology, namely that at least some animals are rational,[24] has seriously undermined Aquinas' denial of animal rationality. So in a sort of reverse logic, if animals are rational then the ontological argument fails. Linzey seems to have been stirred to question the traditional view because of the impact of science. Since science now declares humans to be animals,[25] Linzey wonders how we could not give rights to animals that we have given to humans. Are we really different enough from animals to justify such a disparity of treatment? Linzey answers in the negative. He also sees a contradiction between the way humans accept a variety of differences as insignificant to how we treat each other. Just consider how we have learned to handle differences involved with gender, race, and nationality.[26]

Linzey also employs another approach. He wonders whether even assuming Aquinas's view of human ontology is correct, the mentally in-

22. Newmyer, *Animals, Rights and Reason in Plutarch and Modern Ethics*, 22–23. Aristotle believed that only humans could be deliberative. The culmination of the rationality argument occurred with Descartes, who denied that animals could even experience pain.

23. For a good discussion of the intellectual transition from an organic view of reality to a mechanistic one that occurred in the seventeenth Century, see Martin, "New Ways of Knowing and Being Known," 21–45.

24. Rationality is meant to designate that intellectual ability to deliberate among various choices and to show evidence of directive rather than instinctual behavior. Language is heralded as a primary evidence for rationality.

25. Recently, to better conform classification to evolutionary theory, taxonomists have been adopting a classification system based on phylogeny. This would, of course, effect *Homo sapiens* the scientific classification of mankind. University of California Museum of Paleontology, *Using the Tree for Classification.*

26. Linzey, *Animal Rights*, 5–6.

competent should be considered sub-human. He continued by question-ing whether we could treat the mentally feeble the same way we presently treat animals. As if the argument from consistency lacked sufficient force, Linzey appeals to God's call for Christians to be self-sacrificing by stat-ing that our superiority should make it harder for us to justify our abuse of animals. Linzey proffers that just because a creature is non-rational, it does not follow that the creature lacks moral standing.[27]

Linzey provides one more piece of evidence to help Christians rec-ognize that there is another way to view humanity's relationship to the earth. As we have seen, Linzey is critical of hierarchical Western theol-ogy as espoused by Aquinas. But lest we think that Aquinas' view is the only Christian one, Linzey calls us to consider the perspective of Eastern Orthodoxy, not because it held a different view of dominion or human specialness, but because of how that Church understood God.[28] Eastern Orthodoxy portrayed God and creation in harmony with living things in continuity, rather than disjunctive points on a ladder. Linzey observes that their prayers are more ecological, uniting the spiritual and the physi-cal together.[29] He thinks that an Eastern Orthodox understanding will help us re-imagine our role on the planet.

Linzey says the second way the Church asserted human superiority to animals (and conversely denied the existence of direct human obligations to animals) was to deny that animals were sentient.[30] Sentiency is the ability for an organism to experience pain at a cognitive level. It is more than sim-ply responding to stimuli. This distinction is important for Linzey because he rejects the idea that we have the same obligations to trees and insects that we have towards vertebrate animals. He says a bell rings when struck. But the bell's response to a stimulus does not mean that the bell is sentient. But Linzey quickly moves on, perhaps recognizing that the Church, while not seeing the issue of animal pain as a significant moral issue, never advocated the deliberate and purposeless injury to animals.

27. Linzey, *Animal Rights*, 11–14.

28. Linzey and Cohn-Sherbok, *After Noah*, 92.

29. Ibid., 93ff. Linzey mentions Descartes and his denial that animals experience pain.

30. Descartes, "Animals Are Machines," *Animals and Christianity*, 50. Descartes said animals act naturally and mechanically, like a clock. Ironically, Descartes believed ani-mals did not experience pain to protect God's character. See Young, "Animal Soul," *The Encyclopedia of Philosophy*, 122.

The Church's third claim is that God has granted humanity domin-ion over the animal creation. This argument presented a more significant challenge for Linzey, perhaps because of the impact of the plain reading of the Biblical text. It is at this point that we will look at how CAR activists use Scripture to support their position.

Argument from the Covenant of Creation[31]

CAR activists agree that Genesis provides a template for God's ideal for human behavior, and[32] it is the covenant found there that requires human-ity to see their treatment of animals[33] as a moral duty.[34] Linzey observes how Scripture through the covenant shows us that humanity and ani-mals are morally related.[35] Some passages show how animals and humans share a commonality that is so integrally connected that they cannot be separated. Animal and human destinies are intertwined (Gen 3:15; Ex 9:9; Jer 7:20; Psa 104:10–12).[36] To CAR activists, God's grant of dominion to humanity was not for exploitation and domination, but for a caring role of trust and leadership.[37] Scripture teaches that creation has value to God independent of human interests, and therefore does not exist for the glory of humanity. While recognizing that humans stand at the apex of creation, and thus closer to God by proximity, Linzey says humans are still connected with the rest of creation. Linzey argues that our belief in dominion as conquest of nature came not from a Judeo-Christian world view but from a Manichean[38] notion that nature was evil and needed to be subdued. He rejects any concept of dominion that distracts from God's

---

31. Linzey, *Animal Rights*. 17–18.

32. Young, *Is God a Vegetarian?* 16.

33. In modern scientific nomenclature, the specific identification of many animals in the Bible is profoundly difficult. Fortunately, precise identification to the species level is not necessary. For those interested in a discussion on the identification of Biblical animals see Hope, *All Creatures Great and Small*.

34. Murray, *The Cosmic Covenant*, 114. Though not an animal activist, Murray says compassion towards animals is a religious duty espoused in the Bible.

35. Linzey, *Christianity and the Rights of Animals*, 31.

36. Linzey and Cohn-Sherbok, *After Noah*, 22–23.

37. Hyland, *God's Covenant with Animals*, 17.

38. Carruthers, "Farming in Crisis and the Voice of Silence—a Response to David Atkinson," 60, makes a similar argument.

immanence in creation and His supreme moral rule over it.[39] Unlike other animal rights activists,[40] Linzey's assault on the uniqueness of humans is not to drag them down to the level of just being another animal. Rather, he uses the Christian principle of sacrificial rule to show that humans have moral obligations to animals. For Linzey, the fact that humanity is morally superior to animals should compel us to sacrificially work on behalf of animals, and alleviate their suffering.[41] All these commonalties can be subsumed under the umbrella of "Covenant."[42] Covenant speaks of community, and both humanity and animals are part of a community. The metaphor of community provides CAR activists the interpretive rubric for understanding humanity's dominion over animals. Since Adam and Eve were commanded to be vegetarian, our understanding of dominion should be modified to one of harmony and not killing.[43]

CAR activists base this non-traditional[44] understanding of Genesis by rejecting the two arguments used to support human utilization of animals, namely that humans wield ultimate dominion over animals and are ontologically superior to animals.[45] They proffer that when the Genesis narratives are understood in their entirety, readers will find support for the non-anthropocentric interpretation of dominion.[46] Specifically, CAR activists reject the view that Genesis supports any notion that humanity is both superior and special in respect to animals, which would justify the killing and/or eating of animals.

39. Linzey, *Animal Rights*, 18.

40. Pluhar, *Beyond Prejudice*, 123. The title of her book alone expresses her view of the moral leveling between humans and animals.

41. Linzey, *Animal Theology*, 45–61. Linzey spends an entire chapter discussing his view that mankind is special, but not in a way that supports the notion of privilege and self-service.

42. Linzey, *Animal Theology*, 30ff.

43. Cf. Linzey and Cohn-Sherbok, *After Noah*, 17, 20.

44. Phelps, "The Dominion of Love," 45. He pejoratively names the traditional view, the "Aristocratic Theory."

45. Young, *Is God a Vegetarian?* 16ff.

46. We have to say supports rather than proves, because of Linzey's acceptance (albeit muted) of higher-critical understanding related to Scripture's development. He insinuates that differing traditions competed for supremacy, thereby making Scripture an inconsistent source of authority. See Linzey, *Christianity and the Rights of Animals*, 41. Phelps is more blunt, stating that Scripture is an "amalgam" of divine inspiration and too frequent human intrusion. Phelps, *The Dominion of Love*, 24.

To Western Christians, reared with the traditional understanding of humanity's place in the universe, the CAR claim can seem nothing less than absurd.[47] However, the CAR argument is quite ingenious because, like a gestalt drawing, they are asking us to look at the data from a different vantage point so that we can allow ourselves "to see" the different picture that emerges.[48] Young suggests that the hermeneutical key to properly understand humanity's role in creation rests with Genesis 1:29–30, which says the Garden's first residents were vegetarians.[49] CAR activists draw two critical points from this observation. First, the fact that animals and humans ate only plant material signifies that the Garden exhibited harmony between both animals and humans, and by inference the rest of the planet. Young explicitly states that the Garden was a blessed place lacking violence, oppression, hatred, killing, disease, and death.[50] Second, CAR activists believe that Genesis 1:29[51] limits the scope of human dominion granted in Genesis 1:26–8. Since human dominion did not permit the killing of animals, it follows that the scope of human dominion and power over creation was substantially limited.

Linzey looks at the meaning of dominion from a different perspective. He thinks the dominion mandate really turns on determining whether governing requires humanity's needs to be primary (known as the anthropocentric view), or whether governing requires humanity to consider the needs of humans and creation together (non-anthropocentric view).[52]

47. For an interesting history of vegetarianism in the West see Stuart, *The Bloodless Revolution*.

48. Phelps, *The Dominion of Love*, 33–34. Phelps uses the second of the two great commands, (love your neighbor as yourself, which for him includes the "weaker children" known as animals, 48, as the lens through which all Scripture should be evaluated. Passages that cannot be reinterpreted through this lens are set aside as the result of "noise" during the transmission of inspiration, 83.

49. Young, *Is God a Vegetarian?* 15–16.

50. Support for this beatific view of the Garden is buttressed by appeals to Isaiah 51:3; Ez 36:35 and Rev 21–22.

51. Linzey, *Christianity and the Rights of Animals*, 26; Linzey, *Animal Gospel*, 36.

52. Linzey is not alone in his concern. Christian environmental scientist Richard T. Wright observes that Christians (not involved with the animal rights controversy) hold opposing views on human-environment relations. Some believe that the earth was made for man and it was intended by God to serve human needs. Others contend that the earth is not to be a slave to serve man's desires. Humans are to care for the earth as one cares for a garden. Wright notes that even the motivations behind the two views differ. The former believe that humans should protect the earth because it is important to their needs, a

Linzey supports the second and softened understanding of dominion by encouraging readers to move beyond the meaning of the word *radah* (dominion) and consider the wider context. He rejects the interpretation of *radah* as despotism, saying it is better understood as limited rulership.[53] Another writer suggested that the KJV's[54] translation of *radah* as "dominion" helped distort the word's true meaning as "rule", "govern", or "have authority", adding that the term's use with governments ruling their citizens suggests that *radah* should be understood as ruling for the benefit of one's subjects, not one's enrichment.[55] CAR activists believe Genesis 2:15 limits the scope of human dominion, noting that it tells us that Adam and Eve were to be servants because they were the only species ordered to tend the garden.[56] Activists argue that this assignment means that human rule was not to be self-centered and separated from creation, but connected to creation in altruistic service of other creatures in our service of God.[57] We, like Adam and Eve, were to be tending God's garden, God's way. The issue is not whether we have power, for as Linzey says, we do have power. The issue is, How shall we use that power? Humanity should use its power to serve the animal creation as a servant-king, where we serve not equally in terms of animals, but actually sacrificially in their favor. Thus Biblical dominion, properly understood, cannot sanction humanity's present behavior of eating animal flesh, destroying wildlife habitat, and inflicting suffering upon animals.[58]

Lest one think that the CAR reassessment of Genesis is significantly out of the mainstream, it should be noted that other Christians agree that

---

sort of indirect moral responsibility. The latter says that since creation is to glorify god, then God must value creation on its own right (otherwise why would He call it Good?). To value creation as creation is not a form of idolatry but rather reflects mankind's stewardship responsibility to treat God's property well. Wright, "Tearing Down the Green: Environmental Backlash in the Evangelical Sub-Culture," Np. Parentheses mine.

53. Linzey, *Christianity and the Rights of Animals*, 25ff.

54. *The Holy Bible*, the King James Version of 1611.

55. Phelps, *The Dominion of Love*, 51. Phelps, although not technically a Christian Animal Rights Activist, is cited because his book contains an endorsement from Andrew Linzey which says, ". . . *The Dominion of Love* is an insightful, judicious, and inspiring contribution . . ."

56. Linzey, *Animal Gospel*, 38.

57. Alexander, "Feeding the Hungry and Protecting the Environment," 96

58. Linzey, *Animal Gospel*, 40. See also Linzey, *Animal Theology*, ix., where Linzey says that animal abuse includes killing animals for food and sport hunting.

our dominion should be understood in more egalitarian terms.[59] Philip Schafran claims that dominion should not be seen as domination because creation was good and it lacked anything that would oppose humanity and therefore did not need to be subdued. He translates "rule" and "subdue" as "mastery" and "settle" respectively. He understands Genesis more in terms of egalitarian notions of joint participation with creation, rather than our being monarchial rulers over creation. If those arguments lacked sufficient power to convince, Schafran appeals to Psalm 104 to provide proper hermeneutical balance to temper any understanding that humans have an "exalted position" in the world.[60] He observes that Psalm 104 tells us that God is king over creation, while humanity is just part of the natural order, as demonstrated by the paralleling of humanity with the lions.

Third, CAR activists contend that our dominion must be understood in the context of our being made in the image of God.[61] They argue that the "image of God" (Gen 1:26) statement does not entail the ontological inferiority of animals but should be interpreted as referring to humanity's sense of morality, that we should mirror God's holiness and justice. Linzey opines that Christianity's long love affair with anthropocentrism stems from ". . . an exaggerated interpretation . . . of Genesis 2 . . . ."[62] He argues that while Scripture speaks of humanity's special role, it also speaks of the many commonalties humans have with animals.[63]

Several arguments are presented to support a non-ontological understanding of humanity as an expression of God's image. First, Genesis tells us that animals and humans share a common creator. Humanity is a creature of God just like the animals, and this reality makes us fellow creatures. All of us were created for Christ (Col 1:16).[64] Humans and animals partake of life that belongs to and results from the spirit (*ruach*) of God, as demonstrated by the word *nephesh* (soul) which underscores

59. DeWitt demonstrates this tendency in his excessive emphasis on Genesis 2:15. DeWitt, *Caring for Creation*, 31–32, 43–47. See also Carruthers, "Farming in Crisis and the Voice of Silence—a Response to David Atkinson," 59–64.

60. Schafran, "Is Mankind the Measure?" 92.

61. Linzey, *Christianity and the Rights of Animals*, 25–26.

62. Andrew Linzey, *Christianity and the Rights of Animals*, 55.

63. Linzey and Cohn-Sherbok, *After Noah*, 21–22. Linzey and Cohn-Sherbok make these argument which are summarized here. This writer has chosen to place these points under the rubric of covenant, rather than tacking it on as an additional point, because of Linzey's earlier published statements.

64. Ibid., 55.

this shared reality (cf. Gen 6:17).[65] Mankind's creation was no more special than that of the animals, since both were formed out of the ground (Genesis 2:19), and we share the same blessing as animals, namely to be fruitful and multiply (Gen 1:22, 28).[66] Therefore, it is illegitimate to argue that animals were made just for human use.[67] Second, animals have their own place in creation. Humanity does not have a right to the whole world, nor does the world belong to humanity. Third, God placed animals in relationship to humans as seen in their being created on the same day. Linzey, though recognizing the symbolic nature of naming as exhibiting authority, mitigates its authoritarian implication by suggesting that Adam's naming of animals expressed "a profound relationship and kinship."[68] Fourth, animals are under humanity's care because humanity is commanded to care for the earth in accordance to God's will. On the basis of Genesis 1:29 and 9:3, Linzey proffers that God's original plan for planet-wide vegetarianism required humanity's rule to be servant-based and non-violent. The first couple's dominion was to consist of tending the Garden for not only the benefit of humans but for the benefit of the animal creation as well. Animals and humanity were to live in peaceful and mutual harmony. Fifth, Sabbath being the day God rested demonstrates that God, not humanity, is the goal of creation.[69]

Linzey says creation has value irrespective of human interests; it has value in and of itself.[70] This value stems from its relationship to God, not mankind. Linzey clearly is walking a tightrope here. He wants to affirm that humans stand in special proximity to God, but does not want to raise human significance so as to deny interconnectedness with broader creation and thereby, justify humanity's use of animals. The Fall initiated the appearance of violence, which then grew in depth and scope until God ultimately had to destroy the planet with water.[71] Our failure to properly understand dominion, Hyland says, has caused us to damage the very environment we need to have rule over.

65. Ibid., 30.

66. Ibid., 31. These comments are echoed by Hyland, *God's Covenant with Animals*, 16–19.

67. Hyland, *God's Covenant with Animals*, 14f.

68. Linzey and Cohn-Sherbok, *After Noah*, 21.

69. Ibid., 21.

70. Linzey, *Animal Rights*, 16–17.

71. Hyland, *God's Covenant with Animals*, 18–19.

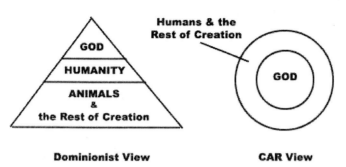

Fig 1. Dominionist vs. CAR View of Human Animal Relations

All diagrams are simplistic. However, these images express the key contrast between the Dominionist and the CAR view of humanity's relationship to the world. Domionists see humans as separate and over animals; CAR activists see humas and animals as fellow citizens under God.

In any event, CAR activists' central concern lay with their belief that humanity has a duty to value creation for itself and not just for its instrumental or utilitarian value for serving humanity's interests.[72] Linzey wants us to see animals not as solely given to humans in an exclusivist instrumental sense, but rather as including the final cause of their existence being for God.[73] Linzey strenuously asserts that the value of animals to us and their value to God are two completely separate issues, for God alone is the fount of their significance.[74]

Argument from the Fall & Noah Narratives

Christian animal rights activists link the Fall and Noah narratives in order to explain why humans and beasts no longer live in harmony.[75] Their approach to the Fall narrative is primarily theological rather than exegetical, as their interest lay only in the broad sweeps of the narrative than in the gritty details. They identify three significant elements in the Fall account that explain how violence occurred between humanity and animals, and

72. Linzey, *Animal Rights*, 16–17.

73. Linzey and Cohn-Sherbok, *After Noah*, 121.

74. Linzey, *Animal Gospel*, 37.

75. Linzey, *Animal Theology*, 81; Young, *Is God a Vegetarian?* 57.

thereby broke the divinely willed harmony in the cosmos.[76] First, the Fall broke relational harmony, not just between God and humanity and between humanity itself, but also between humanity and the entire order of creation. They specifically cite the conflict between the woman and the serpent to illustrate the loss of harmony between humanity and animals (Gen 3:15). This relational breach means that creation is now no longer unambiguously good in God's view. Second, creation, although still valuable, became devalued (Gen 3:17). The power God gave to creation for good and service to Him is now turned against creation itself through violence. CAR activists observe that it was the violence within creation that caused God to destroy the earth in the flood.[77] Humanity is singled out for special rebuke because only humans have the ability to choose their behavior. Young takes a slightly different view and suggests that human meat eating was involved in the meaning of violence (see Gen 6:11–12 in parallel with Lk 17:27). He even goes so far as to proffer that animals became corrupted by becoming carnivores (Gen 6:12//6:17).[78] This violence brings us to a third point, namely that the Fall led to despair, and explains Paul's comments that creation now groans as in travail (Rom 8:20–21).[79]

As with the Creation accounts, CAR activists believe a contextual understanding of the Noahic accounts actually supports an animal rights view. The ark demonstrated God's concern for the animal creation in that He provided a way for land animals to survive the deluge. They also find support for their view of humanity as animal protector by Noah's construction of the ark.[80] Finally, they see commonality between humans and animals affirmed in God making a covenant with both animals and humans, not just humans alone (Gen 9:9–10).

It should come as no surprise that Linzey and other CAR activists understand God's grant of permission to eat animal flesh as condescen-

---

76. Cf. Murray, *The Cosmic Covenant*. Murray proffers a view that ancient Near East culture believed that humanity was to maintain stability in the cosmos by obedience and cultic ritual. Instability was identified by social and environmental chaos.

77. Hyland, *God's Covenant with Animals*, 89–90. He links human and animal violence together.

78. Young, *Is God a Vegetarian?* 43–44; Anderson, *From Creation to New Creation*, 143. Anderson also suggests predation may be in view here.

79. Linzey, *Christianity and the Rights of Animals*, 11–14.

80. Linzey and Cohn-Sherbok, *After Noah*, 76. It says, "We know so well the saga of Noah and his ark that we frequently fail to grasp its radical, ecological message that all life exists in a covenanted relationship guaranteed by God." Young, *Is God a Vegetarian?* 47.

sion rather than a behavioral recommendation. CAR activists do not believe Genesis 9:3ff. supports a view that God happily granted mankind the right to kill animals. The Noahic covenant's removal of the prohibition against meat (Gen 9:3), in their view, demonstrated God's permissiveness to humanity's violent nature,[81] or perhaps out of necessity after the flood damaged earth. Linzey interprets the prohibition against eating blood as signifying that God owned the life and, therefore, affirming its value (Gen 9:4).[82] The life of the animal belonged to Him, and animal killers were accountable to God for their actions. Phelps adopts a more rabbinical reading, suggesting that the command against eating blood was God's way of reminding humans that killing animals was shameful.[83]

Interpreting the Noahic covenant as God's condescension to human violence becomes the lens by which CAR activists interpret all later passages. Scriptures that speak of animal and human relations are then identified as being pro-animal or anti-animal on the basis of how they fare when viewed through the Noahic Covenant. Linzey uses this hermeneutical lens to great effect, as it helps him to defuse objections before they develop too much momentum. This approach is quite ingenious. If God only conceded humanity the ability to eat meat, then it should be no surprise to see laws suggesting that God wanted to mitigate the inherent violence that humans would inflict on His animal creation. For example, Linzey sees Scripture supporting the notion that God cares for animal wellbeing and enshrined it covenantal language as seen in the Noahic covenant (Gen 9:15). Linzey does not delve deeply into the exegesis of these passages, but rather cites them in various circumstances.

Evaluation of the Argument from the Covenant of Creation and the Fall

As noted in chapter 1, the question of humanity's ideal relationship to animals is part of the larger question of our relationship to the earth/nature/environment. CAR activists oppose the Dominionist view on account of its mechanistic, monarchial, and utilitarian worldview of Genesis

---

81. Young, *Is God a Vegetarian?* 127f. Hyland says that God's comment about humanity eating animals was simply a statement of fact as in humans will kill animals rather than an instance of God granting permission or His blessing to our consumption of animals. Hyland, *God's Covenant with Animals*, 25–26.

82. See also Young, *Is God a Vegetarian?* 60ff. Young says the ban on blood also shows that human dominion was limited, and that God saw animal life as an important matter.

83. Phelps, *The Dominion of Love*, 99.

that justifies treating the world as an object to be used and controlled. In contrast, CAR activists believe that humans should view the world as having intrinsic value (versus utilitarian value), working in compassionate harmony with nature.[84] At this point, the question of whether or not the CAR activists have accurately portrayed the Church's understanding of dominion will be set aside.[85] Instead, I will investigate the central issue of whether the CAR activists have properly characterized Scriptural teaching about human-animal relations as teaching humans to refrain from lethal behavior toward animals.

Linzey and others make a number of points to which all Evangelicals should willingly concede. First, all should hold that the early chapters of Genesis are foundational for a Christian environmental doctrine. The creation account should shape and guide our actions and behavior toward the wider non-Christian world.[86] Second, all Christians should agree that humanity's dominion ought to be circumscribed by God's plan for the planet. Humanity's use of the planet's resources ought to satisfy human needs in the service of God (1 Cor 10:23—11:1). Whatever the precise meaning of humanity's being made in God's image, all parties hold that humans were God's functional representatives to the earth, as this notion was commonly understood in both Egypt and in Mesopotamia.[87] This functional representation also included a moral aspect, in that humans

84. At its foundation, the debate rests on one's model of proper human-nature relations. Categorization of the various models is difficult, but two will be presented to facilitate an understanding of the issues in the controversy. One scheme identifies three types of human-nature relationships: A. man subjugated to nature, B. man in harmony with nature, and C. man exercising mastery over nature Adapted from Brown, *The Ethos of the Cosmos*, 15. Brown cited Ronald Simkins' nature to culture models. A value-laden model recognizes: 1. nature is only valuable because of its usefulness to humans, 2. nature is equal in value as humans, and 3. nature has intrinsic value as nature because God made it. Bube, "Do Biblical Models Need to Be Replaced in Order to Deal Effectively with Environmental Issues?" 90. It would be fair to say that CAR activists fall under categories B, 2, and 3, and are in opposition to views C and 1.

85. I think a strong case could be made that the CAR activists have conflated human actions with Church approval, and have therefore made the Church's position into a straw man.

86. Haas, "Creational Ethics Is Public Ethics," 2.

87. Walvoord and Zuck, *Dallas Theological Seminary: The Bible Knowledge Commentary*, 1:29; Walton, *Ancient near Eastern Thought and the Old Testament*, 194–95.

were to represent God's qualities as a relational being.[88] CAR activists are also correct that less ontological significance should be placed on God breathing the breath of life into humans because in Egypt, all sentient life received their vitality from the "breath of god."[89] Nor does a semantic review of *nephesh* (soul) provide any support for ontologically separating humans from animals, because both animals and humans share in *nephesh*.[90] CAR activists are certainly correct in their observation that humans and animals share many commonalties.[91] Both are commanded to reproduce and fill the earth.[92] Both are sustained by the earth and share the breath of life. Both are created by God, and both are indeed good and part of the overall goodness of Creation.

What is less certain, however, is the CAR activists' claim that Genesis does not allow humanity's specialness to justify its killing and/or eating of animals. Put another way, "Is it true that whenever humans kill animals, a disruption in cosmic harmony has taken place?" As will be shown, the evidence suggests that CAR activists have overstated the extent and significance of their contention that God does not wish that humans kill animals. For it appears that Genesis does ground humanity's dominion over animals in our ontological or functional[93] status as being created in God's image. Additionally, it will be demonstrated that CAR activists have ignored evidence that supports a different morality between animals and humans.[94]

Our evaluation will consider the CAR activists' arguments from two perspectives, structurally and lexically. At the structural level, CAR activists have sought to diminish humanity's standing in relation to other creatures because of their desire to eliminate the arguments that justify

88. Walton, *Ancient near Eastern Thought and the Old Testament*, 221.

89. Ibid., 206.

90. Ibid., 213–14. Walton argues that *nephesh* is not something humans have but something that humans are.

91. Linzey, *Animal Theology*, 38. Linzey says he is nervous with the idea that humans have divinely appointed power over animals.

92. It is true that the land animals did not receive a reproductive blessing (cf. Gen 1:22,8). However, this writer will concede this point to the CAR.

93. The various theories of the nature of the image of God in humanity can be categorized as structural, relational, and functional. See Ware, "Male and Female Complimentarity and the Image of God," 15–16.

94. CAR activists do not deny that humans are in a different moral category from animals. They just deny that humanity has the moral authority to kill animals, contending that humans must serve animals. See Linzey and Cohn-Sherbok, *After Noah*, 21.

humanity's killing of animals. I will investigate the scripture to determine if it can support a greater equality between humanity and animals, as the CAR activists assert. Later, I will address the CAR activists' understanding of the terms "image of God" and "subdue and rule", to uncover whether their meaning can be softened as the CAR activists claim.

CAR activists endeavored to blunt the observation that humans were the goal of creation by arguing that the goal of creation was not humanity but the harmony, peace, and rest of Sabbath.[95] Sabbath was the day that God rested, not humanity and certainly not the animals. If Sabbath was the goal rather than the culmination of God's activity in creating humanity, then why did God bother to create in the first place? Nothing could be more harmonious and peaceful than the Trinity remaining in union and bliss for eternity. Furthermore, if Sabbath as the goal somehow diminishes humanity's standing in creation, then why did God call His work "very good" after the creation of humanity rather than waiting until day seven?[96] If CAR activists intend to suggest that the goal of creation was the glory of God, then there is no debate.[97] Although Sabbath may be better translated as "harmony" more than "rest"[98] (Genesis 1—2), the fact remains that we must still determine the character of humanity's role in creation.

Biblical scholarship has demonstrated that Scripture does present its own cosmology, and unfortunately for CAR activists, the cosmology does not support a more democratic view of animal-human relations. Baker has argued that Genesis (and other Scriptures) presents humans as the *"pinnacle of creation."*[99] He observed that Genesis 1 moves to a crescendo, with humans as the end point. Creation is good through the creation of animals but God reserves his higher praise of "very good" after creating

95. Linzey and Cohn-Sherbok, *After Noah*, 20. Argument possibly gleaned from Moltmann, *God in Creation*, 197.

96. Cf. John 5:17

97. Thanks for this idea goes to personal comments by Mark D. Mathewson, "Dissertation Review."

98. Ross suggests that "cease" and notes that God is enjoying and celebrating His accomplishment. To my thinking this could be understood as supporting the notion of interpreting Sabbath as harmony. Ross, *Creation & Blessing*, 113–14.

99. Ross, *Creation & Blessing*, 112–13; Baker, *In the Image of God*, 12 (italics his). What follows is a listing of Baker's argument found on pages 12–17. Interestingly, Patton says that humans are the *telos* of the primordial birthing but says the question of whether creation was made for humans is still unanswered. Patton, "He Who Sits in the Heavens Laughs," 406.

humans (Gen 1:31). Stated differently, creation only became complete or finished after God made Adam and Eve. One cannot simply claim that this reading flows from an Aristotelian/Thomistic[100] bias, because Psalm 8 suggests a similar hierarchal perspective years before Aristotle or Aquinas. William P. Brown, in his book, *The Ethos of the Cosmos*,[101] explores in great detail Biblical testimony about creation and how its cosmology informed Israel's ethics. He argues that the way the cosmos is structured says something significant about how a community is to be shaped.[102] Although his use of source criticism inhibited his ability to develop an overarching environmental moral rubric,[103] Brown determined that the blessing God gave to humans should be distinguished from that given to the animals because God's blessing of humans integrated procreation and rule. While humans are still connected to the earth, they work *in* creation in order for creation to work *for* them (italics his).[104] Brown does agree with the CAR activist view that humanity's original dominion was bloodless. However, he does modify the more negative CAR assertion on the Noahic covenant by saying that it was not just a concessionary evil, but that it was also a necessary one.[105]

It is instructive to contrast Israel's cosmology with that of her neighbors to see if any further insights on the position of humans in relation to the broader creation can be observed. Here again, the CAR view of diminishing human standing suffers. David Livingston compared the viewpoints of both Egyptian and Mesopotamian creation stories to the Bible's

---

100. In the Medieval ages, Thomas Aquinas strongly supported the notion that humanity's power over animals was divinely decreed and demonstrable by natural reason. As can be expected, Aquinas finds scriptural support for mankind's divinely placed superiority over animals in Genesis 1:26. He claimed that human rule over the animal creation was part of God's original plan, and that the Fall disrupted the quality of animal obedience to mankind. *Summa*, Question 96, Article 1. In other words, animal rebellion to human authority was one of the punishments placed on mankind on account of the Fall. Aquinas does not claim that Adam and Eve ate meat before the Fall, for he believed that humanity was nourished by the "Trees of Paradise." However, he continued, that while humans may not have had bodily need of animals prior to the Fall, they did need to obtain "experimental knowledge" of their natures (reply to objection 3).

101. Brown, *The Ethos of the Cosmos*.

102. Ibid., 10–11.

103. Ibid., 382.

104. Ibid. 43–45.

105. Ibid., 45, 56, and footnote 62.

and summarized his findings. The portion relevant for our purposes has been excerpted in the following table.[106]

Figure 2. Biblical and Ancient Near-East Creation Accounts[107]	
Biblical Creation Account	**Non-Biblical Creation Accounts**
4. Humans to have dominion over earth. Gen. 1:26–29 (Ps 8:6, 115:16, Heb 2:8, 9) Sublime account of first man and wife, created by and subject to Yahweh.	4. Humans to serve the "gods" (other men)—to "feed" them. Sex, violence, physical strength emphasized.

The critical point to be gleaned here is that in the Biblical narrative, the overall tone is one of earth serving humanity rather than humanity serving others. The notion that Adam and Eve were to be worrying about the dietary needs of animals is just foreign to the passage. If Israel needed to distinguish her beliefs from pagan views about the relationship between humans and animals, she could have clearly done so. That she did not supports the Dominionist view of humanity's role in the earth. Note that Israel did not portray animals as emblematic of powerful forces (shamaci theurgy), or identify them with gods (Egyptian theology) or combine animals into spiritual-human-animal gods (Hinduism).[108] Alexander Heidel, commenting on the Mesopotamian creation accounts, concurs. He investigated the manner in which the *Enuma Elish* and the Scripture described mankind's creation and role. He observed that both accounts have the creation of humans as the culmination of the creative activity of the divine figures. In terms of Genesis, Heidel says that the creation of humanity is the story's culminating point. However, Heidel cited one key difference, namely humanity's role.[109] In the Babylonian account, humans were created to serve the gods in the sense of being a breadwin-

106. Livingston, "Creation Stories of the Ancient near East," 86.

107. For more details on Egyptian, Mesopotamian, and Israelite views on dominion see Manahan, "A Re-Examination of the Cultural Mandate," 143–207. On page 207, Manahan notes that biblical and Mesopotamian literature differ on humanity's place in the cosmos.

108. Patton, "He Who Sits in the Heavens Laughs," 404–5.

109. Heidel, *The Babylonian Genesis*, 119–20, 127.

ner for them (*Enuma Elish* Tablet VI:123–131). Although humans had some sense of dominion in that they could build temples, Heidel stated that the concept was poorly described in comparison with Genesis 1–2. Note, however, that Heidel overstated this contrast; when commenting on 2:15 he said, "But this work obviously was in his own interest; the Lord God did not ask for any returns."[110] While true in that God does not need humanity's help to survive, God did require human obedience and implicitly its worship.

We have seen that CAR activists believe that humans should refrain from any activity that involves killing or eating animals. But their interpretation overlooks a third option, namely that a vegetarian diet (Gen 1:30) does not address the issue of whether Adam and Eve had the moral authority to kill animals.[111] Killing an animal is a separate act from eating it. Furthermore, it is a major leap to move from the idea that Adam and Eve were not to kill or eat an animal to the notion that they were to serve animals. At issue here is the ideals held by the interpreter. Ultimately, one has to decide whether to let the text guide us, or whether we guide the text.[112]

A lexical analysis of Genesis reveals that the nature of humanity's role in creation was more complex than what CAR activists have stated. First, humanity has a unique relationship towards God and the animal kingdom that supports a hierarchical view of humanity's rule over the animal creation. Note how the writer tells the creation story from the assumption that domesticated animals (Gen 2:19,20)[113] are perfectly normal and not a negative representation of humanity's sinful domination of nature (Gen 1:24–5).[114] Genesis 2:18–20 goes even further by emphatically asserting that animals were helpers to humanity.[115] The point being, while the ani-

110. Heidel, *The Babylonian Genesis*, 121.

111. Von Rad, *Genesis*, 61. Von Rad makes a similar leap, turning a prohibition against eating into a prohibition against killing.

112. Snoke, "Why Were Dangerous Animals Created?" 122–23. Snoke makes a similar comment on the issue of whether animal death is bad or not.

113. The juxtaposition of *bahamot* (animals) and *hayah shadah* (beasts of the field) in Genesis 2:19, 20, 3:14,and others supports the translation of the NASB of *bahamot* as cattle (domesticated animals) and over against beasts of the field meaning wildlife. See also Koehler et al., *The Hebrew and Aramaic Lexicon of the Old Testament*, Entry 1089.

114. Tucker, "Rain on a Land Where No One Lives," 10. Tucker explains that Hebrew text recognizes distinctions between animals, distinctions based upon whether they were domesticated or not.

115. Ibid.

mals were deemed not suitable for the role of a mate, they were still helpers for humans, albeit at a lower significance. The assumption is that there is a hierarchal view of creation in terms of rule, not just moral capability, a view reaffirmed by Adam's naming the animals.[116] Further, Genesis 1:30 can be understood as God taking responsibility for the care of wild animals off humanity's shoulders because they could feed themselves.[117]

The writer of Genesis also suggests a hierarchy of creation by the way creatures are described in their creation. God spoke inanimate objects into existence, but he formed the land creatures. Even here, however, the human creation was qualitatively different from that of animals. Genesis 2:7 specifically tells us that God breathed the 'breath of life' into Adam. There is also greater intimacy involved in the narration of Adam's creation as compared to that of the animals. Both creatures were created out of the ground, but the Bible only mentions that humans were 'formed' out of the dust of the ground.[118] In fact, Linzey has stretched the biblical evidence to suggest that we are essentially bigger brothers to the animals.[119] He overlooked how Genesis provides us with a number of distinctions between animals and humans, and that these are not just differences in number but differences in kind.

Genesis treats humans as special because only they carry the moniker of being made in the image of God. Consider Genesis 1:26. Then God said,

> Let Us make man in Our image, according to Our likeness; and let them rule over the fish of the sea and over the birds of the sky and over the cattle and over all the earth, and over every creeping thing that creeps on the earth (NASB).[120]

116. Patton, "He Who Sits in the Heavens Laughs," 432. Patton correctly says that God using His surrogate to name the animals means that He had interest in animals. But she does not negate human authority, as she notes that through naming animals, Adam assumed God's role to them. Murray, *The Cosmic Covenant*, 100. He says that Adam's naming exhibited the kingly quality of wisdom. See also Ware, who explains that the naming of animals demonstrates that humanity's authority over animals derived from God. Ware, "Male and Female Complimentarity and the Image of God," 17.

117. Cf. Calvin, *Commentaries on the First Book of Moses Called Genesis*, Commentary on Genesis 1:30. *hayyah* Koehler et al., *The Hebrew and Aramaic Lexicon of the Old Testament*, Entry 2817. definition 1.

118. Brown observed the subtle way the text distinguished humans from animals by humans being made from fine soil. Brown, *The Ethos of the Cosmos*, 137–38.

119. Linzey, *Christianity and the Rights of Animals*, 46.

120. *NASB*. All Biblical quotes will be from the NASB unless noted.

The verse begins with some cryptic words[121] about humans being made in the image of God. The more classic phrase, "in the image of God," is used in the following verse.[122] This phrase occurs only one more time in the O.T. (Gen 9:6; The N.T. has 1 Cor 11:7 & Jms 3:9). In all contexts, the phrase is used to emphasize the importance of humans.[123] CAR activists neglect to wrestle with the significance of humans being made in the image of God. Clearly Genesis sees humans as significantly more than animals. At no time does Scripture identify animals as being "creatures made in the image of God." (cf. Psa. 8). Second, God developed a relationship with humanity on a personal and individual level as well as corporate, but He never established individual, interactive, and communicative relationships with animals.[124] Any argument that appeals to the laconic nature of O.T. narrative as a viable reason for the lack of God-animal relationship[125] would have to explain how out of nearly 230 Greek and Hebrew words for animals, the Bible, both Old and New Testaments, does not record pet names and instead speaks of animals in terms of species or kinds rather than as individuals.[126] The silence argument fails to convince, given the lack of God-animal relationships in the rest of Scripture.

In light of the diversity of concepts expressed in Genesis about mankind's uniqueness, it comes as little surprise that theologians have debated

---

121. *Zlm* "image" and *dmut* "likeness." While they appear to be references to physical shape it is obvious that something else is meant here.

122. These comments should be taken as mere truism. Even a brief search of any theological library will present a researcher with a wealth of writing trying to explain the meaning of the phrase "image of God."

123. A cursory look at the lexicon entry for "image" supports this view. Koehler et al., *The Hebrew and Aramaic Lexicon of the Old Testament*, Entry 8011. See also Brueggemann, *Genesis*, 83.

124. Busell, *A Systematic Theology of the Christian Religion*, 139. He says that humanity being created in the image of God (not in the image of the beast) means that humans were created for fellowship with God.

125. This writer does not deny that God speaks to animals or that God is detached from animals. Certainly Scripture shows that God has ordered animals to perform actions (1 Kgs 17:14; Rev 19:17) and provides for them (Ps 104). But nowhere in Scripture does it show that God maintains an extended communicative relationship with animals on an individualized basis.

126. Cansdale, *All the Animals of the Bible Lands*, 13. It should also be noted that the point being made is not that the Bible never speaks of animals as an individual or specifically (cf. Balaam's donkey), but rather the nature of that singularity does not suggest animals are so special that humans should not kill or utilize them.

about what aspects actually constitute humanity being made in God's image. Does the meaning of God's image support what Dominionists wish it would, namely an ontological justification for humanity's killing and eating of animals? Baker provides five theories or models employed to describe the nature of God's image in humans:[127] 1. Image as inner quality; 2. Image as God-human relationship; 3. Image as dominion; 4. Image as God's representative; and 5. Image as sonship.

Image as inner quality view argues that there is something about humans which animals lack. This inner quality must correspond, albeit in an analogous way, with God's nature. Historically, this view has argued for rationality, spirituality and the like as what separates humans from animals and joins us with God. Image, according to the God-human relationship view, suggests that image ". . . is not in the similarity between the subject (God) and His reflection, but in what the subject wants the mirror to reflect."[128] Barth extended Emil Brunner's notion of the God-man relationship to that which occurs between man and woman. Leonard Verduin understood image as dominion. This interpretation focused on the immediate context of Genesis 1:26, where after the statement regarding God's image, humans were given authority over creation. Image, therefore, is one characterized by power over something, and the inherent ability to execute that power. Image as God's representative, espoused by G.C. Berkouwer, contends that image entails holiness, for humans are to be holy as God is holy (Lev 11:45; Mt 5:48; Col 1:15; 3:10). H.D. McDonald argues that all the aforementioned ideas can be subsumed under the heading of sonship. He notes that sonship language was used with Adam (Lk 3:38) presenting an interesting framework to understand Christ and the significance of Adam's power. Baker argues that all of the evidence is best explained by the inner quality argument. He explains that the dominion understanding of image fails because it confuses the effect with the cause. Although intrigued with the relationship argument, Baker says we can have a relationship because the moral and intellectual qualities within us permit such a relationship. Sonship and relationship views, relying on elements of inner qualities, are really confusing effects with causes.

Moises Silva has persuasively argued that our difficulty understanding the phrase "What is this image?" stems from the question being rephrased

---

127. Baker, *In the Image of God*, 36–40. The explanations of the following theories are Baker's.

128. Ibid., 37.

as "What is the image of God *in* man?" (italics his).[129] He says it is not too far off the mark to understand that God's image in humanity must be understood in the totality of what it means to be human. He points to the real possibility that what we call anthropomorphisms such as those found in Psalm 94:8–9, could actually be re-characterized as theomorphisms.[130] Silva recognizes, however, the limits of this sort of argument because he concedes that animals also have eyes and ears. So he probes deeper and asks if Genesis 1 and 2 provide any contextual clues to help us understand what it meant when it spoke of the image of God. Silva acknowledges that humans have dominion as only humans till the earth. But he does not believe that image is semantically equivalent to dominion. Rather we should recognize that our image gives us the ability to have dominion. The solution for Silva lies in language, as communication is the key element of how God's image is manifest in humans. He does not deny that animals communicate, and even points to research showing how much communication can occur among primates. Nevertheless, he claims that animals lack the unbridled breadth of communication available to humans. He says it was Adam's communication and language ability that put his naming of the animals into proper context. Silva explains that Adam could not rule the earth unless he understood it. He needed to organize what he saw, and language helped him accomplish that. Silva then provides a quick summary of language, that it is: 1. intrinsic to God's being, 2. evidence for Adam and Eve as distinctive creatures made in God's image, and 3. connected to Adam and Eve's rule over creation.[131] Silva continues and provides further evidence for the importance of language by noting its connection to sin, Tower of Babel, and the many passages condemning falsehood and God's redemption by sending His Word, Jesus.

Baker finds much significance in the way humans are described, namely being made in the image and likeness of God (Gen 1:26). Humanity holds a superior position over the animal and plant kingdoms. Our dominion is not to destroy or devastate, but rather to utilize for our own needs and for God's glory. Turning to Genesis 2, Baker argues that humans are a material masterpiece. God formed humans and then imbued them with the breath of life that also exists in animals. In Adam's

129. Silva, "God, Language and Scripture: Reading the Bible in the Light of General Linguistics," 205.

130. Ibid., 206.

131. Ibid., 206–7 and footnotes.

naming of the animals, Baker finds evidence to support the essential rationality of mankind. God's command for Adam to name the animals also stood as an object lesson to drive home the point that humans are unlike the animals. Only a woman is suitable for man (Gen 2:20–5). Her suitability is underscored by: a. she comes from man, b. she is a helper of his kind, and c. she can unite with Adam as one flesh, connoting their sexual compatibility. Next, their moral innocence suggests a moral aspect to God's image. Finally, humans are creatures of immense value as stated in Gen 9:6, as shown in that there is no death penalty for killing animals (see also Psa 8; Eccl 7:29; Rom 9:21; 1 Cor 11:9; 1 Tim 2:13).

Finally, we have the issue of the nature of humanity's dominion. Even if we have proven that humans are ontologically different than animals, we have not determined whether this ontological distinction justifies human use of animals. Brueggemann says

> . . . the task of 'dominion' does not have to do with exploitation and abuse. It has to do with securing the well-being of every other creature and bringing the promise of each to full fruition. (In contrast, Ezek. 34:1–6 offers a caricature of the human shepherd who has misused the imperative of the creator.).[132]

Brueggemann continues and says that humans are to work for creation's interests, and even be like Christ in "laying down their lives for the sheep."[133] Scholars have endeavored to soften the harshness of dominion by either reducing the scope of human rule or the severity of that rule. Christians, including Evangelicals, have not been immune to these idelogical currents.[134] Smarting from Lynn White Jr.'s stinging indictment of Christianity,[135] Christians revisited Scripture to reassess their own understanding con-

132. Brueggemann, *Genesis*, 32–33.

133. Ibid., Wood et al., "Christian Environmentalism: Cosmos, Community, and Place," 3. They say that "God's desire for human beings to flourish is subsumed within (but not replaced by) his desire for all of creation to flourish."

134. The author recognizes that his summation here suffers from the weaknesses of generalization. The Church's relationship to environmental issues is not monolithic. See Schafran, "Is Mankind the Measure?" Endnote 1 for a listing of texts related to the subject.

135. White Jr., "The Historical Roots of Our Ecologic Crisis," 1205; Fox, *Toward a Transpersonal Ecology*, 5; Kearns, "Saving the Creation: Christian Environmentalism in the United States," 55; Bouthier, "Religious Leaders Weigh in on Responsibility toward Environment,"Np; Fox, *Toward a Transpersonal Ecology*, 5f. For a critique of White's assessment read Wright, "Responsibility for the Ecological Crisis," 851–53.

cerning its teaching about human-nature relations.[136] They concluded that Scripture did not support the view that humanity was given *carte blanche* power over creation, and was therefore in harmony with the concerns and goals of environmentalists.[137] In light of this finding, Christians began to speak of "stewardship" rather than "dominion" as the appropriate meaning behind God's creation mandate.[138] Stewardship was understood as the utilization of resources wisely and/or at sustainable levels. Christians also began to pursue environmental work with a new sense of calling, seeing their endeavors as part of God's call for creation care.[139] Today several Christian views of the environment have been identified, demonstrating that Christians have started to work on the subject.[140]

Yet, for the most part, the foundational question concerning the extent of human dominion was not raised beyond generalities exhorting Christians not to abuse the earth. Christians, and even the larger secular society, did not recognize that the suffering inflicted on non-human sentient life by human activities was a problem that needed consideration, let alone discussion. Christians believed that God granted humans the moral right to use all of the earth's resources, including minerals, plants, and animals, as long as they were extracted in an environmentally appropriate manner. Environmentally appropriate extraction was understood to mean sustainable acquisition, with due concern for the protection of individual human health and safety, and the collective continuance of plant and animals as species.[141] Christians, and the public at large, did not

136. See Schaeffer, *Pollution and the Death of Man*, 1:57–69. Schaeffer reprinted White's article. Davis,"Ecological 'Blind Spots,'" 274. Davis says that the renewed evangelical interest in the environment began in 1970.

137. Evangelicals have gone out of their way to reject any understanding of dominion as exploitation even though they neglect to explain in concrete ways what exploitation actually looks like. See Bube,"Do Biblical Models Need to Be Replaced in Order to Deal Effectively with Environmental Issues?" 90; Schafran, "Is Mankind the Measure?" Np. Other examples may be found in references cited elsewhere in this paper.

138. See DeWitt, *Caring for Creation*, 43ff.

139. An example of this can be seen in the recent statement on global warming. Hansen et al., *Evangelicals and Scientists on Global Climate Change*, Np.

140. Kearns, "Saving the Creation: Christian Environmentalism in the United States," 56. Kearns identifies three Christian views as, Christian stewardship ethic, Eco-justice ethic, and Creation spirituality ethic. Ball,"The Use of Ecology in the Evangelical Protestant Response to the Ecological Crisis," 33. Ball identifies four Evangelical ecologic ethics, Wise Use, Anthropocentric Stewardship, Caring Management, and Servanthood Stewardship.

141. Environmentally appropriate extraction from nature is called "Ecological eco-

take up the challenge of the Deep Ecologists. The public still believed that humans belonged at the top of the ecological pyramid.

Tucker says that dominion was given to humans over the animal life on the earth but not over the earth itself. This, he believes, will somehow militate against a despotic rule over the earth. However, a few lines down shows that Genesis 1 clearly establishes a hierarchy. So if humanity can rule the animals, which rule the earth, does it not follow that humanity also rules the earth just as a corporate president rules the janitor at the bottom of the corporate ladder?[142]

CAR activists want to interpret *radah* "to rule" in the sense of serving.[143] Linzey argued that the traditional reading of the word *radah* has been rejected by "scholars" for three reasons. 1. Humans are given control over creation and the power to use it but not given absolute power over it. They cannot have despotic rule. Their authority is to mimic the morality of God. 2. Humanity was to be king in the sense of king in God's service.[144] 3. Humans are commanded to be vegetarian. Thus their power was limited to being vegetarian. Phelps took a somewhat different tack and argued that rulers are expected to rule for the benefit of their subjects. "In saying that we have dominion over nonhuman animals, the author of Genesis is telling us that they are analogous to citizens under our governance."[145]

These are certainly nice sounding words, but are they an accurate reflection of what the Bible wanted to convey when it used the verbs "rule" (*radah*) and "subdue" (*chabash*)? The verb "to rule" occurs 22 times in the Old Testament, and in every case the idea of "authority over" is found with the connotation of authority in the face of opposition. It is also a word never used with animals doing the ruling. Stated simply, *radah* is a term of the power to compel obedience.[146] God empowers humanity

---

nomics" in King and Woodyard, *Liberating Nature*, 6–7.

142. Tucker, "Rain on a Land Where No One Lives," 7.

143. Linzey, *Christianity and the Rights of Animals*, 25f; Linzey, *Animal Theology*, 34.

144. Linzey says that man had authority over animals as designated by the naming of the animals. However, he says, Adam also named Eve so he was meant to live in harmony with the created order. Linzey, *Christianity and the Rights of Animals*, 25f. This writer would agree, but note that Linzey has made a category mistake as Adam never married an animal. So it is very likely that Adam's authority over the animals was of a different order than his authority over his mate.

145. Phelps, *The Dominion of Love*, 51.

146. Keil and Delitzch, *The Pentateuch*, 152, suggest that mankind's original rule was less forceful than after Genesis 9:1–7. Animals served willingly and man had

to rule, *radah* (Qal form), when accompanied by a direct object with a *beyt*, which clearly means to rule in the sense of power to compel behavior.[147] Consider the way the construct is used with Solomon's rule in 1 Kings 4:24 and in 9:23, with the corvee officers (see also Isa 14:2 and Ezek 29:15). It is true that the level of force could vary, as insinuated by adverbs of force and severity found in Ezekiel 34:4.[148] But *radah* still connotes the idea of power over, with the ability to compel. Genesis 1:28 continues this rulership theme. While containing the verb *radah*, it now adds a new verb, *chabash*, "subdue." In every other use in the Old Testament, the word carries the idea of placing another entity in a servant role, again referring to humans only (cf. Mic 7:19 where God will 'subdue' our iniquity).[149] Military usage predominates, and it does so prior to any reference to the Fall.[150] This fact is even more significant when *mashal* (to rule), which occurs in the same context, could have been used (see Gen 1:18).[151] Linzey seems to not understand that Adam and Eve's transgression of God's law is even more egregious because as God commanded[152] them

---

power over creation which was lost after the Fall. Of course the question is why God had to wait till the flood to express the fact that man was to be feared by the animal kingdom. Could it be that God wanted animals to fear Noah and his sons so as to give them a fighting chance to reproduce? Otherwise wouldn't these same animals have been imprinted and thereby tamed by Noah?

147. Koehler et al., *The Hebrew and Aramaic Lexicon of the Old Testament*, Entry 8680.

148. Manahan's observation that the level of force employed must be understood contextually, as the level of opposition varied. Manahan, "A Re-Examination of the Cultural Mandate," 221.

149. Schafran. Endnote #8. Schafran's contention that the word's meaning in Genesis must be understood in a less authoritarian way is a classic example of special pleading.

150. Von Rad, *Genesis*, 60. Von Rad says, "The expressions for the exercise of this dominion are remarkably strong . . ." See also Ross, *Creation & Blessing*, 113. and Oswalt, "*Kabash*," 1:951. Oswalt says that the word in Gen 1:28 implies that creation will not easily do humanity's bidding. Murray, *The Cosmic Covenant*, 99. Murray's comments that *kabash* must be understood in a limited, non-exploitive, and non-arbitrary way does not detract from the point being made here because he still recognizes that it involves taming the earth, even under vegetarian restrictions. See also Manahan's discussion of the verb. Manahan, "A Re-Examination of the Cultural Mandate," 224–26.

151. Culver, "*Mashal* III," 1:534–35. *Mashal* has a much broader range of meaning from dominion to management.

152. Tucker, "Rain on a Land Where No One Lives," 6. Tucker says without argument that Genesis 1:28–29 is not a commandment but a blessing. It is unclear to me that the two points have to be mutually distinct.

to rule the animal kingdom. Linzey assumes there was perfect harmony in the Garden, a harmony of non-carnivorous animals. While there are a number of arguments available to dispute whether dangerous animals and/or animal death resulted from the Fall,[153] the fact is there was at least one animal, the Serpent, that was not in harmony with Adam and Eve or God. It could be insinuated that Adam and Eve were too kind to the Serpent. They should have expelled the Serpent from the comfort and protection of the Garden. Dare one say that the Serpent should have been killed for blasphemy?[154] Another problem with the CAR interpretation lies in its assertion that these nuances negate the traditional meaning of *radah*. All of creation was given to humanity under God's authority. The point of Genesis is not that mankind was to rule as an absolute despot; rather it was to show the extent of power mankind had over Creation, a power given by an omnipotent God.[155]

Let us turn to the next part of the CAR argument, namely the assertion that Christians should work for the well-being of every sentient creature, including animals. We will begin by granting the CAR view that Adam and Eve were vegetarians.[156] In one way, the vegetarian interpretation scores a major point for the CAR view. It would be reasonable to think that if God's original plan was for humanity to be vegetarian, then it is possible that we should continue to strive toward that goal. However,

153. See Snoke, "Why Were Dangerous Animals Created?" 122–24. Although Snoke's denies that Romans 8:22 refers to the Fall, his other arguments are quite compelling. See also Alexanian, "Are Dangerous Animals a Consequence of the Fall of Lucifer?" 237; and Phillips, "Did Animals Die before the Fall?" 146–47.

154. The present writer wishes to thank Dr. Meredith Kline for the inspiration for this argument.

155. Manahan puts it well in saying, "The activity of man when done in loyalty to his Creator means continued well-being for creation. When man moves in disobedience to his Creator, there is an absence of well-being in creation (Gen 3:7–24). [paragraph] The activity of man within creation is restricted only by his relationship to his Creator. Manahan, "A Re-Examination of the Cultural Mandate," 230 (brackets mine).

156. While arguing from silence has many difficulties, it should be noted that Genesis never says "Don't eat animals nor does he say don't kill animals." Adam and Eve were probably vegetarians, but this vegetarian view is often claimed by CAR proponents on the basis of reading the content of Genesis 9:3 back into Genesis 1–3, something that they fail to do with the comments of the Second Adam, Jesus Christ (Mk 7:18f; see also 1 Timothy 4:1–3). John Calvin believed that humans were permitted to eat meat prior to the flood. Calvin, *Genesis*, 9:3ff. Kidner, *Genesis*, 52. Kidner suggests that God only meant to show that all life depended on plants rather than a statement that Adam and Eve were vegetarian.

while diet would certainly limit the meaning of "rule", diet says nothing to prohibit Adam and Eve from exercising lethal dominion over the animals. The vegetarian interpretation only stops Adam and Eve from eating the animals they killed. To suggest that Adam and Eve were prevented from killing animals for food would be a legitimate option; however, killing animals to protect crops would also be an option as well. It is very plausible that Adam and Eve would have had to express painful, if not lethal, dominion over animals in order to protect their crops.[157] The Garden was the Lord's, but, unlike pagan creation accounts, the Garden of Eden was built for humanity to have fellowship with God[158] and not to simply be the place where humanity fed the deities. The Garden was also a microclimate, which, as McNeill notes, is the reason for human success on the planet. Humans, unlike most animals, adapt nature to meet our needs.[159] Mankind impacts nature by shortening the food chain in order to grow more food. When we understand that humans impact their environment, we learn that we also create an imbalance that parasites can exploit. Humans must intervene to adjust that imbalance to prevent parasites from overwhelming our work. For example, high concentrations of fruit trees are attractive to animals seeking an easy meal. Humans have to intervene and exclude and/or remove them so as to prevent them from stealing the desirable fruit. While some CAR activists may acknowledge the moral legitimacy of killing animals for crop protection, they would think it should be rare. Frequently, animal activists call humans to modify their behavior for the sake of the animals and their homes.[160] The problem is how one thinks Adam and Eve would have done this sort of animal rights calculus, given that every human birth would reduce the area and food available for animals. Even a non-cursed creation would still result in the deaths of animals, through the loss of habitat as human population expanded and consumed more resources. One way to bypass this dilemma would be to envision a world in which animal birth rates were mystically tied to

---

157. For a less nuanced view on the human right to protect crops and property see Phelps, *The Dominion of Love*, 177.

158. Wallace, "Garden of God," 2:906; "Eden, Garden Of," 2:281–82.

159. McNeill, *Plagues and Peoples*, 46–47, 59.

160. Linzey, *Christianity and the Rights of Animals*, 141. He even goes so far as to say, "We have to wonder whether God's right is served by the ever increasing numbers of human beings that every day lay *exclusive* claim to more and more of this *common* earth." (Italics his).

human population growth. As human populations grew, animals would have fewer young. The only other option would be God creating a world with unlimited growth potential, perhaps space travel.

Genesis tells us that God permits people to enjoy the fruits of their labor. CAR activists correctly state that humanity's dominion should be characterized by stewardship. But they forget that responsible steward-ship may involve culling and forceful imposition, as denoted by words "rule" *radah* [161] and "subdue" *kabash*. [162] God's allowance of coercive domin-ion makes Adam and Eve's failure to evict or even kill the Serpent even more egregious. [163] Furthermore, even conceding the view that pre-Fallen humans were exclusively vegetarian, the question regarding their need to protect the Garden from animals seeking to partake of the garden's produce remains. [164] God placed Adam in the Garden with the obligation for him "to cultivate and keep it." (Gen 2:15). CAR activists are correct to assert that this command modifies the dominion command in Genesis 1. However, they overstate the extent of the modification. For the command "to keep" [165] involves violent force as seen in the word's use of the angel guarding the garden to prevent Adam and Eve from returning (cf. Gen 2:15 and 3:24, as both use *shamar* in the Qal inf construct). Even if the Fall never occurred, competition between human and animal interests would have had to take place eventually, given the finitude of the earth's available resources. [166]

Second, the CAR view improperly diminishes the differences be-tween humans and other sentient creatures. It is true that humans have many similarities with animals, such as being souls (*nephesh*) and having

161. Keil and Delitzch, *The Pentatuech,* 152, suggest that man's original rule was less forceful than after Genesis 9:1–7 because prior to the Fall animals served willingly. Their view could be correct. But it is also possible that God wanted animals to fear humanity for their own survival. Otherwise wouldn't these same animals have been imprinted not to fear humans?

162. Cf. Oswalt, "KABASH," 1:430; Culver, "*MASHAL III,*" 1:534–35. It is significant that m*ashal* was a lexical option, but not chosen by the writer of Genesis.

163. I wish to thank Dr. Meredith Kline for the inspiration for this argument.

164. This writer is open to Moltmann's identification of humanity's role as "justices of the peace," provided that we have the power of the sword (Rom 13:4). Moltmann, *God in Creation,* 188.

165. See also Koehler et al., *The Hebrew and Aramaic Lexicon of the Old Testament,* Entry 9773.

166. To suggest otherwise requires one to postulate such a fantastic set of circum-stances that one wonders how to respond.

bodies. However, Genesis 1–2 clearly shows that humanity stands at the apex of creation. Humanity alone is "in the image of God," (see also Gen 9:6; 1 Cor 11:7; Jms 3:9); a phrase that, as we have seen, emphasizes the importance of humans.[167] Humanity's significance is underscored by God's having an interactive and communicative relationship with individual humanity; a reality that does not exist with animals. In light of humanity's privileged position, it is perfectly legitimate to understand that humans have been granted authority over creation in the sense of being able to exert coercive and lethal control over the animals.

Evaluation of the Argument from the Noahic Narratives

If CAR activists are correct that Genesis 9:1–3 constituted God's condescension to human violence, it still does not prove that simply the act of killing animals prior to the Flood was always forbidden. Abel offered a lamb to sacrifice, and it would not be difficult to imagine that other believers continued the practice (Gen 4:4). God clearly smiles upon Noah for his sacrifice offering (Gen 8:20ff). For CAR activists to suggest otherwise (as will be seen in the discussion on the sacrificial system below), is simply a result of their arbitrary bias against all the relevant Biblical data. Nor does the CAR view help us to understand, as Calvin observes, that animal skins were used prior to the flood, so that humans had some access to animals.[168]

More significant is the CAR activist belief that animal abuse began after the Fall and/or was part of the violence God was objecting to when He punished the world by water. A few problems emerge here with this thesis. First, animals cannot corrupt themselves.[169] So it is unclear why God would punish animals for something that they could not help. Under the Dominionist view, the animals were killed because of federal headship

---

167. The point being that despite humanity's similarities with animals, humanity holds a unique position in creation.

168. Calvin, *Commentaries on the First Book of Moses Called Genesis*, Comments on Genesis 1:29. The footnote by the editor states that if the sacrifices were holocausts, then only the skin would be available for human use.

169. Keil and Delitzsch, *Pentateuch*, 89. They say of Gen 6:10–12, "The corruption proceeded from the fact, that *"all flesh"*—i.e., the whole human race which had resisted the influence of the Spirit of God and become flesh (see v. 3)—*"had corrupted its way."* The term "flesh" in v. 12 cannot include the animal world, since the expression, "corrupted its way," is applicable to man alone. The fact that in v. 13 and 17 this term embraces both men and animals is no proof to the contrary, for the simple reason that in v. 19 "all flesh" denotes the animal world only, an evident proof that the precise meaning of the word must always be determined from the context."

(cf. Rom 5:15–21; 1 Cor 15:22).[170] The sin of leaders frequently impacts subordinates. Second, Anderson suggests that while violence is a disease in God's creation, the focus is on human violence, not violence within the animal or natural kingdoms.[171] It is unclear whether or not predation was a result of the Fall. It could very well be that the issue was not death, but whether death served humanity or whether humanity served death.[172] Furthermore, the CAR activitsts use of the Noahic narrative fails to be substantitve enough to overthrow the Traditional understanding of humanity's dominion over the animals.

---

170. For a brief explanation of Federal Theology see Collins, "Federal Theology," 413–14.

171. Anderson, *From Creation to New Creation*, 144–45; 158–59.

172. See an extended discussion on this in Snoke, "Why Were Dangerous Animals Created?" 117–25. Thanks to Dr. Meredith G. Kline for his insight.

3

The CAR Movement's Argument
from Old Testament Scripture
Part 2

CAR ARGUMENT FROM THE O.T. SACRIFICIAL SYSTEM

THE ISRAELITE SACRIFICIAL SYSTEM presents a significant challenge to the CAR activist's view of human-animal relations.[1] Linzey looks at Genesis 8:20–22 with particular amazement as he openly wonders how God could love animals and yet savor their deaths.[2] In light of this challenge, CAR activists use three tactics to deflect the significance of the pro-sacrifice passages. First, they suggest that God never ordered sacrifices, as insinuated by anti-sacrificial comments made by later prophets (Isa 29:13; Jer 7:22; Amos 5:25). Second, they assert that God permitted sacrifices as a cultural concession.[3] Finally, CAR activists reinterpret the significance and meaning of sacrifice altogether.

Phelps adopts the first tactic.[4] He openly cites passages where God is claimed to have enjoyed and/or commanded animal sacrifice (Gen 4:3–5;

---

1. Webb, *On God and Dogs,* 66. He says, "The difficulty with animal sacrifice is that it contradicts our perception of God's character and design for creation." Yet Webb has little trouble condemning notions of God's immutability as Greek rather than Hebrew thought, 55.

2. Linzey, *Animal Theology,* 104.; Linzey, *Christianity and the Rights of Animals,* 40–41; Young, *Is God a Vegetarian?,* 46. Young just denies that God delighted in the sacrifice and says it was just a figurative way to say that God accepted it. God does not desire or need food (Ps 50:13).

3. Young, *Is God a Vegetarian?* 67f.

4. Ibid., 71. Although Young recognizes the idea of empty sacrifices, to say that sacrifice without accompanying change of heart amounts to murder is just too fantastic to engage.

8:20–21; Ex 29:15–18; Lev 1:14–17; 8:22–8; Psa 20:3; Lk 2:22–24).[5] Phelps just appeals to America's love of the underdog by saying that these passages were just the "official" position. He then proceeds to cite a variety of passages which appear to question the official doctrine regarding God's approval of animal sacrifices (Isa 1:11–17; 66:3–4; Jer 7:21–23; Amos 5:21–5; Mic 6:6–8; Psa 40:6).

Evangelicals may dismiss Phelp's argument as a typical example of liberal selective reading. However, Phelps offers a different challenge. He rejects the Evangelical interpretation that the Prophets were not condemning sacrifices per se, but sacrifices done in an *ex opera operatum* manner. Phelps derides this interpretation by calling it the "empty sacrifice" theory.[6] He gives three reasons why the empty sacrifice theory should be rejected.[7] First, it conflicts with the plain reading of Scripture. Phelps, taking a page from the literal Bible reading of his upbringing, states that the prophets called for repentance *instead of* sacrifice not *in addition to* (italics his). If the prophet's words were not clear enough, he points to the fact that some actually said the sacrificers needed to repent because they sacrificed as their hands were covered in blood. Second, he argues that Isaiah 1:11–17; 66:3–4, Jeremiah 7:21–3, and Amos 5:21–25 never believed that God ever commanded sacrifices.[8] Phelps sees their comments as internal proof that "static" interfered with Israel's understanding of God's real revelation. Finally, Phelps wants us to follow Christ, who summarized the law in two great commandments (Mt 22:36f) that were devoid of sacrificial import.

Regarding the second tactic, Young says that it was a way, although not God's ideal, that God tolerated as sacrifice was a meaningful way for Israelites to encounter God. Young also emphasizes that even in sacrifice the Israelite model was different, and that God sought "to wean humanity away" from the practice.[9]

Linzey takes the third approach by redefining the significance and meaning of the sacrificial passages. He believes the solution lies in rejecting the common notion that sacrifice is destroying something valuable

5. Phelps, *The Dominion of Love*, 74–77, 82.

6. Ibid., 77–83.

7. Ibid., 77–84.

8. Young, *Is God a Vegetarian?* 74. Young concurs stating, "God did not originate the idea of sacrifices and we suspect was never entirely pleased with it."

9. Ibid., 68–69.

(such as an animal) to placate God's wrath. Instead, Linzey thinks that sacrifice should be understood as giving something to God. The death of the animal is not in focus. Linzey quotes Eric Mascall's statement, "There is no suggestion that God is glorified by the destruction of his creature, for if it could be literally destroyed there would be nothing left for him to accept and transform." Linzey continues by saying that sacrifice is the idea of freeing the animal's life to be with God. As if sensing the need to bolster his argument even further, Linzey cites Isaiah 1:11 noting that God was tired of Judah's sacrifices. Elsewhere Linzey highlights that underneath all the pro-sacrificial language, Israel had a minority who recognized that sacrifice was not the answer to remove sin.[10] Webb spends little time addressing the issue of Old Testament sacrifices, choosing to simply cloud the issue by detailing various theories to justify the ultimate purpose of sacrifice. His real goal is to get to the New Testament period, where animal sacrifice has ended. As for the Old Testament, Webb says the Hebrews, like everyone, had to update their views on sacrifice.[11]

EVALUATION OF THE CAR ARGUMENT
FROM THE O.T. SACRIFICIAL SYSTEM

We should begin by noting Kimberley C. Patton's caution that studies of sacrifice reveal an intense bond between the offerer and the victim, and that simply labeling sacrifice as a sign of oppression inappropriately bars us from a deeper understanding of the role of animals in such systems.[12] CAR arguments concerning animal sacrifice are either incredulous or provide an example of special pleading.[13] Most troubling is the manner in which they readily dismiss passages that contradict their theology, or contend that there is some sort of inherent contradiction between various

10. Linzey, *Animal Theology* 105.

11. Webb, *On God and Dogs,* 144–46

12. Patton, "He Who Sits in the Heavens Laughs," 403.

13. DeVaux, *Ancient Israel: Religious Institutions,* 2:414.ff. A brief comparison of Roland DeVaux's section on Sacrifice shows that Linzey has overlooked a great deal of information on Israelite sacrificial theology and practice. He also ignores the possibility that God could create something to be destroyed. If so, then the destruction of an animal or tree or something else is part of its purpose. Ladd, *A Theology of the New Testament,* 426 mentions a theology by V. Taylor that sounds very similar to the one used by Linzey. Essentially Ladd quotes James Denney by saying, ". . . blood in separation from the flesh does not mean life but death, . . ." 426.

ideological groups that were not sufficiently harmonized by later editors. Scripture provides a number of rationales for the negative comments it makes about sacrifices. Zohar contends that the Pentateuch does not separate a repentant heart from the act of sacrifice.[14] Some of the passages cited by CAR activists actually recognize the simple truth that God would rather have His followers obey Him than offer penal sacrifices (1 Sam 15:22).[15] For example, the CAR activist use of Psalm 40:6 fails to recognize the context in which those words were said. The point there is that God would have much rather had David's obedience than the sacrifice after the fact.[16] Hauret explains the relationship between the sacrificial rite and interior attitude well. He says, "The rites serve to make interior sentiments visible: . . . "[17] He continues by explaining that the later prophets did not provide any real innovations, noting that the heart of the offerer was always primary (cf. Ex 19:5; 24:7).[18] Sometimes, the CAR activist neglects to read the wider context of the passages to see that condemnation of sacrifices is not in view. Linzey took such a myopic approach when observing that Isaiah condemned sacrifices.[19] He failed to take the time to notice that if his understanding of Isaiah was correct then Isaiah must have been a tortured soul, as he predicted that the Egyptians would eventually worship the true God by offering sacrifice (Isa 19:21; *zebah*). Why would Isaiah, an alleged critic of sacrifice, proclaim that Egypt would begin sacrificing? Even Isaiah 34:6 has the Lord sacrificing the peoples of Edom.[20] So either

14. Zohar, "Repentance and Purification," 614.

15. For a succinct explanation on how to harmonize apparently conflicting passages on sacrifice see M'Caw and Motyer, "The Psalms," 476–77.

16. Jobes, "The Function of Paronomasia in Hebrews 10:5–7," 188.

17. Hauret, "Sacrifice," 453.

18. Or in the case of Amos 5, the contrite heart of the offerer was at least an essential part of the sacrificial offering. See Davies, *The Gospel and the Land*, 80–81.

19. Linzey, *Christianity and the Rights of Animals*, 41. What is ironic here is how Linzey cites a scholar who points out that the prophets were condemning empty ritualism. See also Thompson's claim that the prophets never "rejected the Jerusalem cultus entirely." Thompson, "Hebrews 9 and Hellenistic Concepts of Sacrifice," 573. Thompson is citing G. von Rad, *O.T. Theology* and also J. R. Brown *Temple and Sacrifice in Rabbinic Judaism*. Even Young accepts the idea that many of the anti-sacrifice passages of the prophets were actually condemnations of empty ritual. Young, *Is God a Vegetarian?* 69.

20. Wolf, "Zebah," 1:235, says *zebah* means slaughter here. While not rejecting the idea of slaughter, the present writer wonders if the term *zebah* was used to emphasize that God would make his peace through death (cf. p.233 which notes that the noun *zebah* is used frequently with peace offerings).

Isaiah forgot what he wrote some several chapters earlier, or Isaiah did not write it, or some other speculative theory. In the final analysis, CAR activists take a theory and then read scripture through that theory, and thereby ignore all contrary evidence.

Second, these interpreters neglect to read the Old Testament with Christian revelation in mind. Kidner keenly says the following on Psalm 40:6's comment that God did not desire sacrifices, "After such a deliverance, what offering can one bring...?"[21] He continues showing that David had in mind the end of all sacrifices with the coming of the Messiah, as confirmed by Hebrews 10:5–10.

Third, the CAR activists' view of sacrifice tries to make the problem of sacrifice go away by saying it is a mysterious unexplainable event, insinuating it was done by ignorant ancients. While we probably do not know all the dynamics behind God's command for sacrifices, we can reasonably infer some. Linzey reduces the nature of the death involved in sacrifice and instead appeals to some strange notion that the basic idea of sacrifice was not destruction but rather giving the animal to God.[22] First, he boldly denies the doctrine of propitiation, namely that Christ's sacrifice required blood and that it was necessary to turn back God's wrath. He writes,

> The Sacrifice of Christ was not a propitiation demanded of Christ by an angry God. On the contrary, it was the free offering to God the Father in the cause of love for fellow creatures. It is the sacrifice of love freely given, and not the sacrifice of blood required, that is the distinctly Christian understanding of this matter.[23]

Young states, "It may be that God does not demand satisfaction for offending divine holiness or transgressing the law as much as God gives us freedom to cooperate in restoring relations by removing guilt."[24] How Linzey or Young respond to Hebrews 9:22's citation of Leviticus 17:11 or Roger Nicole's landmark work on propitiation,[25] one can only speculate.

Fourth, the CAR view overlooks the fact that sacrifices were to cost the penitent something. Israel existed in an agricultural economy (cf. 2 Sam 24:24). The killing of livestock required one to lose economic power

21. Kidner, *Psalms 1–72*, 159.
22. Linzey, *Animal Theology*, 104.
23. Ibid., 110.
24. Young, *Is God a Vegetarian?* 74.
25. Nicole, "C.H. Dodd and the Doctrine of Propitiation," 117–57.

and security. Sacrifice, thereby, could truly express the penalty of sin and the cost of rectifying the situation. In this sense, the death of an animal as a consequence for human sin was tragic. If the CAR activists only had this notion of sacrifice in mind, then they would be on the mark. The problem is they even condemn animal sacrifice when done not for sin but as part of worship as in a peace offering. While significant overlap of the meanings of the various sacrifices probably existed, it is reasonable to note that it is highly unlikely that they were never used for non-atoning circumstances.[26] Whether or not animal sacrifice would have occurred prior to the Fall is a question that Scripture has not answered. The CAR argument that Christ's sacrifice, being the greater for the lesser, constitutes a model for humans to sacrifice their energies for animals (as individuals not collectively as species) stands as a principle without Biblical warrant.[27] Even the story of Jepthah's daughter stands as a tragic result of his foolish vow (Judg 11:30ff).

Perhaps what is lost in the discussion about sacrifice, including animal sacrifice, is the importance sacrifice played in Old Testament worship. Chafer keenly observes that,

> The altar is one of the most important features of Old Testament doctrine. Man was taught by divine instruction (Exod 20:24–26) that the altar represents no work of his own hands. It is the sacrifice on the altar which is blessed of God to the benefit of his soul. It is most significant that the divine instruction respecting the building of an altar follows immediately upon the giving of the Decalogue.[28]

The altar was not just an ancillary notion of worship that Israel copied from her pagan neighbors. Rather it was a key element in her relations with God.

CAR ARGUMENT FROM THE LAW, WRITINGS & PROPHETS

CAR activists contend that many passages demonstrate that God's concern for animals continued to be made manifest despite the significant impact of the Fall. Generally, these passages Fall into four main categories,

---

26. Beckwith, "Sacrifice and Offering," 1042. Beckwith is too cautious here.
27. Linzey, *Christianity and the Rights of Animals*, 43ff.
28. Chafer, "Soteriology," 15.

but we will only need to discuss three:[29] restrictions on human use of animals either by rules demanding humanness or, limiting the kinds of animals humans may eat (kosher laws); passages suggesting a preference for a vegetarian lifestyle; and the model of Eden.[30] Ultimately, their goal is to blunt the Old Testament's substantial record of animal killing by showing that through all that bloodshed, God still kept the candle of compassion toward animals lit for all to see. In this way, even though God conceded to us the ability to kill and eat animals, we were still obligated to recognize that animals suffer,[31] and treat them appropriately as His creatures.

Passages Viewed As Supporting Humane Treatment of Animals

CAR activists contend that a number of passages should be interpreted as exhorting compassion. Young asserts that Scripture is replete with passages showing that God cares for the animal kingdom, and that the laws related to compassion flow from that concern.[32] The kosher laws are used by CAR activists as a negative proof. They argue that the laws demonstrate God's concern for animals because the dietary restrictions are to limit the extent of human use of animals.[33] For simplicity, passages will be listed along with a brief explanatory note to draw attention to their role in the discussion.

---

29. The fourth category includes passages that suggest animals suffer. The present author, unlike Descartes, does not deny that animals feel pain and discomfort. The issue for the present author is not the fact that animals experience pain but rather its moral significance. For example do animals suffer in that they have a continued state of consciousness and personal identity that enables them to experience and anticipate suffering? Also, how much suffering must an animal endure before humans must seek to stop it? Since our concern is on the treatment of animals rather than whether they suffer, this category will not be discussed. It is more prudent to concede the point to the CAR movement.

30. Webb, *On God and Dogs,* 22. He says the dietary laws put restraints on gluttony (Lev 11–15) and the unrestrained violence of the pre-diluvian period, and provide a glimpse of the garden.

31. Linzey and Regan, *Animals and Christianity,* 6–10, 42–45, 85–86, 116–17, and 152–55.

32. Young, *Is God a Vegetarian?* 83f. Passages cited include, Gen 9:8–17; Psa 145:9, 16, 17; 36:6; 104:10–14.

33. Ibid., 82–83.

Gen 24:14 watering of camels,[34]
Gen 24:31 camels given a place of their own,
Gen 33:13–14 Jacob responsible to care for the flocks,[35]
Exod. 23:5 helping the laden ass,
Lev 22:28 don't kill a mother and her young on the same day,
Lev 25:6–7 Sabbath rest extended to livestock (cf. Ex 20:8–11),
Num 22:21ff. Balaam's ass,[36]
Dt 14:21 You are not to boil a young goat in its mother's milk,
Dt 22:1 returning a wayward ox,
Dt 22:6 don't take mother and eggs on the same day,
Dt. 22:10 don't plow with an ox and donkey in the same yoke,
Dt. 25:4 don't muzzle the ox,[37]
Psa 104:14 God grows food for cattle,
Prov 12:10 a righteous man cares for the life of his beast,[38]
Jonah 4:11 God cares for the Nineveh's animals.

In light of these passages, CAR activists believe that God wanted His people to treat animals responsibly. For them, God's call for compassion for animals after the Fall confirms His original ideal of humans not killing or harming animals at all. Therefore, since modern mankind no longer needs to kill animals to live, we must avoid harming animals whenever possible.

Evaluation of the Interpretation of Humane Passages

CAR activists are right in their claim that Scripture does teach of God's concern and care for the animal kingdom (Psa 104:14; Jon 4:11). Likewise, in obedience to God, humans should mirror God's behavior in this area as a way to honor Him.[39] At issue, however, is whether that concern translates into abstinence from killing, utilizing, or otherwise subjugating animals to serve human needs and desires. For example, a number of passages used to support compassion toward animals can be easily understood in terms of the owner's self-interest. Livestock was a valuable commodity in the

---

34. Webb, *On God and Dogs*, 23.

35. Ibid., 24.

36. Webb, *On God and Dogs*, 23.

37. Linzey and Cohn-Sherbok, *After Noah*, 23–24; 31–32.

38. Webb, *On God and Dogs*, 24.

39. One need only review God's command for Israel to "be holy" as He is holy to recognize that God wanted His people to mirror His character on earth (Lev 11:44, 45; 19:2, 24; 20:7, 26).

ancient Near East. Treating animals poorly would be the moral equivalent of carelessly throwing money away (Gen 24:31; 33:13; Dt 22:10).[40]

Other passages are not so clear in supporting the CAR view. For example, several passages focus on helping your neighbor whose animal is either overburdened or lost (Ex 23:5; Dt 22:1). The command perfectly fits with God's command to love your neighbor as yourself. The primary focus of the command is not the animal; it is the owner of the animal who is in need of help. The same could be argued for the command to rest the animals on the Sabbath. The focus lies not with the animals as it stands that if the animals are forbidden to work it would be difficult for humans to work as well (Ex 20:8–11; Lev 25:6–7).[41] Since God's rationale behind the prohibition of boiling young in its mother's milk (Lev 22:28; Dt 14:21) remains unknown,[42] despite Talmudic interpretations to the contrary,[43] the passage supports neither view. The same could be said for the rationale behind the kosher laws. Scholars have tried to find a unifying principle behind the restrictions, but despite their best efforts they have been unsuccessful.[44] To endeavor to explain the kosher laws as God's attempt to move humanity towards vegetarianism, or at least slow down humanity's carnivorous cravings, is to argue beyond the Biblical evidence.

Even the story of Balaam's ass (Num 22:21ff.) does not directly address the issue of animal abuse the way CAR activists wish it would. Balaam is not condemned for beating his donkey per se, he is condemned for not recognizing that his beating (perhaps cruelly)[45] of a previously

---

40. Webb, *On God and Dogs,* 24. Webb is on stronger ground when he claims that the Hebrews were to be more concerned about the animals directly under their care. Strangely, Linzey condemns treating animals properly for self-serving reasons, calling it "enlightened self-interest." Linzey, "A Reply to the Bishops," 171.

41. It is also possible that God had concern for both the domesticated animals' well-being and that of the humans. But this dual interpretation does not detract from a Dominionist interpretation because the underlying right of humans to coerce animals to do serve human needs is still upheld, contrary to the CAR view.

42. Nelson, *Deuteronomy,* 181. Nelson suggests that since the parallel used to support a rejection of Canaanite religious practice has been discredited, perhaps the command refers to the unnatural mixing of the realms of life and death. Interpreters for the now discredited religious view include Thompson, *Deuteronomy,* 179. and Von Rad, *Deuteronomy,* 102.

43. Linzey and Cohn-Sherbok, *After Noah,* 31.

44. Sprinkle, "The Rationale of the Laws of Clean and Unclean in the Old Testament," 645–53. Sprinkle lists a number of rationales behind O.T. laws, including hygiene and distance from paganism.

45. Wenham, *Numbers,* 170–71. Wenham says Balaam beat his donkey viciously three

perfectly obedient animal should have struck him as odd. The seer obviously did not see the signs very well.[46]

More troublesome for the CAR view are the number of passages where harm was brought to animals and portrayed in a decidedly neutral and sometimes positive way. Take for example, the concept of the ban (*herem*) by which Israel was to completely destroy both human and animal life in a condemned city (Dt 13:12–15). One of the reasons expressed by the Biblical writer behind Saul losing his throne was attributed to his *failure* to destroy the Amalekites and their livestock (1 Sam 15:2–3). At minimum, these passages suggest that animal life, including human life, was by no means sacrosanct. Instead, they underscore the idea that animals were property in that they were to be destroyed along with the humans in the ban. Even if the CAR activists argued that the destruction of both animals and humans suggested an underlying equality or parity, their position would not be enhanced. First, humans, not humans and animals, are performing the judgment. Second, the people of God are expressing dominion over those outside of the family of God.

God's command for Joshua to hamstring the horses of the Hazor presents even further difficulties (Josh 11:6).[47] The context suggests that Joshua crippled the horses after Israel's victory in the open field.[48] Although Scripture fails to mention which form of hamstringing was performed,[49] the lack of tactical benefit of hamstringing the horses as opposed to humanely killing them, raises the question of God ordering cruelty.[50] Clearly,

---

times in violation of Prov 12:10. *NaCaH*, in the hiphil, connotes to smite, sometimes in a very negative way. Koehler et al., *The Hebrew and Aramaic Lexicon of the Old Testament*, Entry 6175.

46. Ibid., 170. Wenham explains that animals were considered omens in Mesopotamia. See also Way, "Balaam's Hobby-Horse," 682–86. He explains that the reversal theme occurs in both the Numbers passage and Dier 'Alla Plaster Text.

47. See also 2 Sam 8:4; 1 Chron 18:4 which record that David hamstrung all the horses, save those needed to pull 100 chariots.

48. Callaway and Maxwell, "Settlement in Canaan: The Period of the Judges," Np.

49. Horses can be hamstrung in two different ways; one allows the horse to walk and the other makes the affected limb useless. See Research Staff of the Equine Research Publications, "Rupture of the Gastrocnemius Tendon," 222–23. and Research Staff of the Equine Research Publications, "Rupture of the Achilles Tendon," 223.

50. It is possible that God wanted the horses hamstrung rather than killed in order to have the horses continue to consume foodstuff; thereby diminishing the city's food supply. It is also possible that killing the horses would have been more noticeable and alert the inhabitants of a pending attack. Two other passages use the same word (Gen 49:6; 2

the horses needed to be disabled to prevent Israel from relying on them. Hamstringing a horse prevents it from pulling a chariot. But in light of the harm, why not just kill it? Young's observation that Jacob condemned the hamstringing of oxen (Gen 49:6–7)[51] actually supports the idea that utility play a role in guiding human behavior towards animal treatment. Oxen were valuable assets to an agricultural economy, and had no offensive military value. Hamstringing oxen was just foolish on multiple levels.

God's command not to muzzle working oxen is heralded as a proof text against animal cruelty (Dt 25:4).[52] The argument states that God forbade humans from the cruelty of withholding "wages" from working animals. Verbruggen, in a recent article, contends that this and other proffered interpretations do not fit the context. He says that the passage is actually requiring renters of oxen to treat rented property in a responsible way. When oxen were rented, the renter would be strongly motivated to minimize the rental costs by denying food to the working oxen. The renter had an economic interest in sending the oxen back to their owner hungry, forcing him to bear the cost of feeding the animals. A modern analogy would be renting a car with a full tank of gas and then returning it with an empty tank. In other words, says Verbruggen, the focus of the passage is economic, not humaneness.[53] This economic interpretation also has the advantage of making better sense of Paul's statement in 1 Corinthians 9:9.

The point is that a wholistic approach to Scriptural testimony requires one to re-characterize God's concern for animals in order to properly nuance one's understanding of the totality of Scriptural teaching. As can be seen, Scripture does not support the CAR view that humanity has a duty to avoid all harm to animals.

Sam 8:4). David did a similar thing but saved a few for his chariots.

51. Young, *Is God a Vegetarian?* 85.

52. Von Rad, *Deuteronomy*, 154. Von Rad says, ". . . springs, like the rules in Deut. 22:4, 6, from an animal-loving attitude."

53. Verbruggen, "Of Muzzles and Oxen: Deuteronomy 25:4 and 1 Corinthians 9:9," 703–4.

Excursus on Proverbs 12:10

Proverbs 12:10 stands as one of the premiere passages for CAR activists, as they contend that the verse condemns animal cruelty. Yet a survey of commentators shows that most have not vigorously evaluated the passage.[54] Most only touch on the issue of cruelty or compassion;[55] and/or interpret the parallelism as a general contrast between the wicked and the righteous.[56] Although beast here probably means domesticated animal,[57] without any associated modifiers it can refer to all land animals, wild and domestic. Proverbs is trying to show, however, that a contrast exists between the righteous and wicked treatment of animals. In my opinion, the issue is not that the righteous treat animals well, so how much better they must treat mankind, or that the wicked can treat animals better than people. Rather the sage uses the word play in the second colon to call into question the wicked's "compassion"[58] for animals or people. The word translated cruelty (*'akzari*) occurs only 8 times in the O.T.[59] Since righteous people "know" (*yada*) their animals, they can thereby implement the best treatment of the animal based on clear thinking, rather than sentimentality.[60] The point is that a righteous person knows well enough how to treat animals, and that culling them may be in the best interests of all, both human and animal.[61]

---

54. Keil and Delitzsch, *Proverbs*, 1:185–86 is a notable exception.

55. These commentaries only touch on the issue of animal compassion. McKane, *Proverbs*, 452. Kidner, *Proverbs*, 1964). 96. Oesterley, *The Book of Proverbs*, 92–3. Carson, *New Bible Commentary*, Np. Garrett, *Proverbs, Ecclesiastes, Song of Songs*, 131.

56. Plaut, *Book of Proverbs*, 145.

57. Brown, et al., Brown-*Driver-Briggs Gesenius Hebrew and English Lexicon with an Appendix Containing Biblical Aramaic*, 96–97.

58. Brown, et al., Brown-*Driver-Briggs Gesenius Hebrew and English Lexicon with an Appendix Containing Biblical Aramaic*, 933.

59. Oswalt, "'Akzari," 1: 436. Prov 5:9; 11:17; 12:10; 17:11; Jer 6:23; 30:4; 50:42; Isa 13:9.

60. Brotzman, "Man and the Meaning of Nephesh," 407ff. Brotzman's comments that *nephesh* here means "appetite" suggesting that the righteous person takes care of the dietary needs of the animal does not diminish this proffered interpretation.

61. For an interpretation that I believe supports my view that humans should be concerned with animal feelings (just not supremely so) see Keil and Delitzsch, *Proverbs*, 1:185–86. Garrett places the passage within a three verse inclusion (Prov 12:9–11). He says ". . . that a good man cares for those who provide for him, even if they are only animals. The wicked only exploit." Garrett, 131.

Passages that Suggest a Preference for Vegetarianism

CAR animal activists contend that God's preference for vegetarianism can be found elsewhere in the Old Testament. Four passages are worthy of review: Israel's craving meat in the wilderness (Num 11:2), descriptions of Israel's ideal diet (Dt 8:7–10; Jer 29:5; Amos 9:14; Hos 2:22), Daniel's diet (Dan 1:5–16), and Elijah being provisioned with bread (1 King 19:5–8).[62] Numbers 11 refers to Israel's call for meat during the Wilderness wanderings (Ex 16; Num 11:4).[63] What strikes the CAR writers is that although the focus is primarily on gluttony, the object of the gluttony is meat. They contend that the Biblical writer has connected gluttony with the consumption of meat in a subtle way to remind the Israelites that eating animal flesh is not God's ideal. The concept is heightened, they argue, given that Israel, being fed manna (reputed to be vegetarian by design), got weary of God's provision. Webb finds support for the aforementioned interpretation in that way that God grants Israelites permission to hunt in the Promised land (Dt 12:20; if they crave meat). He observes that the same verb for crave used in Deuteronomy 12:20 also occurs in Numbers 11:4.[64] Webb believes by using the same negatively nuanced verb, the writer of Deuteronomy was reminding Israel that meat eating was not God's ideal.

CAR activists also appeal to the frequent descriptions of Israel's diet as regularly consisting of vegetable products. This reality coupled with the positive results of Daniel's diet when he refused to eat King Nebuchanezzar's meat is proffered as a subtle reminder of the blessings resultant of pursuing God's ideal. Young recognizes that the ravens sent by God to feed Elijah provided him with animal flesh and bread (1 Kgs 17:6). But he observes that God only provided Elijah bread before his journey to meet God at Mount Horeb. He then asks,

> Does this imply that the Israelites perceived something unholy about killing for food? Does it suggest that we should abstain from flesh before seeking God's face in worship and prayer?"[65]

---

62. Young, *Is God a Vegetarian?* 98–99. Webb, *On God and Dogs,* 21. Dietary laws, contends Webb, provide us with a glimpse of the garden. Webb even finds a representative supporting the vegetarian ideal in Daniel 1:15. Webb says Daniel supports the notion that eating less meat is beneficial for health, both physical and spiritual, 22

63. Phelps, *The Dominion of Love,* 102–3.

64. Webb, *On God and Dogs,* 21,137.

65. Young, *Is God a Vegetarian?* 99.

CAR activists use these passages to suggest that since the bulk of Israelite diet was vegetarian, we too should follow their example.

Evaluation of Passages that Suggest
Preference for Vegetarianism

In regards to Israel's craving of meat in the wilderness, the CAR activists make an interesting observation. While it is true that the same verb root occurs in both passages, CAR activists neglected to mention that Scripture uses the verb in two different forms, hithpael (Numbers) and piel (Deuteronomy). According to one lexicon, the piel form means "desire" (cf. Dt 12:20; 14:26; 1 Sam 2:16), while the hithpael implies "crave" in a negative sense (cf. Psa 106:14; Prov 21:26).[66] Unfortunately for the CAR activists, their argument actually backfires, as Deuteronomy 12:20 actually portrays the opportunity for Israelites to hunt as a sign of God's bountiful blessing for them, not as a concession to their sinful desires.

Nor do the passages suggesting the dietary ideal work to help the CAR case. First, animals need plants as much as people do, due to trophic levels. If plants cannot grow, neither can animals, so it is logical for Scripture to emphasize plants. One need only look at the connection in Jeremiah's account of a serious drought in Jeremiah 14. There he notes how the plowman cannot work nor can the calf remain in the field (Jer 14:5). Jeremiah was providing a classic description of Israel's farming, which was a mixture of cattle and agriculture. To understand the passage in a manner other than a Dominionist model would have to account for Jeremiah's strikingly Dominionist statement in 27:4–6, where God states His universal ownership and right to give the land and its animals to whomever He deems worthy. Second, the CAR activists, in their vegetarian ideal interpretation of Deuteronomy 8:7–10, fail to account for the entire context, for verse 13, speaks directly about flocks.[67] As for Amos 9:14, it is ironic that the CAR activists fail to mention that Amos, a true prophet of God, was a herdsman (Amos 7:14). Nor does the story of Daniel's vegetarian diet help the CAR's case, as the point of the story

---

66. Koehler et al., *The Hebrew and Aramaic Lexicon of the Old Testament*, Entry #214.

67. One could also ask that if vegetarianism was God's ideal then why were Reuben and Gad, with their large flocks, never condemned for being herders? (Num 32:1).

is God's blessing his obedience in not consuming food that was unclean and/or sacrificed to idols.[68]

The argument concerning the feeding of bread to the prophet Elijah suffers from being an argument from silence. We can only speculate as to why meat was not part of Elijah's fare as God prepared him for the journey to Horeb. Fasting is a Biblical principle, but it is so not because of anything inherently wrong with the food or that some foods cause us to more distant from God (as CAR activists like to suggest).[69] Rather fasting is to help us focus our energies on God.[70] Even those taking a Nazirite vow had no prohibition against eating meat (Num 6). Alternative explanations could be offered that are just as reasonable. For example, bread would be more easily kept for the long travel where refrigeration would be lacking (cf. the Gibeonite deception in Josh 9:5).

Consumptive Use of Wildlife in the Old Testament

Unsurprisingly, CAR activists tend not to discuss the references to hunting and trapping[71] (both fall under the heading known as the consumptive use of wildlife), saying that there is very little information about these activities in Scripture.[72] Those outside the CAR camp tend to agree that hunting "was not a common occupation in ancient Palestine,..."[73] It could even be argued that Scripture looks askance at hunting because the two

---

68. Even Collins, who suggests that Daniel went beyond Torah restrictions, says the issue was ritual purity. Collins, *Daniel*, 142.

69. Webb, *On God and Dogs*, 22. Webb says Daniel 1:15 supports the notion that eating less meat is beneficial for health, both physical and spiritual.

70. Belben, "Fasting," 364.

71. The present writer begs the reader's indulgence here. While the focus of the present paper is on trapping, discussion of hunting has to be included due to the lack of precision in the literature. Cf. Rakow, *Hunting & the Bible*, 13. Additionally, at this point, the issue is not so much the manner in which wildlife is taken, rather the debate at this point rests with whether wildlife may be taken at all.

72. Webb, *On God and Dogs*, 135. Webb does state, though not as a significant point, that there is remarkably little about hunting in the Bible.

73. Harrison, "Hunting, Hunter," 491.

hunters mentioned (Nimrod in Gen 10:9;[74] and Esau in Gen 25:27; 25:34; Heb 12:16) are portrayed in a negative light.[75]

Tom Rakow, in an interesting little pamphlet,[76] makes a rather compelling case that hunting was probably more common in ancient Israel than previously recognized. He employs three forms of evidence to support his view. First, Scripture explicitly mentions hunting (cf. Judg 14:5; 1 Sam 17:34; 1 Kgs 4:23), hunting tools (Gen 27:3; Prov 1:17; Eccl 9:12; Amos 3:5), and uses hunting imagery (1 Sam 26:20; Prov 7:21–23; Lam 3:52; Isa 51:20).[77] Second, Scripture acknowledges the importance of hunting by providing rules for hunting, such as the prohibition against blood, (Lev 17:13–14) and the species that could be taken (Dt 12:15; 14:5). Finally, the lack of abundant references to hunting in Scripture[78] does not

74. Kidner, *Genesis*, 107. Kidner considers the hunting reference to be a positive one, yet later notes the irony that Nimrod's kingdom culminated with the Tower of Babel. Nor does awareness that Nimrod was the progenitor of the Canaanite line help the pro-hunting view. Ross, *Creation & Blessing*, 229.

75. Mobley suggests that the issue is that Esau represents the nature/outsider/wild man and Jacob the culture/societal member/stable. However, in Scripture wild man does not equal outsider in the negative sense. Wild men, like Samson, and Elijah can stand as outsiders against an evil cultured society. Mobley, "The Wild Man in the Bible and the Ancient near East," 227ff.

76. Rakow, *Hunting & the Bible*.

77. Trapping imagery is also employed, particularly for birds (see Ps 124:7; Hos 9:8; Amos 3:5). Hope mentions Sirach 11:30 and describes how partridges were trapped. Hope. 155. Every trapper would immediately recognize the importance of setting traps at pinch-points along trails (Job 18:9–10). Cf. Har-El, "Jerusalem & Judea: Roads and Fortifications," 12. It is also worth mentioning that Cartledge in his translation of Herodotus 7.85 speaks of a nomadic group called the Sagartians. This group, of Persian ethnicity, had an unusual way of fighting in battle. Herodotus records that they would ride up to the enemy and throw a rope with a noose at the end. Whatever the noose could grab would then be pulled toward them and destroyed. The importance of Herodotus' account here lay in determining how the Bible uses the term snare. Typically it is understood as referring to trapping animals. But could it be that at least some of the passages refer to a tactic in war? It is possible, given that snaring is frequently found in Davidic/warrior psalms (Psa 18:5; 14:19), that the Psalmist had this cowboy fighting technique in mind and used less metaphorically than we thought? Cartledge, *Thermopylae*, 237.

78. Scripture lacks the hunting lists characteristic of Assyrian royal annals. Perhaps the following provides a reason for the relative lack of hunting statements in Scripture. Since Anat was a bloodthirsty goddess who hunted (CTCA 18.1.22–31), and Baalism did permit wild animals as sacrifices, it is possible that the Bible writers did not speak much of hunting out of a desire to maintain a sharper separation between pagan and Israelite activity. Clifford, "Proverbs Ix: A Suggested Ugaritic Parallel," 300. Albright, *Archeology and the Religion of Israel*, 77, 92–93. Hittite texts also speak of offerings of hunted beasts

prove hunting was not employed. He explains that even today there are thousands of Christians who hunt, yet if one perused Christian literature little mention of hunting would be found.

Archeology also supports Rakow's assertions. Abraham Terian, commenting on Isaiah 51:20, cites archeological findings (some dating back to the third to fourth millennium B.C.) to show that the net referred to in this passage actually refers to hunting kites designed to capture wild gazelles.[79] The point being that hunting, even as late as Isaiah's time, was a common occurrence and not condemned. Even though the kites may have had been used for herding livestock does not necessarily eliminate their role in hunting, as they were located in antelope habitat and accompanied by hunting imagery. Bottom line, Terian says "... they ... would have constituted a vivid representation of hopeless activity, suffering and death."[80]

Readers should also be reminded of the large number of O.T. passages that signify the culture's awareness of trapping. For example, snaring is frequently mentioned.[81] While snaring is used in both literal (Psa 91:3; 124:7; Hos 9:8; Amos 3:5) and figurative ways (Dt 7:16; Judg 2:3; Eccl 7:26; Jer 5:24[82]; Ez 12:13), the frequency of the concept demonstrates that snaring was sufficiently well known to be meaningful to hearers throughout Israelite history. Israel's awareness of animal capture also goes back to its roots. Lambdin argues that fowling (*peh*) as used in Psalm 124:7 and elsewhere, is actually an Egyptian loanword.[83] Unsurprisingly, since the Levant sits on a major bird migratory flyway,[84] archeology also supports his claim as examples of Egyptian fowling practices have been uncovered.[85] The authors describe a type of bird trap that allows trappers to set

---

to their gods. See Mobley, "The Wild Man in the Bible and the Ancient near East," 225.

79. Terian, "The Hunting Imagery in Isaiah 51:20a," 468–69.

80. Ibid., 467–68.

81. Logos Bible Software. Search revealed 53 occurrences from 10 base Hebrew words.

82. Although scholars differ, it is interesting to consider the possibility of understanding God as "the trapper of Babylon." See Huey, *Jeremiah, Lamentations*, 413; Bright, *Jeremiah*, 342, 354.; Holladay, *Jeremiah 2*, 419.

83. Lambdin, "Egyptian Loan Words in the Old Testament," 153.

84. Lipkind et al., "Review of the Three-Year Studies on the Ecology of Avian Influenza Viruses in Israel," 89.

85. Luce et al., "Archeological News and Discussion," 414.

several of the traps (thereby permitting multiple catches) and then lure the birds to the traps by mimicking bird calls.

SUMMARY

It should be clear at this point that the CAR activists have not demonstrated that the O.T. denies or condemns humans the right to utilize animals for human purposes. Only an arbitrary and selective reading of Scripture can possibly support an animal rights conclusion. Rather, as Tucker and others have shown,[86] Scripture portrays animals in different ways. First, animals are portrayed in a positive manner in that they are useful to people as they provide power, food, and clothing. The fear and dread of animals is not due to our extensive authority over them, although limited by the respect for life displayed in the prohibition against eating blood, but the fact that we are the top of the food chain (Gen 9:2–3). Tucker explains that the Bible also portrays animals in a negative light. While the lion, bear, and eagle symbolize strength, courage and freedom (2 Sam 17:10; Prov 30:18–19, 30–31; Isa 40:31), they are also portrayed as dangerous (Amos 3:8, 12; 5:19). Finally, regarding Isaiah 11:6–9,[87] he agrees that the point of the passage is that there will be a time when the world will be safe for domestic animals.[88]

However, all the views that the CAR contend for should not be rejected outright. They are correct that human power has divinely established limits. Sabbath, the hunting restriction of Deuteronomy 22:6, and others all provide boundaries for extent of human activity. Scripture does teach that God has concern for animals (Psa 147:9 and Job 38:39).[89] Where CAR activists go astray is by their blanket assertion that nature is not to serve humanity. It is one thing to say that God forbids humans from doing whatever they wish with creation; it is another to say that God did not place creation under human authority. Tucker's understanding of Job as an illustration of the limits of human power is instructive. But even he over-reaches when he asserts that all of creation is not to serve humanity[90] because his view of service is too narrow. To say, as Tucker does, that humans can control domesticated animals but wild animals are beyond our

---

86. Borowski, "Animals in the Literatures of Syria-Palestine," 289–96.

87 Tucker, "Rain on a Land Where No One Lives," 10–11 and n.22.

88. Ibid., 12.

89. Ibid., 14.

90. Tucker, "Creation and the Limits of the World," 13–14.

control ignores the question of whether humans have the right to place wildlife under our control, however control is defined. Nature can serve humanity by being beautiful and reminding us of its powerful creator, who deserves our worship. Tucker is correct that only God can control wildlife and that the wild ass is free and human society does not have to domesticate it. But to argue that Job 38–9 is a direct challenge to the human drive to control wildlife goes beyond the evidence, because there is no way that the Bible presents the view that eagles scavenging on bodies should not be stopped (Job 38:39). Tucker is also correct that Psalm 104 tells us that animals have their place, and that God provides their food.[91] He is also correct to observe that humans have power over the earth, and to withdraw from that power is as dangerous as overreaching with it. The Bible represents both responsibility and the limits of authority, as demonstrated by its connecting morality with nature (Hos 4:1–3).[92]

Patton explains the problem well by noting that AR activists call Aquinas' views anthropocentric and hierarchal because they neglect to consider that Aquinas said those things because he believed that it was God (not humanity) who established the hierarchy. She continued by explaining it is not that the monotheistic religions denigrated animals and made them worthless, it was just that humans were so much more valuable.[93] The following diagram was created as a visual expression of her suggestion that the traditional hierarchical view is too simplistic. God does have a direct relationship to the animal kingdom, unmediated through human agency. In this regard, then, the CAR critique has assisted us in developing a better understanding of human-animal relations that properly accounts for the diversity of Old Testament revelation.

91. Ibid., 15f.

92. Tucker, "Creation and the Limits of the World," 12–13.

93. Patton, "He Who Sits in the Heavens Laughs," 406–7.

Figure 3. Patton's View versus a Dominionist view of humanity's relationship to animals.

Patton's View: God is in the center, humans still have a superior position over animals but God also has a direct relationship to animals as well.

Dominionist View

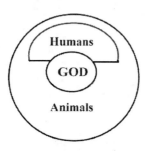

We now turn to the N.T. to see if it can provide the evidence that the CAR needs to support their view.

4

The CAR Movement's Argument
from New Testament Scripture

THE CAR MOVEMENT'S ARGUMENT FROM THE GOSPELS

CAR ACTIVISTS APPEAL TO the words and deeds of Jesus, to show that He planted the seeds of an animal rights theology that Christians should follow. Scripture shows that in word and deed, Jesus cared about animals. Therefore, Christians, by following Christ, need to care for animals and work toward restoration because cruelty is atheism.[1] The evidence CAR activists employ falls into two main categories. The first category includes specific instances where Christ demonstrates His concern and/or relationship to the animal kingdom in a way that is antithetical to the Dominionist model. The second category, called the "Generosity Paradigm," argues that Christ as God's gift of the greater serving the lesser, provides a model for human behavior to follow in regards to animals.

Under the first category, CAR activists ask us to consider the significance of animals in Christ's earthly ministry. The first sign they point to is Christ's being laid in a manger, a cow feeding trough (Lk 2:6–7),[2] at His birth. More importantly, activists appeal to Christ's testing in the wilderness. They believe that Mark 1:12–13 meant to show that Christ was beginning His work to restore broken creation.[3] Parables constitute the second sign. They suggest that Christ's frequent use of animals in his parables exhibits great concern regarding their well-being, even if com-

---

1. Linzey, *Christianity and the Rights of Animals*, 105; Linzey and Cohn-Sherbok, *After Noah*, 9–10. This statement is from a theologian named Humphry Primatt who in 1776 wrote *The Duty of Mercy and the Sin of Cruelty*.

2. Webb, *On God and Dogs*, 25.

3. Linzey, *Animal Theology*, 135; Webb, *On God and Dogs*, 25.

passion for animals was not the primary purpose of the parable (Lk 13:15; 15:4; Mt 12:11//Lk 14:5).[4] Christ's statements about God's providential care for sparrows and the feeding of birds substantiates an inclusive understanding of God's love, namely that God also cares for non-human creation (Mt 6:26//Lk 12:24; Lk 12:6–7).[5]

For the third sign, CAR activists appeal to Christ's cleansing of the Temple (Mt 21:12–13; Mk 11:15–17; Lk 19:45–46; Jn 2:14–16). They believe the cleansing constituted an example of animal liberation for two reasons. First, by driving animals out of the Temple, Christ saved them from death on the sacrificial altar.[6] Second, in quoting Jeremiah 7:11 in His rebuke of the money changers, Christ was actually appealing to the passage's broader context in which Jeremiah condemns sacrifice. In effect, Jesus was condemning animal sacrifice. For additional support, Linzey notes that the Gospels do not show that Christ or His disciples participated in animal sacrifices, and that His actions here expressed continuity with earlier prophetic denunciations of sacrifice.

The second category is known as the "Generosity Paradigm."[7] Linzey says Christ exemplified this principle in the way that He, the greater, gave Himself for the weaker. The mere fact of the incarnation is, for Linzey, evidence of this paradigm, because God humbled Himself by taking the form of a servant.[8] The incarnation showed that God's lordship was made manifest by serving. Pointing to the *kenosis* of Philippians 2:5ff, Linzey says Christ sacrificed His glory to take on the form of a servant. As Christ gave of himself for the Universe (*kosmos*), we too are to follow His moral example and give sacrificially; the greater for the lesser (cf. Mt 25:35–37).[9] In later writings Linzey is more emphatic, arguing that God is present in weakness.[10] Therefore, as representatives and followers of Christ, we are to minister to the "least of these", meaning we must sacrifice for those creatures weaker than us, which for Linzey includes animals.[11] In light

---

4. Webb, *On God and Dogs*, 25.

5. Linzey, *Animal Theology*, 35; Webb, *On God and Dogs*, 25. Webb also cites Mt 23:37.

6. Linzey, *Christianity and the Rights of Animals*, 42; Phelps, *The Dominion of Love*, 87–88.

7. Linzey, *Animal Theology*, 39.

8. Linzey, "The Place of Animals in Creation: A Christian View," 131.

9. Linzey, *Animal Theology*, 54f.

10. Linzey and Cohn-Sherbok, *After Noah*, 80.

11. Linzey, *Christianity and the Rights of Animals*, 44.

of this principle, Linzey believes that Christians are to fight for the rights of animals.[12] He strenuously contends that God desires to redeem creation of parasitical living, namely eating of animal flesh.[13] In a striking statement, Linzey says, "There can be no lordship without service and no service without lordship. Our special value to creation consists in being of special value to others."[14] CAR activists argue that Christ's example of self-sacrifice provides the preeminent example for us to reject anthropocentrism and support animal rights or, as Linzey calls it, the concept of "Theos-rights" (which suggests God has given these rights to animals).[15]

CAR activists do acknowledge some difficulties with the actual actions of Jesus as represented by Scripture and historical reconstructions. To the objection, "What about Christ's diet? Did He not eat fish?" Linzey responds that discipleship is not merely imitation because Christ was not a static example.[16] Linzey explains that Jesus had to exist in a particular setting, and as such could not resolve or engage every problem which faced him, such as the role of women, veganism, or home-rule. Christ was in fact limited.[17] Linzey continues in his attempt to diminish the impact of Christ's perceived anti-animal behavior by suggesting that Christ was not morally perfect.[18] Young adopts a less radical approach and simply acknowledges that Jesus probably ate fish but notes that we should not be thinking in terms of the historical Jesus anyway, as God speaks through His word, not historical reconstructions.[19] If that was not convincing enough, Young justifies Christ's actions on the principle of accommodation (1 Cor 9:22). Ultimately, Young concludes that the answer rests in the inscrutability of God and says that Christians follow the risen Christ,

12. Ibid., 70f.

13. Ibid., 76. While Linzey favors a vegan life-style, he explicitly avoids the pitfall of absolutism. He rejects the idea that the issue at hand is black and white, to kill animals or not to kill them. Rather he is proffering a more nuanced idea that says we need to think that killing animals is immoral unless done under dire circumstances, such as starvation or self preservation. See Linzey, *Animal Rights*, 33.

14. Linzey, *Animal Theology*, 33.

15. Ibid., 24.

16. Ibid., 86f.

17. Ibid., 87.

18. Ibid., 133. Linzey cites Christ's statement that no one is good except God alone (Lk 18:19; Mt 19:17; Mk 10:18). On page 134, he further nuances the point by providing alternative explanations.

19. Young, *Is God a Vegetarian?* 3, 9.

presumably which is opposed to the earthly one.[20] Phelps argues from silence saying that nowhere does it record that Christ ate lamb, nor does it say that fish was a regular part of His diet. Phelps even makes the fantastic claim that Christ never killed boatloads of fish (cf. Lk 5), calling such a passage a legend that Luke inserted into the text.[21] Phelps suggests that Christ's calling the Disciples to become "fishers of men" is actually a call to stop killing animals (Mk 1:17).[22]

EVALUATION OF THE CAR MOVEMENT'S ARGUMENT FROM THE GOSPELS

The CAR activists are certainly correct when they highlight the number of passages where Christ speaks of concern for animals. All Dominionists, traditional as well as the modified version mentioned in the previous chapter, should agree that animals have value. At issue is the CAR hard disjunction that killing and/or eating animals constitutes a cruel and abusive treatment of God's creation. Scripture taken in its entirety suggests that the CAR position exhibits the logical error known as a "false disjunction."[23] Additionally, the CAR activists are correct in saying that following Christ does not mean becoming exactly like Christ in every way. After all, Christ did not call everyone to suffer the shame of martyrdom or not enjoy the bounties of marriage. But what the CAR position neglects is that while *carte blanche* mimicking may not be required, it is altogether another matter to suggest that mimicking Christ could be immoral.[24]

A closer inspection of the CAR interpretation of several passages also needs to be explored. Christ was born in a stable and laid in a manger (Lk 2:7). Yet this fact does not proffer the ideal of non-violent and non-anthropocentric harmony with animals as the CAR activists suggest. Instead it shows that Christ, the Lord of Creation, could not find a place in hu-

---

20. Ibid., 12–13.

21. Phelps, *The Dominion of Love*, 108–11. Phelps will only concede that Christ took a nibble of a fish to prove he was truly raised from the dead (Lk 24:42f).

22. Ibid., 111.

23. Carson, *Exegetical Fallacies*, 94ff.

24. The phrase "image of Christ" occurs only once in the N.T. (2 Cor 4:6), but the idea that Jesus was a model for Christian behavior is a key one in the N.T. Paul even says elsewhere that the Corinthians should follow him as he follows Christ (1Cor 4:16; 11:1). This holds firm even if Furnish believes this particular passages focuses more on the Gospel and Christ's death and resurrection. See Furnish, *2 Corinthians*, 248f.

man society.[25] Furthermore, Christ's being in a stable would actually show that Christ was in harmony with humanity's use of the animal creation to serve humanity's needs. The argument could easily be reframed to show that Christ's parents (over whom God had sovereign control) employed anthropocentric thinking by making His bedding needs take priority over the livestock's need for a place to eat.[26]

CAR activists' appeal to Mark 1:13 as a proof text to support Christ beginning His mission to repair creation can be seriously doubted. Heil[27] presented a significant critique of the interpretation that Christ was in harmony with wild animals during His wilderness trial. Heil's argument can be summarized as follows: He questions the notion that Christ's work in the wilderness was as the second Adam called to repair the first Adam's failure. Heil finds the parallels to be too inadequate to sustain that position, and provides several reasons to support his point. 1. Adam was driven out of the Garden after his temptation, but Christ was driven out before. 2. No mention of the 40 days in the Garden. 3. Adam was tested in the Garden, but Christ was tested in the desert. 4. God brings animals (wild and domestic) to Adam, but Christ was only exposed to wild animals. Heil explains that if Christ was to restore creation, we should read that the wild animals were with Him rather than vice versa. Instead, the Greek term *therion* (wild beasts) actually has a negative nuance, suggesting hostility, rather than a positive nuance suggesting docility. 5. Heil notes that Christ as a second Adam is not found as a theme anywhere else in Mark.[28]

Instead, the chiastic structure of the passage, both in content and grammatical clues, supports the view that wild animals were to be contrasted with angels.

> Mark 1:12–13 (NASB)
> A [12] And immediately the Spirit impelled Him *to go* out into the wilderness.
> B [13] And He was in the wilderness forty days being tempted by Satan;

---

25. Marshall, *Commentary on Luke*, 107. Marshall also notes that animals are not even said to be present at the time. 106–7.

26. For discussion on the meaning of "manger" see Fitzmeyer, *The Gospel According to Luke I–IX*, 408.

27. Heil, "Jesus with the Wild Animals in Mark 1:13," 63–78.

28. Ibid., 64–65.

B¹ and He was with the wild beasts,[29]
A¹ and the angels were ministering to Him.

Heil explains that Mark wanted to parallel Christ not with Adam but with Israel and her time in the wilderness. Jesus becomes the antitype of Israel as the Son and Servant of God. Heil provides three main arguments in support of his view. First, Mark 1:2–3 parallels Israel's experience as seen in other O.T. passages (Ex 3:20; Isa 40:3; Mal 3:1). Second, Mark 1:9–11 and Christ's baptism parallels well with Isaiah 42:1; 63:7–64:8 and Jeremiah 38:8–9, 19–20. Third, Mark 1:12–13 parallels Israel's time in the wilderness (Dt 8:1–16; Psa 77:19, 24–25; Wisdom 16:20; and Psa 90:11–13 LXX). The Psalm 90:11–13 passage is most interesting in that the Psalmist says that God will protect His chosen one from dangerous animals, including poisonous snakes. Finally, this context fits better with the following Marcan narrative that Jesus is the "stronger one."[30]

As for the argument from the generosity paradigm, CAR activists cannot provide one concrete example of Christ ever giving in a sacrificial way to animals during His earthly ministry, either before or after His resurrection. Christ's behavior towards animals provides an example of lordship that is diametrically opposed to what Linzey wishes to suggest.[31] In fact, the Evangelist's extensive use of parallels from Genesis 1 in John 1 exhibit a clear attempt to convince readers to identify Jesus Christ with the Creator of the world.[32] Therefore, logically speaking, if Christ is identifiable with the creator of the universe (i.e. Yahweh), and Jeremiah 27:5ff says that Yahweh can give animals to the service of whomever He chooses, then could it not be said that Christ's use of animals should be understood as a demonstration of His right to give animals in service to whomever He chooses?

Christ fails to support an animal rights agenda, both negatively and positively. Negatively, Christ is remarkably silent about condemning the amount of meat consumed by His fellow Jews. For example, priests ate a diet known for its high meat content. They ate so much meat that they

29. Ibid., 66. Heil explains that the term "with the animals" does not suggest that the wild animals were subordinate to Christ. Instead, the phrase means 'in the presence of.'

30. Mobley, "The Wild Man in the Bible and the Ancient near East," 228. Mobley says that Christ being with the beasts means that he was an outsider in terms of the contemporary culture.

31. Linzey, *Animal Theology*, 17.

32. Lioy, *The Search for Ultimate Reality*.

actually suffered health consequences from it.[33] Christ failed to condemn Jerusalem's livestock market[34] which provided the Temple with all the animals necessary for sacrifice. In other words, humanity's shared commonalities with animals do not seem to make Jesus change his behavior toward the animal kingdom.[35] First, Christ kills[36] fish for the sole purpose of demonstrating His power and possibly enriching the disciples (Lk 5). Second, Christ commands the disciples to fish in order to obtain tax money (Mt 17:27). What is significant about this story is not whether the fish died (one critic did suggest the disciples threw the fish back), but the fact that Christ would permit a fish to suffer the pain and stress of being hooked[37] and removed from its natural environment simply to remove a coin and pay a tax. In effect, the disciples' fishing activity is analogous to "Market Hunters," those who capture wildlife for profit. Would it not have been better and more moral (from the CAR's perspective) if the Lord created the money out of thin air? Even if someone argued that Christ wanted to rescue the fish from the suffering of having a coin in its mouth, why does that meaning seem absent from the story? Third, Christ allows demons to enter a herd of swine (Mt 8:31ff). The swine respond by jumping into the Sea of Galilee and drowning. It is understandable that Christ, in His humanity, could not foresee that reaction on the part of the swine. But what is telling is that He appears to be totally unconcerned about the deaths of these pigs. Christ made no effort to try and rescue them personally or by proxy through His disciples. More significantly, these pigs died in a manner deemed inhumane.[38] Fourth, Christ rides a young donkey even though He could have walked (Mt 21:1–5). In Luke 5:14, Christ also commanded a recently healed leper to kill animals to fulfill the sacrificial requirements of Leviticus 14:30ff. It could also be argued that in light of Jesus' activity and sumptuous dining around the Galilean

33. Jeremias, *Jerusalem in the Time of Jesus*, 26, 106, 170.

34. Ibid., 47–49.

35. Contra Linzey, *Animal Theology*, 10–11.

36. While not immediately the cause of the death of the fish, Christ was the ultimate cause in that He guided the disciples to change their behavior resulting in the large catch. The assumption of the passage is that Christ created a miracle here, a miracle that led to the death of a large number of fish.

37. Balz and Schneider, *Agkistron* "Fish-Hook," 1:20.

38. American Veterinary Medical Association, *AVMA Guidelines on Euthanasia*, 22, 27.

area (Mt 11:19),[39] it would have been very unlikely that any refusal to eat fish would have been mentioned by His Pharisaical enemies.[40] The point being made here is not that all these passages provide great evidence for Christ's theology of animal use. The point is that if CAR activists want to infer from Christ's behavior to develop a theology of animal use, then they must consider all of His actions.

Linzey argues that Christ had to be a redeemer in a particular historical context, and so was unable to deal with every issue. But this view is perilously close to asserting that Christ could not perfectly live up to God's ideals[41] If Christ could not live up to those ideals, has not Linzey insinuated that Christ sinned or failed to live up to God's ideals? Or are we to suggest that God's moral law changes? It is one thing for Christ not to deal with every aspect of oppression and liberation, and another for Christ to participate in the oppression that He was supposed to ameliorate.[42] In other words, why did Christ refrain from owning slaves but still engaged in the oppression of animals (as the CAR activists define the term)? Perhaps better stated, "Why did Christ help and encourage others to cause animals to suffer?" For example, after healing the leper (Mk 1:40–45), Christ instructed the leper to fulfill the commands of Moses (Lev 14:1–44), which included sacrifice. Phelps' assertion that Christ knew the leper would sacrifice anyway and therefore conceded to let him go with

39. Chancey and Porter, "The Archeology of Roman Palestine," 180.

40. Arguments from silence are fraught with problems. However, not all arguments from silence should be rejected. Sometimes an event or deed is not mentioned in Scripture because it is assumed. For example, Scripture clearly teaches that Christ cooked fish, helped the disciples catch more fish, asked them for fish, and encouraged them to eat fish (John 21). The fact that Scripture does not record that Christ ate fish Himself would seem to be beside the point, as it would assume He did. Even if Christ's personal choice was to abstain from eating fish (and other meat) as CAR activists suggest, the passage shows that the risen Christ had no problems with encouraging others to eat fish.

41. See Linzey, *Christianity and the Rights of Animals*, 101 where on this page, Linzey says, "Even the Son of Man appears to accept his own part in the falleness of the world. . . . No human being can live free of evil."

42. Contra Linzey, *Animal Theology*, 132–37. Linzey in these pages discusses four basic ideas of handling the difficult problem of Jesus and His use of animals. Linzey prefers the one which suggests that Jesus had to kill fish due to necessity, as Galilee didn't provide enough protein. It should come as no surprise that Linzey provides absolutely no evidence for this contention. Patterson, "Galilee," 537. Patterson says that Lower Galilee, where most of the Gospel narratives took place, has considerable stretches of feral land. It exported olive oil, cereals, and fish from Galilee. I should also point out it could produce swine; see Luke 8.

the instruction "do not tell anyone"[43] flies in the face of the imperative verbs in verse 44, (go, show, and offer).

Another troublesome element for the CAR view lies in the result of redaction criticism from Luke. Luke was intensely concerned about the poor and marginalized. Yet researchers have observed that those who produce food, both animal and plant, are placed in a positive light (Lk 2:15; 15:4ff).[44] It would be unlikely that those who produced animal food would be portrayed positively, if God's intent all along was for humans to maintain a vegetarian diet.

The CAR argument regarding the Temple cleansing does not help their position either. Although Christ did overturn the tables of the dove sellers (Mk 11:15), and flogged those selling oxen, sheep, and doves (Jn 2:14–15), the Evangelists seem to direct Christ's anger at how the Temple area was converted into a shopping mall, rather than the particular product being hawked.[45] Furthermore, Christ was likely upset by illicit business practices as insinuated by His condemnation of the money changers as constituting "a den of robbers" (Lk 19:46; cf. Jer. 7:11).[46] Christ's anger at the dove sellers provides additional evidence regarding the financial nature of Christ's rage. Doves (were turtledoves equivalent to doves?)[47] were allowed for the poor. They could be trapped and given that way.[48] Kremer appeals to Malachi 3:1–6 that Christ wanted temple worshippers to exhibit different priorities.[49] Note that Malachi 3:6 mentions oppression of the poor. If Christ was against the use of animals in the sacrificial

43. Phelps, *The Dominion of Love*, 85–86. Additionally, Christ was completely capable of telling people not to sin when their past behavior made it extremely likely that they would re-offend (Jn 4:18ff).

44. Grimshaw, "Luke's Market Exchange District: Decentering Luke's Rich Urban Center," 42.

45. Wright's interpretation of Christ's actions as a condemnation of the politicization of the temple does not help the CAR interpretation either. Wright, *The Challenge of Jesus*, 65–67.

46. Walvoord and Zuck, *The Bible Knowledge Commentary*, 2: 279.

47. Hope, *All Creatures Great and Small*, 124ff.

48. Brewer, "Hunting, Animal Husbandry and Diet in Ancient Egypt," 453–55. Trapping birds was and is not that difficult to accomplish. See also Luce et al., "Archeological News and Discussion," 414. Bird trapping must have been common because a Judean molded lamp found primarily in Judea and southern Palestine portrayed images of baskets or a bird-trap. See Chancey and Porter. 184.

49. Kremer and InterVarsity Press, *The IVP Bible Background Commentary: New Testament*, Jn 2:15.

system, he could have easily said this along with condemning the pecuniary nature of the activity.[50] Jeremias' citation of Josephus' (Ant 20.205) statement that Ananias (in office A.D. 47–55) was the "great procurer of money and that the Temple was going to ruin"[51] supports a financial reason for Christ's righteous indignation.[52]

Finally, if killing or harming animals is wrong, or not God's perfect will, then Christ's perfection is in doubt (Heb 9:14) as He was directly and indirectly involved in the infliction of death and suffering upon animals.[53] If Christ's perfection is in doubt, then the N.T. teaching that Christ is our example also comes under question. For as Lampe cogently remarks, "As incarnate, he is the pattern of man in his intended relationship to God."[54]

THE CAR MOVEMENT'S ARGUMENT
FROM APOSTOLIC TEACHING

Christus Victor[55]

Like various Christian environmentalists,[56] CAR activists draw heavily on the notion of the Cosmic Christ because in doing so they can further reinforce a brotherhood between animals and people, and reduce the traditional focus that salvation is for humans only. A number of passages are drawn upon to support this idea that Christ came not just to save humans but to reconcile all creation, including animals (Rom 11:36; 1 Cor 15:22–

---

50. Walvoord and Zuck, *The Bible Knowledge Commentary*, eds. 2:157. This commentary suggests that part of Christ's concern was the way the market activity crowded out the Gentile worshipers and caused incredible foot traffic as people used the Temple area as a short-cut.

51. Jeremias, *Jerusalem in the Time of Jesus*, 49.

52. Chilton argues that the *Targum Zechariah* 14:21 statement "there shall never again be one doing trade in the sanctuary of the LORD of hosts at that time" predicts a time when there will be no more middlemen between the offering and the offerer. He believes that Jesus' actions were motivated by this prophecy. Chilton, "Should Palm Sunday Be Celebrated in the Fall?" 86.

53. Mt 8:32; 17:27; 21:1–5; Lk 5:4–6; Lk 5:14/Lev 14:30ff; cf. Lk 5:33 where Christ is accused of letting His disciples eat well, which probably involved abundant meat consumption.

54. Lampe, "The New Testament Doctrine of Ktisis," 460.

55. Aulen, *Christus Victor*, 4. He defines *Christus Victor* theology as Christ's victory over evil and the reconciliation of all creation.

56. Santmire, *The Travail of Nature*, 202ff.

28; Eph 1:9–10; Col 1:20;[57] Jn 1:1–3). Linzey suggests that the doctrine of reconciliation extends beyond humanity. Linzey cites Ephesians 1:9ff to support his view that Christ's work included cosmic reconciliation. What is critical to remember is that this work of Christ's is not just a historical or future work, but a present one in that Christ is actively sustaining all things (Heb 1:3). Moltmann characterizes Paul's logic as follows: if Christ is the creator of all, both human and non-human, then He must be the Savior of all.[58] Thus if Christ is to reconcile everything, then Linzey sees Christ's sacrifice as the model for us to understand how all human-creation relationships should be structured, namely for the greater to give of Himself for the lesser.[59]

If Christ is reconciling the cosmos, then the cosmos must be in some sort of estrangement from God. Linzey and other CAR activists believe that Roman 8:20–21[60] tells us that the earth is suffering and in need of redemption. As we saw in chapter 1, CAR activists consider themselves as an expression of the environmental movement. They believe that the earth is suffering under the dagger of an environmental crisis which desperately needs healing and restoration. Moltmann notes that our mechanized view of the world has displaced the Spirit's work in creation. The Spirit wants to unify us with the earth, as illustrated in Creation's groaning with us.[61] The CAR movement believes that part of the groaning of creation is humanity's consumption and abuse of animals, which began with the Fall. Since Christ came to reconcile "all things" (*ta panta*) to Himself, Christians need to participate in that reconciling process. Linzey goes further by asserting a relationship between Christ and the world that borders on pantheism. We have already seen his belief in animal-human relations due to our shared creaturely status. But Linzey says that since all things were created

57. Linzey, *Animal Theology*, 87.

58. Moltmann, *God in Creation*, 94–95. Linzey also argues that the incarnation signifies God's yes to creation and that it is "not a *necessary* implication." that Christ only saw value in humanity (italics his). Linzey, "The Place of Animals in Creation: A Christian View," 118. Young, *Is God a Vegetarian?* 149. Young takes a different approach. He focuses on Christ's conquest of death. Drawing heavily on Moltmann, Young believes the victory over death heralded by Christ's resurrection will apply to all of God's creatures.

59. Young, *Is God a Vegetarian?* 106. Perhaps Linzey's unstated belief here is that the Church, which exhibits the manifold wisdom of God (Eph 3:10), would eventually come to know the implications of Christ's reconciliation in all its cosmic dimensions.

60. Linzey, *Christianity and the Rights of Animals*, 13–14.

61. Moltmann, *God in Creation*, 98, 101.

by Christ, Christ is in all things and God is therefore one with creation.[62] God, in the Trinity, has incorporated creation into the Godhead by the incarnation. Thus Christ's death reconciled the world, and by that Linzey understands to include the animal creation too.[63] He even suggests, albeit quietly, that Christ died to reconcile animals and all creation to Himself.[64] Linzey's criticism of Barth's overemphasis on the differences between humans and animals results in a failure of Christ to bring redemption to creation because, "that which is not taken up cannot be healed."[65] Linzey even goes so far as to say that working to relieve nature from suffering and futility is the most fundamental liberation of all. Through Christ we are to help create the peaceable kingdom as prophesied in Isaiah 65:24ff. Finally, Christ, as the Logos, means that He was creatively involved in the making of animals and is thus concerned for them as various parables suggest.[66]

62. Linzey and Cohn-Sherbok, *After Noah*, 76–77.

63. Ibid., 68–70. Linzey relies on a few passages that are difficult to interpret, such as Col. 1:20 (and through Him to reconcile all things to Himself, having made peace through the blood of His cross; through Him, *I say*, whether things on earth or things in heaven. (NASB)); Eph 1:10 (with a view to an administration suitable to the fullness of the times, *that is*, the summing up of all things in Christ, things in the heavens and things on the earth. In Him (NASB)); and Romans 8:19ff. (Linzey, *Animal Theology*, 157. Verses are cited on this page of notes. Linzey mistakenly cites the verse as Rom 8:28f [see footnote 37 on p. 157]) Linzey's contention is that Romans 8:19 refers to human and animal groaning, and he is not alone. He is also not alone in holding that Christ is going to reconcile animate and inanimate creation. See House, "The Doctrine of Salvation in Colossians," 334. Ryken et.al., *Dictionary of Biblical Imagery*, 31. Hawthorne et.al., *Dictionary of Paul and His Letters*, 322. *A priori*, I have no problem thinking that all created things on earth figuratively groan under the penalty of sin brought on by mankind's sin both in Adam and presently. What is interesting is that the killing of animals is not mentioned as the fundamental expression of the problem as to why creation is groaning. However, a closer look at *ktisis* may lead us in a different direction. Lightfoot, *Acts–1 Corinthians*, 4:156–57 says that the "all creatures" refers to gentiles or the heathen world. Certainly Lightfoot is not the last word, but it is interesting that a fully human understanding of all creation is posited here. Linzey and Cohn-Sherbok, *After Noah*, 83–84.

64. Linzey, *Animal Theology*, 98. Linzey and Cohn-Sherbok, *After Noah*, 77, 79, 83–84. Psalm 36:6 is even cited with the insinuation that ultimate salvation for a beast is in view.

65. Ibid., 9–11.

66. Ibid., 81–82. Linzey even appeals to the sacraments to support the notion of God's unity with creation. He says sacraments are effective only because the world is sacramental. The Holy Spirit's union with the Virgin Mary connected matter with Spirit in perfect co-operation. Linzey explains that God's actions are neither bound by creation or exclusively tied to humans.

Webb draws upon passages suggesting harmony between animals and holy men as illustrative of the work of the Cosmic Christ, which we can imitate.[67] He points to Job 5:22–23 as supporting the notion that wisdom brings peace between animals and people. He also says that the harmony that righteous living brings is behind the idea of snake handling in Mark 16:16 and Luke 10:19, not to mention later church tradition.

Evaluation of Christus Victor

The redemptive impact of Christ's work for all of Creation is not substantially disputed, provided redemption does not include Satanic forces (which are beyond redemption) or heaven (which does not require it).[68] There is much to commend the view that Christ's redemption of the world corrected the parallel figurehead of Adam, whose sin broke the world.[69] The problem is, "What was the extent and significance of that redemptive act?" Two questions are in play. First, "Are the CAR activists correct to assert that the Fall resulted in human predation of animals?"[70] Second, "Does Christ's redemptive act seek to end humanity's consumptive and predatory use of animals?"

Both of these questions are contained in the controversy over the meaning of Romans 8, namely, is creation's groaning[71] the earth's response to the specific human activity of exploiting the animal creation, as suggested by CAR activists, or something else? Hahne eloquently and succinctly explains the relationship between humanity's Fall and its effect on the non-human creation.[72] He contends that Paul's use of corruption (*pthora* in Rom 8:21) refers to the decay, death, and destruction, as in the transitoriness of life.[73] He appealed to Isaiah 24:4, 7, where the LXX uses

---

67. Webb, *On God and Dogs*, 171.

68. Hahne, *The Birth Pangs of Creation*, 1. see also Moo, "Nature in the New Creation: New Testament Eschatology and the Environment," 449–88.

69. Haas, "Creational Ethics Is Public Ethics," 17.

70. Ibid., 12–15, 20. Haas actually says, "Our stance toward development of human life and the rest of creation is one of suffering love, whereby we use our ruling power to liberate and empower fellow humans, and to liberate non-human creation from the destructive effects of sin." Regrettably, he does not detail what that liberation of non-human creation concretely means, i.e. the animals.

71. The writer recognizes that Paul's language here is anthropathic in nature.

72. Hahne, *The Birth Pangs of Creation*, 3–4.

73. Moo, "Nature in the New Creation: New Testament Eschatology and the

pthora (corruption), to show that Isaiah believed human sinfulness impacted creation negatively. Hahne explains, "Although Genesis apparently limits the punishment of death after the Fall to humanity, Paul extends it to all of creation in Rom. 8:21."[74] On its face, it would appear that Hahne's research of the question accords with a CAR view.

However, I believe that the evidence can support a different understanding. First, consider that Hahne concurs with the notion that the Fall subjected creation to futility because it prevented creation from fulfilling its mission.[75] From that basis, the issue Isaiah was describing is not the death resulting from humanity's extraction of food and resources from creation, per se; it is the environmental death and destruction that occurs during societal chaos. The earth is groaning because its death is wasted, in that it could not fulfill its purpose of serving humanity.[76] If a vine suffers because its fruit is not harvested (Isa 24:7), is it not likely that creation can groan because the animal kingdom is not able to serve humanity the way it should? Fitzmeyer says that "*phthora* (corruption) denotes not only perishabilty and putrefaction, but also powerlessness, lack of beauty, vitality, and strength that characterize creation's present condition (parenthesis mine)."[77] My point is that it is not altogether clear that the mere existence or reality of death in the animal creation is what Paul had in mind when he said that creation was groaning. It could be the existence of meaningless death by disease, starvation, and natural disaster, not death caused by human activity, provided that the animal's sacrifice served humanity's purpose as God intended.[78]

Additionally, it should be mentioned that the section upholds an anthropocentric interpretation of Scripture and Christ's redemptive work. Paul notes that the salvation of creation is tied to the destiny of human salvation.[79] Reicke argues that the N.T. employs a polarity of Good and

---

Environment," 461. Moo believes *pthora* refers to death.

74. Hahne, *The Birth Pangs of Creation*, 5.

75. Ibid.

76. Kline, *Kingdom Prologue*, 1:41–43. Kline believes that before the Fall, death existed in creation (including animals) but that it served humanity. After the Fall, humanity served death.

77. Fitzmeyer, *Romans*, 509.

78. Hodge, *Commentary on the Epistle to the Romans*, 272. Hodge says this question is a vain one.

79. Fitzmeyer, *Romans*, 508–9.

Evil, and that in this vein, Paul's use of specific words provides clues as to whether the creation he refers to is being spoken of in a positive or negative light. Thus Paul's reference to creation's groaning actually refers to the negative view of creation as longing for a day when humans would be freed from the negative polarities of earthly existence. Reicke's comments are worthy of being quoted in full,

> The importance of this triumph of Christ for mankind was especially developed in the Epistle to the Romans. Adam lost the glory or image of God, but the atonement in Christ gives the believer a new righteousness (Rom 3:3–25). Because of Adam's sin, mankind became mortal (5:12) and the universe subject to vanity (8:20), but in his intensive prayer Paul felt the longing of the creation for the freedom of the believers (8:21–23) who are independent of all polarities dominating material existence (8:35–39). Among these polarities Paul mentioned life and death, present and future time, zenith and nadir as the dimensions of existence, time and space, and in addition referred to different principalities which control the material universe (8:38–39). He wanted to prove that no oppressive factors in nature and society can impede the universal victory of God's love in Christ."[80]

The second issue is that Paul refers to a future hope, not a present reality. Christians do not hope in vain because we have the Holy Spirit as a down payment of the future reality. But the restoration of creation remains a future event.[81] This brings us to the already-not yet nature of the Kingdom of God. The CAR activists, in their desire for a predatory-free existence, actually exhibit an over-realized eschatology. Even if we, for the sake of argument, concede that God will bring about a world free of animal death, it does not mean that it is His will for us now.[82] The CAR activists are correct in saying that our experience with the Spirit of Christ should lead the faithful to make responsible use of all God's property. It is certainly true that not all killing of animals by humans is justified. But that is a far cry from saying that humanity may not kill or eat animals.

---

80. Reicke, "Positive and Negative Aspects of the World in the NT," 365. For an even more emphatic discussion explaining that God saves the world by saving humanity, see Lampe," The New Testament Doctrine of Ktisis," 449–62.

81. Achtemeier, *Romans*, 143. See also Hodge, *Commentary on the Epistle to the Romans*, 269.

82. For a discussion of the all-ready and not-yet nature of the Kingdom of God see Bright, *The Kingdom of God*, 215ff. Ladd, *A Theology of the New Testament*, 66–67.

Additionally, as I have noted previously, Christ's work to put all things under His feet (Heb 2:8–9) must be understood in light of His earthly ministry and actions.[83]

Eschatology and the Symbol of Eden

CAR activists place a great deal of hermeneutical emphasis on the eschatological hope prophesied in the O.T. and grounded in God's redemptive work in Christ. Since Christians are to be living according to the principles of the next age, CAR activists endeavor to convince people that the future is one where humans and animals coexist in non-lethal harmony. Three arguments are employed to support this view. The first argument appeals to the interconnectedness of human and animal destinies, the second appeals to animal nature and spirituality, and the third to God's compassion (which has already been addressed above).

CAR activists argue that Scripture affirms the doctrine that humanity and animals share a common destiny. What affects one group affects the other.[84] "The peaceable kingdom reflects the Hebrew concept that the history of humanity is inextricably bound with the history of the earth."[85] When the knowledge of God is manifest, peace follows; where such knowledge is lacking, chaos strikes.[86] To support this view, Young cites a number of scriptural examples to illustrate the connection between animals and humans. First, animals are implicated in human judgment (Jer 7:20). Second, animals and humans mourn before God (Jon 3:6–9),[87] look for deliverance from God (Rom 8:18–23), and are sustained by God (Psa 104:27–31). Third, animals will participate in human restoration (Psa 36:6; Joel 2:21–2), and this peace will not just occur among the human community but also between humans and animals (Ex 34:25–9).[88] Since

---

83. Ross, *Creation & Blessing*, 113.

84. Eaton, *The Circle of Creation*, Np. Although not at all scholarly, Eaton's short book does show how animals play a role in the story of Scripture. Linzey, *Animal Theology*, 34. Linzey cites the Noahic covenant (Gen 9). Linzey does not mean that animals and humans are inseparable but he does see the two groups as bound by the covenantal relationship. Linzey, "The Place of Animals in Creation: A Christian View," 128.

85. Young, *Is God a Vegetarian?* 144.

86. Ibid. 141–42.

87. Other passages can be cited where the Bible connects human and animal lives, such as Joel 1:15–16,18; Jn 4:9–11; Lk 12:24, 27.

88. Young, *Is God a Vegetarian?* 145. He even makes the remarkable claim that for the

death has been conquered in Christ and will be banished in the resurrection (Isa 25:7; Hos 13:14; 1 Cor 15:26, 54–57; Rev 21:4), Christians must be against the death of all creatures, for Christ taught us pray that God's will in heaven be present on earth (Mt 6:10).[89]

CAR activists also point the prominence of Edenic imagery to support a connection between human and animal destinies.[90] If humans obeyed God then they were blessed agriculturally, which is interpreted as a return to the first Garden. Disobey and you will be ejected from the Garden and experience famine. They interpret prophecies concerning the future peaceable kingdom as a renewal and return to the harmony of creation's Edenic beginnings. Since the Garden had animals, Activists see the agricultural metaphor as another clue for God's concern for animals (Hos 4:1–3; Zech 1:2–3; Joel 1:18).[91] The most significant passage that uses Edenic imagery is the messianic prophecy of Isaiah, where he foresees a day when the lion will lie down with the lamb (Isa 11:6–10; 66:3ff. see also Ezek 34:25–9; Hos 2:18).[92] Linzey and others frequently mention that Isaiah's vision of the lion lying with the lamb heralds a time when God will stop animal predation, which justifies human predation.[93]

The second argument used to connect human and animal destinies is the assertion that animals have the ontological capacity to have their own spiritual relationship with God, and therefore will be in heaven.[94] The statement that both humans and animals share the Hebrew designation of being *nephesh hayah* is offered as proof of the ontological compatibility of

---

prophets killing of any kind would be antithetical to the peaceable kingdom.

89. Young, *Is God a Vegetarian?* 143–44, 146.; Phelps, *The Dominion of Love*, 63. Phelps suggests that the passage actually teaches that animals will be present in heaven.

90. Edenic imagery arguments were placed here, rather than in the O.T. chapter, because of their connection with eschatology and restoration of creation.

91. Webb, *On God and Dogs*, 21.

92. Young, *Is God a Vegetarian?* 83, 145. Young says this passage shows God promising animals a future free of killing, and humans will adopt vegetarianism.

93. Linzey, *Christianity and the Rights of Animals*, 33, 103–4.; Widyapranawa, *The Lord Is Savior*, 70. where he tells of how the Davidic king will restore "shalom" to the earth in an Edenic manner of friendliness.

94. Phelps, *The Dominion of Love*, 57f. Cf. Patton, "He Who Sits in the Heavens Laughs," 408. Patton says that animals are religious in ways that echo human religiosity and in ways idiosyncratic to their species. She also recognizes three ways God relates to animals: compassion and special regard, communication and mutual awareness, and animal veneration, 409ff.

humans and animals (Gen 2:7, 17). Since animals and humans share the same life force[95] they should have comparable future existences.

Finally, Linzey, who is less sanguine about the existence of animal souls,[96] prefers to base his belief of animals in heaven on an argument from theodicy.[97] He thinks that given all the suffering that animals endure, if they do not go to heaven the doctrine of God as a compassionate being would be besmirched[98] (Jn 4:9; Mt 10:29).

Evaluation of the Eschatological and Symbol of Eden Arguments

CAR activists correctly believe that God cares about the earth and all its inhabitants, and that this care will be exhibited in a future earthly restoration.[99] Sadly, Christians have, from time to time, overemphasized other-worldly salvation to the detriment of the physical world[100] as characterized by the hymn, "This World is Not My Home."[101] Additionally, activists are correct to say that there is a connection between animals and humans, as we saw above in the comments regarding *Christus Victor*.

Nevertheless, a number of difficulties still accrue to the CAR position. The problem with their first eschatological argument is not that a link between animals and humans does not exist; it is that the link is not as strong as the CAR activists contend. They wrongly assume that the world to come matches the Garden.[102] This parallelism is not only highly speculative, it is also highly unlikely. For example, marriage occurred in the Garden but will not occur in the next age (Gen 2:22f; Mt 22:30). If

95. Ibid., 58.

96. Linzey, *Christianity and the Rights of Animals*, 36–38. He appeals to Eccl 3:19–20.

97. Lewis, *The Problem of Pain*, 140–43. Lewis spoke of the possibility that domestic animals may be in heaven because certain animals (say a dear pet) becomes part of the human's train.

98. Linzey, *Christianity and the Rights of Animals*, 37–38. Linzey, *Animal Theology*, 100. Perhaps he could appeal to Isa 43:20 where God says the wildlife will glorify Him in response to the waters in the desert.

99. For an excellent survey of the arguments in support of a renewed earth see Middleton, "A New Heaven and a New Earth: The Case for a Holistic Reading of the Biblical Story of Redemption," 73–98.

100. For a brief review of the environmental impact of premillenialism see Truesdale, "Last Things First: The Impact of Eschatology on Ecology," 116–22.

101. Brumley, *This World Is Not My Home*.

102. Berkhoff, *Christian Faith*, 171. Berkhof argues that it isn't referring to a return to the original state of creation. Contra Jewish expectations see Jeremias, "Paradise," 5:767.

marriage, a bond established by God from the beginning and reaffirmed by Jesus Christ and the Apostle Paul, will not exist in the consummation, why should we expect the CAR activists' view of human-animal relations to take place? Middleton correctly shows that God desires to restore His "creational intent" for humanity and the world, which includes those changes which occurred through humanity's cultural development.[103] Haas does not doubt that the Garden was perfect in the moral sense; what he questions is whether the Garden was perfect in the sense of complete.[104] The Garden was morally perfect, but must the new creation be a mirror image of the first? Haas does not think so. The point being, that as God moved creation to its culmination, He made room for humanity to fulfill the cultural mandate of Genesis 1:26–28. God will not simply return creation to a perfect original state, He will correct its wayward direction.[105] To return to the original state would reject the cultural achievements humanity has accomplished.[106] It is for this reason that Isaiah's lion and lamb scenario does not necessarily enlighten us about life in the first Garden.

It is also troubling that the N.T. understanding of "paradise" has a different emphasis than what CAR activist suggest. They want to focus on the externals, as did Jewish scholars, whereas the N.T. focuses on paradise as being with Christ (Lk 23:34; 2 Cor 12:4; Rev 2:7).[107] The fact that "paradise" is a Persian loan word also muddies the significance for CAR activists, because for the Persians, paradise referred to a cultivated hunting park encircled by walls.[108] Certainly the role of hunting is not front and center in the N.T.'s use of paradise, but if we accept the Septuagint's

103. Middleton, "A New Heaven and a New Earth: The Case for a Holistic Reading of the Biblical Story of Redemption," 76.

104. Haas, "Creational Ethics Is Public Ethics," 6–8.

105. Further evidence for this can be seen in the author of Hebrews, who in 11:10 and again in verse 16, tells of Abraham looking for God's city. The city theme is also taken up in Revelation 21:2, 10, and 22:14. (*polis*—see Balz and Schneider, *Polis "City,"* 3:129.) An urbanized future is not what most animal rights activists envision as God's ideal.

106. Haas, "Creational Ethics Is Public Ethics," 13; Moltmann, *God in Creation*, 207–9. He says the goal of creation is not a return to paradise (which cannot be achieved because time can only be expressed with change). Rather the goal of creation is the glory of God, those possibilities opened by the Spirit. He continues that the idea of returning to perfection contradicts the Bible's messianic goal. (Isa 43:18ff.).

107. Jeremias, "Paradise." 5:772–73. See also Lioy, *The Book of Revelation in Christological Focus*, 127.

108. Cartledge, *Thermopylae*, 47–48.

use of the term as informing the N.T.'s use, then an ideal environment for the benefit of humans is certainly in view.[109]

Another issue is that the passages used by CAR activists to support their vision of the peaceable kingdom, can be reasonably interpreted in other ways. For example, they ignore the high probability that Isaiah is proclaiming a day when predators, the bane of herdsman and shepherds,[110] will be eliminated, and that Mankind will again gain its proper place as servant king of the earth.[111] These Isaiah passages that refer to the coming kingdom are all written from the perspective of human interests. The benefits apply to the humans, not to the animals, unless you are a prey species. Rimbach points out that

> In the animal imagery of the OT the ferocity of the lion, the wolf, and the bear as predators is common. The leopard/panther is mentioned six times: three times its stalking prowess (Jer 5:6; Hos 13:7, and, by implication, Isa 11:6), but also its speed (Hab 1:8) and its beautiful pelt (Jer 13:23).[112]

Attention to these sorts of details should come as no surprise if, as Dever claims, pastoral nomadism constituted 10–15% of the total population in the land of Israel right up to modern times.[113] These pastoralists were not isolated from society but connected to the sedentary population through trade.[114] Livestock was an important element in Iron II Israel (1000–586 B.C.). Dever argues that the circular plans found in nearly all sites in this period were to keep marauders (both animal and human) out, and animals inside.[115] Furthermore, citing Lawrence E. Stager's evalu-

109. Bietenhard and Brown, "Paradise," 2:761. This is how the present writer understands the significance of the term "garden."

110. Readers should not ignore that farmers also have to be concerned about wildlife depredating their crops; a reality that is assumed in Psalm 80:13. If the experience of farmers in the United States is comparable to Israelite farmers faced, then feral hogs were a considerable threat, see "Feral/Wild Pigs: Potential Problems for Farmers and Hunters,"1–4.

111. A closer look at Ezek 34:28–29 accords with the present writer's understanding of Isaiah 11. Ezekiel touches on two great threats to a shepherd's security, war and predators, which he poetically mentions in a beautiful chiasm.

112. Rimbach, "Bears or Bees? Sefire I a 31 and Daniel 7," 566.

113. Dever, *Who Were the Early Israelites and Where Did They Come From?* 157.

114. Ibid., 180.

115. Ibid., 163.; Job 30:1 provides evidence that dogs were used to help guard flocks from predation. Hope, *All Creatures Great and Small*, 41.

tion of the pillared four-room house, the inhabitants raised livestock.[116] The point of all this is that if Isaiah wanted to espouse a vegetarian, non-predatory world, he should have, and could have, chosen clearer and more robust language available to him.[117]

Second, there is little doubt that creation bears a heavy burden under the curse which was caused by mankind.[118] However, to suggest that humans should simply turn back the clock to the Garden or fast forward to the *eschaton* causes CAR's theology to suffer from being an over-realized one.[119] Like the Corinthians who pushed for celibate marriages, CAR activists want a meatless diet for humanity. They have, in effect, placed a burden on Christians that Christ did not give (cf. Mt 15:11), and elevated a personal preference to a moral ideal. In so doing they raised questions concerning the character of Christ, who did not meet their standard.

The point of all this is that as humans submit to God's moral law, their changed behavior will result in an external benefit to creation.[120] Again CAR activists agree. They too want to see a future where God's rule turns back the cause of Creation's groan (Rom 8). The problem, however, is that Scripture does not recognize that human dominion over the animals is a problem that needs fixing.

But what of the notion that Christ instituted the beginning of a peaceable kingdom in which Christians should work toward a goal of non-violent relations between man and beast?[121] This is the same sort

116. Dever, *Who Were the Early Israelites and Where Did They Come From?* 163–64.

117. Cf. Silva, *Explorations in Exegetical Method*, 53. Despite the problems of "semantic neutralization" and lack of verbal precision, words capable of supporting an animal rights view were available to Isaiah.

118. H. H. Esser, "Creation," 1:385. Esser writes, "Man is the goal of creation. Therefore, the state of creation is determined by him. All created things look to man as their hope is in man to alleviate the suffering caused by him. All creation is dependent on the restoration of the right relationship between God and his representative in the created world. This can only occur with God's intervention."

119. See Fee's explanation of Corinth's over-realized eschatology in Fee, *The First Epistle to the Corinthians*, 12, 268ff.

120. Haas, "Creational Ethics Is Public Ethics," 9, 13.

121. It should be noted that the term "non-violent" is not perfectly clear. If violence is understood as direct 'physical' action against an animal's well-being then the term is clear. However, if the CAR activists are actually emphasizing harmony, as in humans and animals living with the well-being of both in mind, then readers should know that even non-killing behaviors such as bird watching can result in harm to some species and benefit others. For example, the high visitor traffic to one park was implicated for the

of argument used by Evangelical social progressives, who acknowledge that Jesus was not a violent revolutionary but rather a mustard seed revolutionary. Evangelicals should agree that Christ's actions and teachings were "revolutionary." Christ directly challenged social norms regarding Sabbath, and made statements that criticized Temple authority.[122] Christ's statements that would have an impact on animal use cut for and against the CAR view. On the one hand, Christ's assault on Temple authority can be interpreted as a criticism of, or at least the ending of, animal sacrifice. However, on the other hand, Christ's abrogation of food laws undermines the CAR position. Wright suggests that Christ's words as recorded by Mark cannot be projected to Mark's time (Mk 7:14–19). Christ spoke cryptically, for if He spoke more bluntly a riot would have likely ensued. Instead Christ set, as Wright calls it, "time bombs" against symbols of Jewish separation from paganism.[123] The bottom line here for CAR activists is that they have overstated how revolutionary Christ's teachings and actions were. Christ did not condemn a carnivorous diet; He actually said the Jewish dietary laws (which CAR activists believe God established to promote, among other things, humane treatment of animals) were passing away. It would appear that Henry's point is that their view of Christ needs to be balanced. Henry says,

> Yet we must not overstate the formidable threat that Jesus' alternative of the new social organism posed for existing worldly society. ... It seems far-fetched to interpret taking up the cross and hating one's own life for Christ's sake as a warning by Jesus that his fate and that of his disciples will be crucifixion as revolutionaries ... Christ nonetheless establishes a new social reality (2 Cor 5:17) or, as *The New English Bible* puts it, "a whole new world." The universe is seen in redemptive perspective through God's stupendous provision for overcoming human alienation, and the church of the redeemed community proffers to longstanding enemies an invitation to reconciliation.[124]

---

decline in bird diversity. Adams et al., *Urban Wildlife Management*, 107.

122. Wright, *The Challenge of Jesus*, 58–65.

123. Ibid., 60–61, 65.

124. Henry, *God, Revelation, and Authority*, 4:528–29.

THE CAR MOVEMENT'S HANDLING
OF DIFFICULT PASSAGES

As with the O.T., CAR activists recognize that several N.T. passages pose grave counter-arguments for their view that the Bible supports animal rights.[125] Apart from Phelps,[126] who dismisses Paul as a consummate compromiser, Webb[127] and Young endeavor to mitigate the negative impact of Paul's comments regarding food and animals in various ways.[128]

Meat and the weaker brother
Romans 14:1–23

Webb believes Paul's comments in Romans 8:19–22 show that he understood that creation was frustrated. Webb contends that the real issue behind Romans 14 was political and not dietary. He says in Roman society (first century A.D.) to be a vegetarian could be understood as a critique of pagan culture, which would have placed wealthy Christians in a difficult situation when it came to business meals. These Christians would find it incredibly awkward to refuse to eat the meat offered by a wealthy pagan client. Webb concludes saying, "Paul's advice 'nicely serves the interests of a few socially elevated members of the group by permitting them to ignore the religious dimension of civic life.'"[129]

Meat offered to idols
1 Corinthians 8–10

Phelps presents a rather unusual argument for Paul's comments regarding the eating of meat offered to idols. He says that since Jews were evicted from Rome by Claudius in A.D. 50, all the Jews that remained had to maintain a low profile. Therefore, he contends, they could not operate ko-

---

125. Young, *Is God a Vegetarian?* 80–81. Young accepts the idea that the N.T. understood the dietary laws as signs which were fulfilled in Christ, thereby transforming holiness into an internal from an external reality. Nevertheless, Young believes that while food does not ritually separate us from God, Christians have a moral obligation to use care in what they eat for health, environmental, and compassionate reasons. See pages 81–87.

126. Phelps, *The Dominion of Love*, 160–63, 170f.

127. Webb, *On God and Dogs*, 25. It is instructive to note that Webb acknowledges that Paul's theology, as it relates to animals, is "ambiguous."

128. Ibid., 25–28.

129. Webb, *On God and Dogs*, 27. Webb is quoting another scholar, thus the double quotes.

sher butcher shops. But ironically, Phelps does not interpret the passage as a Pauline concession for situation. Instead he claims that food for Paul was neither an ethical nor a spiritual issue.[130]

Oxen
1 Corinthians 9:9–10

Webb criticizes Paul for ignoring the literal reading supporting the O.T.'s concern for animals in his drive to fight legalism.[131] He says Christianity excessively continued the Hebraic desacrilization of nature, with the result that the connection between justice and nature became essentially lost. He claims that the N.T.'s opposition to Jewish legalism, heightened by a belief in the approaching *parousia* (second coming of Christ), effectively put many areas, including animals, outside the moral realm.[132]

Abstinence from Certain Foods
1 Timothy 4:1–5 and Colossians 2:16–17

Young openly takes up this passage by reaffirming his rejection of historical reconstructions.[133] He correctly shows that the KJV translation of *broma* as "meat" is unfortunate as the term has the more general meaning of "food." Young says that Paul's harsh words were not for condemning vegetarianism per se, but rather those who mandated vegetarianism. He makes a similar interpretation of Colossians, saying

> Paul is not really addressing the issue of meat eating or vegetarianism, but rather the transitory status of symbols that pointed to the Messiah. We often forget that one's perception of proper and improper behavior is usually conditioned by one's social location in dialogue with one's symbolic world.[134]

He continues by saying the situations in the N.T. differ remarkably from our own.[135] Young ultimately concludes that Paul does not mandate a diet but rather says our eating must be virtue based. The point is that

---

130. Phelps, *The Dominion of Love*, 171–72.

131. Webb, *On God and Dogs*, 25.

132. Ibid., 24–28.

133. Young, *Is God a Vegetarian?* 115–25.

134. Ibid., 120.

135. Ibid.

eating meat is not forbidden but, in light of the total situation, Young thinks it is likely not advisable, for he considers the activity of eating meat for the modern believer to be "reckless liberty."[136]

EVALUATION OF THE CAR MOVEMENT'S HANDLING OF DIFFICULT PASSAGES

It is telling that a *prima facie* reading of the CAR activist understanding of these passages actually supports the traditional view that food is not a moral issue of ultimate standing. This analysis is also supported by the lack of attention paid to these passages by Andrew Linzey, the leader of the movement.[137] Young's virtue argument related to the eating of meat is more subtle and will be taken up in the next chapter.

At its root, the controversy over food rests on how one understands the interaction between principles and exceptions. CAR activists like to argue in broad trajectories, as it allows them to ignore the specific exceptions to their rules. Even if one concedes their view that the Bible puts believers on a path towards animal compassion, we are still left with the problem of how to justify that position in light of the stark imperatives given by Paul. If Paul cannot be trusted regarding the morality of eating meat, then what other moral rules can or should we ignore? I believe that the hermeneutical principle should be that the principle is circumscribed by the specific. Just as a statute that forbids speeding does not mean that police officials cannot exceed the speed limit, likewise a condemnation of cruelty does not mean that humans cannot eat meat.

Furthermore, it is incredibly ironic that Paul, whose testimony in Romans 8 is heralded as a great passage for animal rights, is the same Paul who utilized leather in his trade as a tentmaker (Acts 18:3).[138] Similarly, Simon the Tanner (Acts 9:43) is not condemned for his work in the animal trade as a preserver of animal skins. In fact, his home is blessed, as the Holy Spirit was poured out there, and Peter realized that food was no longer a factor designating participation in God's family.[139]

---

136. Ibid., 123.

137. *Broma* the word used for food in 1 Tim 4:3 is clearly used to refer to fish in Luke 9:13 see also 1 Cor 8:13 where it is used with *kreas* "meat". Ralph Earle, "1 Timothy," 11:372 says "Paul declared that nothing is to be rejected *'apobleton'* thrown away—occurs only here in the N.T.—if it is received with thanksgiving."

138. Michaelis, "Skenopoios," 7:393–94.

139. Bruce, *The Book of the Acts*, 206; Marshall, *Acts*, 186.

Romans 14

Whether Webb has correctly described the historical background for Romans 14 remains to be seen. However, his point that the issue was political actually supports the interpretation that dietary rules are not about ultimate morality, they are for social harmony. Charles Hodge says it well,

> ... the apostle teaches that it [Christian liberty] is not to be given up or denied; that is, we are not to make things sinful which are in themselves indifferent, ver. 14. But it does not follow, that because a thing is not wrong in itself, it is right for us to indulge in it. Our liberty is to be asserted; but it is to be exercised in such a way as not to injure others.[140]

The problem with the CAR's position lay in its not taking seriously Paul's admonition that food is not something one should be using to judge others. A sad aspect of my work here lies in the fact that I, as a meat-eater, must remind fellow Christians who have chosen vegetarianism that their decision to avoid meat is their own. It is improper to suggest that a meat eater is any less of a righteous Christian than someone who practices vegetarianism.

Abstaining from foods [141]
1 Timothy 4:1–5 and Colossians 2:16–17

It should be no surprise that the CAR activists typically ignore 1 Timothy 4:1–5, given the content and severity of Paul's language regarding those who condemn foods, that those who do so risk falling away from the faith because they listened to demons.[142] Although *broma* can mean food in a general sense, Knight believes that the context suggests a more narrow definition of animal flesh.[143] Whatever the word's precise meaning in this passage, the more important point is Paul's rationale for saying that all

---

140. Hodge, *Commentary on the Epistle to the Romans*, 416 [brackets mine]. Even though Jewett's commentary on Romans diminishes the significance of the weak and strong, he concludes that food is a personal choice as all will be judged by God. Jewett et al., *Romans*, 830–38.

141. The writer has bypassed commenting on the 1 Corinthian passages, as they do not provide evidence against a Dominionist view (1 Cor 8–10) or have been dealt with elsewhere (1 Cor 9:9–10).

142. For a survey of the heretical beliefs held by advocates of vegetarianism since the 1600s see Stuart, *The Bloodless Revolution*.

143. Knight, *The Pastoral Epistles*, 187.

food is good. Paul grounds the goodness of food in the creative act of God (1 Tim 4:3). If that statement lacked sufficient force, Paul accentuates it in the next verse where he applies God's creative goodness to individual members of the class (*pan* with anarthrous noun).[144] Paul is not condemning vegetarianism or kosher observance. Neither is he encouraging gluttony or drunkenness (1 Cor 6:9–12; 11:21–22). Paul is simply rejecting any argument that justifies one's food choices on theological grounds.[145]

Colossians 2:16–17 does not provide any solace for CAR activists either. Paul uses terms that would encompass not only Jewish restrictions but also pagan ascetical ones.[146] Lohse explains that in the ancient world people restricted their behavior and dietary choices in order to become closer to the divine. Paul condemns all of this as being subject to the "elements of the universe" (*stoicheia tou kosmou*), which were conquered by the cross.[147]

Bruce argues that the reason why Paul is so emphatic in Colossians, as opposed to his language elsewhere (Rom 14:13–21; 1 Cor 8:7–13), is due to his defense of Christian liberty against those who are trying to undermine it. In other passages, Paul encourages Christians to respect the differences of those who hold a different ethical sensitivity.[148] The bottom line is that until the CAR activists can provide a cogent reinterpretation of these passages, it seems highly unlikely that the case for vegetarianism as an obligatory or preferable lifestyle for Christians can ever be supported.

2 Peter 2:12 and Jude 10

These two passages, from a CAR perspective, must rank among the most speciesist in Scripture. 2 Peter speaks of animals as being made for the purpose of destruction and Jude calls them irrational. CAR activists could counter that the N.T. writer was simply a child of his age and believed, just like his fellow citizens, that animals were irrational[149] and destined

---

144. Ibid.

145. Lea and Griffin, *1, 2, Timothy, Titus*, 130. I should also point out that cannibalism is not allowed as humans are created in the image of God (Gen 1:26; 9:6).

146. Contra Bruce who believes heightened Jewish law is in force rather than syncretism. Bruce, *The Epistles to the Colossians to Philemon and to the Ephesians*, 113–14.

147. Lohse, *Colossians and Philemon*, 114.

148. Bruce, *The Epistles to the Colossians to Philemon and to the Ephesians*. 114.

149. Keener and InterVarsity Press, *The IVP Bible Background Commentary: New Testament*, 2 Peter 2:12.

for human use.[150] However, again it must be said that for CAR activists to employ such a perspective would provide more evidence that their argument uses special pleading.

SUMMARY

The CAR movement has provided the Church with an important opportunity to reflect upon and refine its historic understanding of Scriptural testimony regarding human-animal relations. Nevertheless, it should be clear that the CAR movement has not demonstrated that the New Testament calls Christians to work for the Peaceable Kingdom as the CARs envision it (Isa 11:6–9). If the New Testament requires Christians to avoid eating meat as well as harvesting animals, the call must be so obscure that only a select group of people are gifted to see it. The essential problem with the CAR movement's view resides with its inability to accept Scripture as God's Word. Patton explains the problem well by noting that CAR activists call Aquinas' views of animals and nature as anthropocentric and hierarchal because they neglect to consider that Aquinas said those things because he believed that it was God (not humanity) who established the hierarchy. She continued by explaining it is not that the monotheistic religions denigrated animals and made them worthless, it was just that humans were so much more valuable.[151]

The CAR view, although damaged, may still make a case based on the principle that all things may be lawful but not all things are profitable. I will take up that issue in the next chapter.

---

150. Bauckham, *2 Peter, Jude*, 263.

151. Patton, "He Who Sits in the Heavens Laughs," 406–7.

5

The CAR Movement's Argument from Ethics

Having reviewed CAR activists' appeal to Scripture, we turn to explore their appeal to moral arguments concerning limitations regarding human use of animals, particularly as they relate to the consumptive use of wildlife. It is critical to understand that the moral arguments stand on their own merits. Although grounded in a Christian ethos, these arguments may still be sufficient to persuade, if not compel, Christian behavior even if Scripture does not mandate the behavior. The power behind these moral arguments stems from the CAR activists utilization of an important Christian moral principle that says, "The right to do something does not mean one ought to do something." As Paul phrased it, "All things may be lawful, but not all things are profitable." (1 Cor 16:12) Kaufman and Braun in their book *Vegetarian as Christian Stewardship* state the issue quite clearly, "If eating animals is consistent with fundamental Christian principles, then there is no problem; if not then Christians should strive to abstain."[1]

CAR activists appeal to several moral principles in their effort to convince people to stop killing and/or eating other sentient beings of the animal kingdom. First, they contend that a compassionate lifestyle should be embraced because meat eating and ordinary violence appear to be connected.[2] Second, vegetarianism, by reducing animal death and suffering, models Christ's compassion for creation. Third, vegetarianism exemplifies godly stewardship of the earth by living more simply, in that vegetarians consume fewer resources. Finally, vegetarianism manifests better individual stewardship in that vegetarianism is a healthier lifestyle for those

---

1. Kaufman and Braun, *Vegetarianism as Christian Stewardship*, 1.
2. Webb, *On God and Dogs*, 44.

who choose to practice it.[3] CAR activists employ these principles in three arguments: the argument from compassion, the argument from restraint (or the "No Need Argument"), and the argument from stewardship[4] in order to convince Christians to reject killing and eating animals.

ARGUMENT FROM COMPASSION

The argument from compassion is the oldest[5] and the most widely used argument by CAR activists.[6] We will discuss the secular version[7] (also known as "Ethical Vegetarianism") of the argument since the Biblical version has already been covered.[8] The argument essentially says it is wrong to: 1. kill sentient animals, and 2. inflict gratuitous harm to them.[9] The central point is the belief that animals can and do suffer both during the process of being killed and in the finality of having been killed. So even if an animal was killed instantly, without warning (to avoid psychological distress) and so quickly that it could not feel pain (to avoid physical distress), the animal's death would still be cruel and immoral because the animal would have been deprived of its right to life.[10]

Perhaps realizing that convincing a meat-eating culture that killing animals is wrong would be inordinately difficult, CAR activists begin this

3. Kaufman and Braun, *Vegetarianism as Christian Stewardship*, ix.

4. Scully, *Dominion*, x–xi.

5. Rudrum, "Ethical Vegetarianism in Seventeenth-Century Britain," 76–86.

6. Since Linzey presents the most comprehensive discussion of this particular argument, what follows is summation of his thought found in the following texts: Linzey, *Animal Theology*, 56–58.; Linzey, *Christianity and the Rights of Animals*, 43–46. Linzey is by no means alone, however. See Dear, "Christianity and Vegetarianism: Pursuing the Nonviolence of Jesus," 1–18.

7. By secular, this writer does not mean to imply that the CAR argument is not informed by religious values. Rather it is just to distinguish the argument's appeal to human understanding of morality rather than to divine decree. cf. Hamilton, "Eating Ethically: 'Spiritual' and 'Quasi-Religious' Aspects of Vegetarianism," 65.

8. Linzey, *Animal Gospel*, 67. Linzey says that cruelty to animals is cruelty to Christ. The argument emphasizes God's immanence in Creation so that as creation suffers God suffers too. Humans, as fellow but morally superior creatures, are called to a ministry of amelioration of all suffering. Just as God was not too proud to humble himself in the form of a servant, so humans should oppose their own selfish arrogance and help weaker creatures.

9. Whittingstall and Linzey, "The Debate: Should We All Be Vegetarian?" 24.

10. CAR activists would also point out that the animal's extended family would suffer the loss too, as Canada geese who mate for life mourn the loss of a partner.

argument by demonstrating the reasonableness that animals can and do suffer just like humans.[11] They carefully exploit the commonsense notion that animals can experience pain and anxiety. We just "know" that animals suffer because they have the sentient capacity to "suffer," unlike plants and inanimate objects which can be mistreated but cannot have a conscious experience of pain. CAR activists also appeal to evolutionary theory and scientific evidence demonstrating the significant qualities shared by animals and humans to blur any distinction between humanity and animals that might be used to diminish the reality or significance of animal suffering. In this way, they undermine the traditional argument that animal suffering is morally inferior to that of human suffering. Their goal is to employ the longstanding jurisprudence principle that similar must be treated similarly; animal activists go to great lengths to reject any notion that humans are qualitatively different than animals in a way significant enough to morally justify humanity's infliction of suffering upon the animal kingdom.[12] Once one concedes that animals can and do suffer in the process of being harvested for meat or other products, CAR activists keenly ask us to consider why we do not feel the need to change our behavior towards animals. For if we are unwilling to inflict injury on a fellow human being just because he/she is of a different race or gender, why should we believe we have the right to inflict injury on animals? To continue to inflict harm upon animals, after granting that they suffer and are not significantly different in a moral way, would constitute the error of speciesism. Speciesism, just like racism, is the prejudicial view and/or treatment of other organisms as inferior. CAR activists also ask us to reflect on the possibility that our previous lack of concern over animal suffering was just the cruel expression of self-serving motives. In this way, their critique is based on the Scriptural principles of doubt about one's self-serving motives and an expansive view of who is our neighbor,[13] and appeal to the Western notion of progress towards individual rights and freedom.[14]

11. I concede that animals are capable of suffering, i.e. that they experience pain and that they can recall and avoid it. For an extended discussion of the awareness of animals see Regan, *The Case for Animal Rights*, 1–81.

12. Linzey, *Animal Rights*, 5, 11–12.

13. This particular observation was stimulated by my reading of Williams, "The Good Life," 51–52.

14. Cone, "Whose Earth Is It Anyway?" 36.

Aside from the moral rightness of the cause of animal liberation, CAR activists quietly suggest that societal adoption of vegetarianism will reduce the incidence of violent crime. The idea is if we stop expressing violence against animals we would not be so inclined to kill each other because the notion of any violence will become abhorrent.[15] Arthur Poletti asks, if we cannot stop violence against animals how can we stop it against humans?[16] The basis of this argument from progression is grounded in the discovery that a high percentage of those involved in violent crime were also involved in animal abuse at an earlier age.[17]

Linzey anticipates and responds to several objections to this argument from compassion. The first argument he considers is the claim that hunting is needed to control the species for its own welfare. He says that if population reduction is necessary it must be done in the most humane method, which hunting does not achieve. Furthermore, hunting, as in the case of the otter, has actually led to the decline of wildlife populations,causing hunting to be curtailed. Finally, hunting is often used for species whose populations have been artificially raised for the purpose of being hunted. Linzey does not think it is right to cause a problem just so you can solve it. As insinuated above, Linzey finds the arguments for hunting as a wildlife conservation measure more difficult to dismiss. He does not like culling as he finds it a profoundly anthropocentric activity in that it flows from an idea that animals are valuable not in and of themselves, but for their value to us. He is also suspicious that conservation is praised only so that populations can become high enough to safely hunt. He asserts that those who proffer conservation of wildlife are also the first to hunt that wildlife.[18]

15. Dear, "Christianity and Vegetarianism: Pursuing the Nonviolence of Jesus," 10; Linzey, *Animal Gospel*, 67.

16. Poletti, *God Does Not Eat Meat*, Np. Strictly speaking, Poletti argues from a Judeo-Christian basis rather than an explicitly Christian position. To argument that hunting allows men a release of their aggression, Linzey tersely says this isn't as much an argument as it is a statement of moral incapacity, which should also be rejected. Linzey, *Animal Rights*, 41.

17. Beirne, "From Animal Abuse to Interhuman Violence? A Critical Review of the Progression Thesis," 45; Hensley and Tallichet, "Learning to Be Cruel? Exploring the Onset and Frequency of Animal Cruelty," 37; Merz-Perez et al., "Childhood Cruelty to Animals and Subsequent Violence against Humans," 556–73; Joy, "Humanistic Psychology and Animal Rights: Reconsidering the Boundaries of the Humanistic Ethic," 109.

18. Linzey, *Animal Rights*, 41.

The second claim that Linzey objects to is the notion that humans are instinctual hunters. Linzey finds this assertion ridiculous, noting that just because nature is red in tooth and claw does not mean that we should be.[19] The third objection is that hunting actually reduces the amount of suffering an animal would endure under natural conditions. Linzey finds this argument also unconvincing for he does not believe that nature is a morally responsible agent.[20] For him, the issue is moral culpability rather than suffering per se.

EVALUATION OF THE ARGUMENT FROM COMPASSION

CAR activists' opposition to animal suffering causes them to condemn a wide variety of human activities. Linzey, whose guiding principle appears to be Albert Schweitzer's "Reverence for Life Ethic,"[21] says humans must work to liberate animals in four key areas: wanton injury (i.e. dog fighting, hunting), institutionalized suffering (i.e. intensive farming, animal experimentation, fur trapping), oppressive control (i.e. zoos, pets,[22] animal damage management), and products of slaughter (i.e. eating meat).[23] Any suffering, even that suffering which brings usefulness to us, is not sufficient justification for harming animals.[24] Clearly, adoption of this perspective would have monumental implications for our modern culture. Although our focus will be on killing wildlife for meat, products, and damage control, it is important to recognize the wide scope of the topic. It is also essential to recognize that while the two premises for the argument from compassion, namely our commonalities with animals and the evil of animal suffering, are intertwined,they each stand on their own merits. For example, even if, as we have already shown, humans are substantially different from animals, the argument from compassion still carries force because it argues for the morality of substantially limiting humanity's use of animals.

19. Linzey, *Animal Rights*, 40.

20. Ibid., 41.

21. Linzey and Cohn-Sherbok, *After Noah*, 104.

22. Webb, *On God and Dogs*, xi, 76. Webb, who disagrees with Linzey on the notion that pets are symbols of human exploitive dominance, believes that pets (i.e. companion animals) can exhibit a symbiotic and non-exploitive relationship of love and mutual respect.

23. Linzey, *Christianity and the Rights of Animals*, 104–46.

24. Linzey, *Animal Gospel*, 66.

It should be readily apparent that argument from compassion is decidedly complex and, at times, compelling. CAR activists, along with their secular cobelligerents, have made great strides in reducing the distinctions between humans and animals.[25] Aside from the scientific research regarding animal intelligence (and the evolutionary assumption that humans are just another animal), ethicists have used the argument from marginal cases[26] to batter the traditional view. For example, in times past theologians would contend that rationality[27] was a key distinction between humans and animals. If that is true, then it would be right to ask, "What should be done with the mentally deficient?" and "Should the mentally retarded lose their place in the human family if it can be shown that a baboon is more rational than a retarded person?" While the distinctions between animals and humans have been substantially reduced, the notion continues to persist. In many ways, it reminds us of the difficulties in defining pornography. Just because one cannot perfectly define it, does not mean one is incapable of knowing what pornography is when one sees it. As noted in chapter 2, Scripture does appear to support a notion that something, called 'the image of God,' separates humans from animals. Linzey identifies it as a difference in the moral abilities of humans and animals. But how can we have this moral superiority or capability unless we have that aspect in our nature to permit it?[28] It should trouble the CAR activists that Scripture never tells of animals receiving the baptism or infilling of the Holy Spirit.[29] Although the force of this observation suffers from being an argument from silence, could it also be that animals cannot receive the Spirit? To use a more secular argument, just as Linzey is morally compelled to wonder why humans have an "empirical" sense

25. The distinctions between humanity and animals have certainly been reduced, but they have not been eliminated. For a brief survey of arguments for the continuation of that distinction see Goddard, "I Think, Therefore I Am: One Author Tackles the Philosophical and Ethical Considerations of Pest Control," 124.

26. Pluhar, *Beyond Prejudice*, 67ff.

27. Linzey, *Animal Rights*, 24. See also Thomas Aquinas and Descartes.

28. This type of argument relies on "The Principle of Sufficient Reason." For a discussion of this principle see Moreland and Craig, *Philosophical Foundations for a Christian Worldview*, 466–68.

29. Linzey, *Christianity and the Rights of Animals*, 65–67. Linzey's use of *ruach* of Genesis to support the notion of a spirituality for animals is a classic case of "illegitimate totality transfer." Silva, *Biblical Words & Their Meaning*, 25; Koehler et al., *The Hebrew and Aramaic Lexicon of the Old Testament*, "ruach" Entry 8704.

of duty to animals in that we desire to alleviate their suffering,[30] it is fair to ask why humans empirically feel compelled to draw a distinction between themselves and animals? Asserting that speciesist attitudes simply justify the oppressor's actions does not solve the problem, because it can also be questioned whether CAR activists feel a false sense of moral duty. CAR activists want to minimize the ontological distinctions between humans and animals in order to convince us to adopt their understanding of animal treatment. However, in bypassing the ontological distinction upon which to base our morality, we encounter a critical ethical problem, namely, "How should we treat animals?" Beisner says it best, "The assumption that common biological evolution necessitates *equal* treatment does not define *right* treatment(italics his)."[31] Beisner also demonstrates the irony involved in an ideology that seeks to reduce the distinction between humanity and animals, while employing the speciesist concept of a humane rather than a beastly ethic.[32] Beisner's observation reveals a number of untenable moral problems that face the animal rights movement. Although an imperfect analogy, the debate could be likened to how we should treat the behavior of drug addicts. The addict is "suffering" withdrawal, but needs money to get another "fix." So the addict asks a family member. Should the family member be compassionate and alleviate the suffering by giving money or be greedy and not give the money?

Nevertheless, this paper will simply concede the argument of distinctions between human and animals and instead move onto the area of the moral significance of animal suffering. Their argument must be addressed in two different ways. The first way is by removing the theological basis that funds their argument. CAR activists are correct to assert that God has the right to have His creatures treated in a certain way.[33] However, the critical question is, how does God want animals to be treated? Scripture does support a distinction between our treatment of domesticated animals (animals under our direct control), and those of the field. While God cares for both wild (Psa 104) and domestic animals (Jn 4:11), Scripture shows our responsibility to each is different (Prov 12:24; Mt 12:11).[34]

30. Linzey, *Animal Rights*, 26.

31. Beisner, "Radical Environmentalism's Assault on Humanity," 7.

32. Ibid., 8.

33. Linzey, *Animal Rights*, 23. See Jeremiah 27:4–6 for a strong claim that CAR activists do not address.

34. Proverbs 12:24 assumes the rightness of hunting because it condemns one for not

Melanie Joy, an animal rights advocate but apparently not a Christian, suggests that the key virtue in play is empathy. Drawing on deep ecology, she wants us to see ourselves as part of an overall integrated world, one in which we have a critical part. By looking beyond our narrow self-interest we begin to see the big picture, increase our capacity for empathy, and grow, in psychological terms, beyond ourselves. She says this is all possible because empathy has no inherent limits.[35]

Certainly Joy has provided us with a way to understand the goals of CAR activists. Empathy is certainly an important virtue. But should it be our guiding moral principle? Barth is instructive here, as he rejects Schweitzer's reverence for life ethic as the supreme guiding ethical principle. Barth says,

> According to him [Schweitzer] the first and last word of all ethics is that life must be respected. Its sum is that to preserve and assist life is good, and to destroy and harm it evil (p. 239) . . . theological ethics cannot accept this . . . Life cannot be for us a supreme principle at all, though it can be a sphere in relation to which ethics has to investigate the content and consequences of God's command.[36]

Barth, though somewhat ambiguous regarding the consumptive use of wildlife,[37] does make a powerful point here. Scripture does not elevate the amelioration of suffering, certainly not animal suffering, as the ethical prime directive. Paul suggests that the highest principle would be the glorification of God.[38] Second, empathy may be infinite, but our capacity to act on it certainly is not. One speculates that the animal right's view of morality follows the pagan version of the golden rule, namely, "do no harm." This is the attitude of non-involvement. The Christian, however, has been given a positive command to do good (Lk 10:27). The Christian, by having to act, will do things that may harm others. But there is no moral pollution in doing so because we have a hierarchal moral system. When two rules conflict, we must abide by the higher principle (cf. Acts 4:19).

---

roasting the catch. The distinction is more clearly assumed in the Bible's talk of shepherds. A shepherd defends the flock by opposing wild animals (1 Sam 17:34f; Isa 40:11).

35. Joy, "Humanistic Psychology and Animal Rights: Reconsidering the Boundaries of the Humanistic Ethic," 120, 122–24

36. Karl Barth, *Church Dogmatics*, III.4:324 [brackets ours].

37. Ibid., III.4: 352–54.

38. Westminster Assembly, *The Westminster Shorter Catechism*, Question #1.

The aforementioned argument undermines the view that animal death is inherently evil, but what about the suffering animals experience in the process of being killed? Few Christians today would reject the claim that animals experience pain. Save the much maligned Descartes who denied that animals feel pain, few on the pro-consumptive use side deny that hunted, trapped, and ranched animals experience suffering. Evangelicals do not subscribe to the Christian Science position that pain and illness are illusions. The controversy centers over the moral significance of that experience for the animal. A victim's experience of pain, while unpleasant, is not always evil. Consider the pain a child feels when he is spanked (Prov 23:13). While harvested animals, particularly wild animals, are not being punished per se, the principle still carries that the infliction of pain in and of itself is not necessarily evil despite its being undesirable for the recipient.[39] The crux is the purpose and reasonableness of the infliction of pain. But Linzey and his fellow animal rights activists demonize suffering to such a degree that the righteousness of God can be questioned.[40] Just as meat eaters are condemned for helping sustain the cruelty of animal killing, so God can be slighted for allowing Satan to cause Job to suffer so horribly (Job 1–2). If power or position grants no rights and only grants responsibilities, how should we understand God? Scripture is replete with ample stories of God unleashing judgment on the world; judgments that caused the deaths of thousands, if not millions of creatures (Gen 7–8; Mt 23:33; 2 Pet 2:4ff). The actions of Christ raise serious concerns as well. He seemed to be unconcerned with the plight of animals, and in fact actually was the ultimate cause for many animal deaths. Data, or revelation, should trump mere logical consistency. In Biblical terms this means, at least in God's eyes, that some human-caused animal suffering does not constitute an evil (assuming it is an evil) that rises to the level of causing moral turpitude in the actor or agent.[41]

Practical issues also have to be addressed. Animals frequently cause human suffering through zoonotic diseases, attacks, crop depredation,

39. The question of whether the infliction of pain is necessary or not will be dealt with later in the paper.

40. Pluhar, *Beyond Prejudice*, 32. Since animals do not learn to improve in a moral sense from suffering, it is asked how God can justify its continuance.

41. Stallard, "The Tendency to Softness in Postmodern Attitudes about God, War, and Man," 92–114. Stallard explains how this softening of attitudes has encouraged some to adopt *Christus Victor* theology over the harsher penal satisfaction theory.

and damaging property.[42] Rarely do CAR activists discuss how to morally respond to animals that negatively impact the interests of humans. For example, when is it justified to kill animals to stop human suffering? Linzey begrudgingly concedes that we may never be free of killing animals. He just says that we should only do so when we have serious justification.[43] It could be fairly said that he adopts a minimalist approach, suggesting that humans only intervene in the animal kingdom when conditions demand a correction. While activists are woefully vague on the details for meeting that criterion, Linzey does provide a few guiding principles.[44] 1. He encourages people to employ habitat restriction as a means of controlling and preventing damage,[45] as could be done through fencing or other forms of habitat modification to prevent the access of wildlife to the property.[46] 2. He reminds readers that culling is often short-lived and often has to be repeated. He wonders if simply responding to the damage would take less effort than that required to kill the offending species. 3. Control, when absolutely necessary, must be humane. 4. Calling animals "pests" is without biological foundation. 5. We must be reminded that the earth is ours and the animals.

While pleased that Linzey at least recognizes the reality of animal damage, the vagueness of his guidelines makes achieving the standard unrealistic. Linzey pays lip service to the idea that humans have to kill animals that interfere with human interests, for he says that killing animals must be avoided even if the animal's activity becomes inconvenient, costly, or even potentially infectious to humans.[47] One can only wonder what his reaction would be to the black plague that swept over fourteenth century Europe, killing an estimated 100 million people.[48] Would he say the

---

42. For a broad look at the economic impact of wildlife conflicts see "Human Conflicts with Wildlife: Economic Considerations," i–180.

43. Linzey and Cohn-Sherbok, *After Noah*, 105; Linzey, *Animal Rights*, 33. Linzey says he does not defend animal life as inviolable. He recognizes that killing may be justifiable in times of starvation, and self preservation. See also Linzey, *Animal Gospel*, 120, where he adds that fur coats may have been necessary at one time, but it now has to be proved that it continues to be necessary.

44. Linzey, *Christianity and the Rights of Animals*, 139–41.

45. As does Phelps, *The Dominion of Love*, 177.

46. Linzey, *Animal Theology*, 130–132. Linzey also believes that farmers can kill animals to protect crops, an idea he sees as an extension of self-preservation, but only when the farmer has tried to mitigate the problem through non-lethal means.

47. Linzey, *Animal Theology*, 43.

48. Lomborg, *The Skeptical Environmentalist*, 55.

rats that carried infected fleas deserved to be treated as innocents, and with compassion? Would he say that habitat modification would be sufficient to protect human health and safety? How, given that rats thrive in human-impacted environments? Perhaps Linzey would concede the rat argument; but how would he respond to the following real-life example? Consider a professional wildlife control firm whose client was so phobic about garter snakes *(Thamnophis sirtalis)* that she hired a wildlife control company to remove them. Since state regulations forbade the translocation of snakes, asking for the snakes to be removed from the property meant the snakes would have to be destroyed. Was this a legitimate use of the CAR exception clause? Should the homeowner have been required to undergo counseling and/or medical treatment to address this phobia? Should the homeowner have been legally compelled to change the habitat around her home so that the snakes would no longer want to live there? But what if making those changes, such as removing bushes and ground cover, reduced the value of her home?[49] Whether one agrees with her decision or not, the question still stands: Why is animal suffering on par with human suffering?[50]

Other issues come into play as well, such as whether or not a cruelty-free or cruelty-reduced lifestyle is even possible, despite Linzey's claim to the contrary? Linzey's assertion that modern agricultural practices allow us the ability "to eat—and eat well" without having to kill sentient creatures is not true. Perhaps Linzey had to speak generally due to the constraints inherent in any public lecture (Linzey's statement came from a lecture).[51] However, the implication from reading CAR activist literature is that adopting a vegetarian/vegan lifestyle is by definition cruelty-free because killing animals is not necessary.[52] Another publication says that adopting vegetarianism "constitutes the greatest possible respect for Creation..."[53] When stated this way one can rightfully ask, "Is this true?" Is a vegetarian

---

49. One should also ask, if knowing the client was poor and could not afford to make the necessary changes to the habitat, would that change the ethical equation?

50. We have not even discussed the moral significance issue of animal suffering from non-anthropogenic sources as raised in the abstract of Morris and Thornhill, "Animal Liberationist Responses to Non-Anthropogenic Animal Suffering," 355–79.

51. Linzey, "Unfinished Creation: The Moral and Theological Significance of the Fall," 26.

52. See Christian Vegetarian Association, *Honoring God's Creation: Christianity and Vegetarianism,* Np.

53. Kaufman and Braun, *Vegetarianism as Christian Stewardship,* 2.

lifestyle inherently more compassionate and respectful to creation than a diet that also consumes animal flesh? The problem is the utilitarian argument lying behind the CAR assertion. They claim that a plant-only-diet kills fewer animals than a meat and plant diet. Therefore, using the Least Harm Principle, namely that one should act in a way which causes the smallest amount of injury to another party or parties, humans must become vegetarians.[54]

At first glance, one may easily think that the vegetarian argument has force. However, a closer look shows that plant agriculture involves a tremendous amount of animal killing. First, animals are killed directly through the loss of habitat when land is cleared for planting. Animals are also killed to protect the crops. Retired wildlife biologist Walter E. Howard, says, "Few people realize that agricultural crops could not survive if all native mammals were treated like endangered species."[55] He continues, noting that contemporary crop production creates vast monoculture environments which have the side effect of actually reducing the diversity of vertebrates capable of surviving. Yet, the few that can survive actually thrive to such an extent that they actually become a pest and endanger the crop, thereby requiring control. Additional problems for vegetarians, particularly those in Western cultures, include that much of their preferred crops have to be transported over large distances[56] from areas with a longer or different growing season. It could be argued that by only relying on a vegetable diet, vegetarians may actually increase the loss of species diversity and loss of animal life being killed in the production and transport of the food. Even the harvest of food kills animals, as can be seen when watching rodents trying to flee from an oncoming combine.[57] Steven L. Davis even argues that it is highly likely that a vegan diet would result in the deaths of more animals than a mixed diet of plants and ru-

54. Davis, "The Least Harm Principle May Require That Humans Consume a Diet Containing Large Herbivores, Not a Vegan Diet," 388.

55. Howard, *Nature Needs Us*, 21, 64, 83f.

56. Vehicles and other forms of transportation kill millions of animals every year. U.S. cars alone are estimated to kill 57 million birds annually. Lomborg, *The Skeptical Environmentalist*, 135.

57. Davis, "The Least Harm Principle May Require That Humans Consume a Diet Containing Large Herbivores, Not a Vegan Diet," 388.

minant animals. The reason is because vegan diets require significantly larger tracts of land to produce the needed crops.[58]

The second way to undermine the CAR point is to ask whether the problem of animal suffering is even a problem. Perhaps the answer can be found in the truth that animals are indeed different and that their suffering is different too. C.S. Lewis made this argument when he distinguished sentience (ability to experience) from consciousness (an enduring sense of the self).[59] So while animals can experience pain, perhaps they have no enduring sense of pain. While an interesting solution, it probably only applies to the lower animals. Animal rights activists have noted that animal avoidance of painful stimuli suggests an enduring sense of self.[60] Additionally, some animals with their heightened senses could, in fact, experience even greater levels of pain than humans exposed to the same situations. This would be analogous to the idea that a prison cell may be painful for a human but more so for a bald eagle who had experienced the heights of aerial flight.[61]

Yet if God is not in the picture, then one would have to wonder where we get this notion that animal suffering is evil. If evolution can be used to support our relatedness and therefore our need for concern about animals, should it not support human use of animals as part of the natural order of things? Certainly evolution, in its brilliant blind wisdom, has deemed that suffering achieves greater differentiation of the species. Without suffering there is no change because there would be no force driving species to adapt and modify. Of course, in an atheistic evolutionary perspective, evil vanishes and becomes nothing more than a negative emotional response to one's own circumstances. Ultimately, the answer can only be resolved by an appeal to some higher authority. In this regard, Van Til's presuppositionalism properly frames the issue. The matter can only be decided on the basis of our view of God. Either we accept God as revealed in Scripture or we accept some other alternative.[62]

---

58. Ibid., 389–91.

59. Lewis, *The Problem of Pain*, 132–33.

60. Pluhar, *Beyond Prejudice*, 29, 34–35.

61. The present writer saw this argument stated somewhere but has been unable to find the source.

62. Van Til, *Christian Apologetics*, 14, 18. The point being made here is that while CAR activists appeal to Scripture, their reasoning and worldview are actually based outside of Scripture.

We now turn to consider the societal impact of vegetarianism, namely the belief that vegetarianism and working to avoid animal death and injury somehow will help create a more peaceful human environment. This argument is an old one[63] but it has been resurrected with the work of social workers and psychologists studying criminal behavior.[64] It is clear that those who exhibit violence against their fellow humans often have perpetrated violence against animals. This fact, however, should not surprise anyone as it is reasonable that people would exhibit their aggression against creatures unable to resist. People do tend to steal candy before they rob a bank. Aside from the problems of determining causal links in human behavior, it should be noted that violence against animals does not necessitate violence against humans any more than have sexual relations with one's spouse necessitates promiscuous activity. Readers should also be cautious about what actions are deemed as being cruel to animals. Skinning an animal alive is fundamentally different than hunting an animal, killing it, and then skinning it. Just as marriage circumscribes the sexual act, sporting ethics provide boundaries to animal use. It should not surprise anyone that those who do not respect boundaries with their fellow humans, failed to respect boundaries with weaker animals.

ARGUMENT FROM RESTRAINT

Another argument, dubbed by this writer as the argument from restraint, has enormous appeal for Christians. At its root, the argument exhorts us to live simply and avoid the siren call of modern consumerism. With this argument, CAR activists draw upon the well of Christendom's idealization of monastic life.[65] Monasticism was a lifestyle in which monks dedicated their lives to limiting their own desires and wants in order that they may endure hardships so as to serve others. The power of this position flows from two poles. First, Scripture harshly condemns gluttony, selfishness, and greed (Amos 4:1f; 6:1ff; Lk 12:21; Rom 1:29; Eph 5:3; Col 3:5). The New Testament pointedly reminds readers not to trust in riches; instead, the rich are called to help the poor (Mt 6:24; 13:22; 19:23–4; 1 Tim 6:17).

---

63. Cartmill, *A View to a Death in the Morning*, 9–11.

64. Hensley et al., "Exploring the Possible Link between Childhood and Adolescent Bestiality and Interpersonal Violence," 910–23; Simmons and Lehmann, "Exploring the Link between Pet Abuse and Controlling Behaviors in Violent Relationships," 1211–22.

65. Schaff, *Nicene and Post-Nicene Christianity*, 3:149, 153.

Additional support is garnered by an intuitive realization that life can be a zero-sum game, that accumulation of possessions for one person means the unavailability of those possessions for others. The second pole is the positive promise of a better way of living, one that is characterized by that childlike faith that God will provide for our needs just as He has for the lilies of the field (Mt 6:28; Lk 12:24).

How this argument relates to our understanding of the human use of animals is quite simple. CAR activists believe that eating meat exhibits the vices of gluttony and greed.[66] Eating meat implied gluttony because it meant that our desire for animal flesh outweighed any concern for the being that had to die to satisfy our palate. Greed was implicated because historically meat could only be afforded by the rich. Eating meat, therefore, meant that one was spending money to feed oneself, rather than spending that money on helping the poor.[67] This argument from restraint is perhaps most aggressively heard in the CAR activists' condemnation of fur coats. For in one simple charge, CAR activists can insinuate the vanity of fur-fashion (with the class struggle between those able to afford fur coats and those who cannot) and defending the "innocent and defenseless" animals.[68]

Lastly, CAR activists also employ a somewhat spiritual argument noting that hunting and trapping are just not necessary anymore. Therefore, to continue to perform these activities amounts to nothing less than a blood sport to satisfy the bloodthirsty and selfish desires of someone's lust for power of vanity (i.e. mounting a deer head on a wall). Linzey strenuously denies that sport-hunting can be justified on the basis that it is a proper means of controlling or managing wildlife populations. He does not believe humans have the right to destroy animals needlessly. Economic profit is not sufficient in his view to be properly considered as a justifying need.[69] He heaps scorn on the management language of modern ecological theory. He says wildlife management practices display a decidedly anthropomorphic view of animals. He continues wondering

66. Hyland, *The Slaughter of the Terrified Beasts*, 73. Hyland says, "...lust for flesh." Webb, *On God and Dogs*, 22; Linzey, *Animal Theology*, 132.

67. In modern times the greed argument has evolved to mean that since we no longer need meat, consuming it should be avoided. For by avoiding meat, we allow another sentient creature to live.

68. Hyland, *God's Covenant with Animals*, 86. Hyland calls fur "among the most gratuitous" of cruelties. See also Young, *Is God a Vegetarian?* 35f.

69. Linzey, *Animal Rights*, 39.

how we have the moral authority to manage other populations when we cannot even manage our own.[70]

EVALUATION OF THE ARGUMENT FROM RESTRAINT

The argument from restraint, which can also be called the 'no need' argument, carries much force in public discourse. At first glance, it seems rather obvious. Why kill an animal if it is not necessary? To follow an alternative path seems to violate the Beatles "Let it be" mantra.[71] This argument also cuts to the core of Christian ethical discussion that has raged in Christendom for centuries. At issue is, "How much freedom do Christians actually have?" Paul's statement that asserted "all things are lawful but not all things are useful" epitomizes the dilemma (1 Cor 6:12; 10:23). On the one hand stands the Scylla of Legalism, with its warning of "do not touch" (Col 2:21). On the other stands the Charybdis, with boundless freedom that violates the call of Christ to follow Him through obedience to His commands (John 15). Scripture does not provide much assistance here, in that the specific topic of sport hunting has not been directly addressed. It could be argued that all the situations in which hunting or trapping have been alluded to were simply sustentative acts, rather than activities for pure recreation. Ultimately, the issue will have to be decided by a Biblically informed conscience that considers the evaluation of a sanctified moral intuition.

From an ethical perspective, human participation in the killing of animals can fall into four different categories. First, human can kill animals directly and intentionally, as would occur in the case of hunting or trapping. Second, humans can kill animals indirectly but with intent, as when humans introduce a predator to control a species causing crop damage. Third, humans can kill animals directly but unintentionally, as happens when a squirrel scampers in front of your moving car, making collision unavoidable. Finally, humans can kill animals indirectly and unintentionally, as exemplified by the unintended effects of DDT on raptors chronicled in *Silent Spring*. CAR activists spend the vast majority of their time opposing category 1 and 2.—mankind does not need to eat meat or wear fur.

---

70. Linzey and Cohn-Sherbok, *After Noah*, 121–24.

71. Linzey, *Christianity and the Rights of Animals*, 18. Linzey actually uses the clause "letting be" as the third implication of his belief in man to be a blessing and not a curse to creation.

The first difficulty one finds with the "no need" argument rests with the limited view of "need." The CAR argument assumes that need is simply a caloric or life-sustaining issue. If the need for calories was the only need, then we would have to agree that there is no need of sport hunting or trapping, at least in much of the Western world. But neither would there be a need for a whole host of foods and activities, such as alcoholic beverages, imported Kiwi fruit, or Madagascar cinnamon. All of these products could be considered luxuries, depending on one's frame of reference. The CAR activists would counter that there is no need for any activity that causes the suffering of another. To suggest otherwise is to confuse compulsion with true need, as, say, the compulsion of a serial killer with that of a police officer. Scully puts the issue more forcefully by saying that arbitrarily compassionate trumps arbitrarily cruel.[72]

While an interesting counter-argument, it fails in two ways. First, there are a number of activities that do cause harm, even if the harm is somewhat less apparent. For example, consider wine and beer. They are not necessary for sustaining life. They also consume land that could be used to produce habitat for animals and nutritional food for people. These beverages also are guilty of causing much harm in the world through the effects of alcoholism[73] and drunk driving.[74] If we are looking for ways to reduce our harming others, it would seem that rejecting alcohol would be very high on the list. What about plate glass windows? Are they needed? In fact, these structures are responsible for more than 250,000 bird deaths daily in the U.S., less than all the bird deaths caused by the Exxon Valdez spill.[75] How about motor vehicles? An estimated 60 million birds die annually in the U.S. just from vehicle collisions.[76] If one counted all the other animals killed by vehicles the results would make the alleged Treblinka[77] of trapping look like a family fight. One could say that drivers do not

---

72. Scully, *Dominion*, 39.

73. National Institute on Alcohol Abuse and Alcoholism, "Health Risks and Benefits of Alcohol Consumption," 5. 7.5 % of the U.S. population are problem drinkers.

74. Centers for Disease Control and Prevention, *Impaired Driving*, Np. With 2006 statistics, someone in the U.S. is injured every 2 minutes and killed every 31 minutes due to drunk driving.

75. Lomborg, *The Skeptical Environmentalist*, 192, 200.

76. Lomborg, *The Skeptical Environmentalist*, 135.

77. Employment of Holocaust language is common among the extreme elements of the animal rights movement.

intend to hit the animals, and that would be true (for the most part). However, it could also be said that hunters and trappers do not desire to catch unwanted animals. So are they morally free of the guilt when they pull the trigger at the wrong moment?

Second, it flows from a myopic view of the nature of humanity.[78] CAR's inability to come to grips with the blessing and responsibility of human dominion forces them to view the implementation of that dominion over the animals as profoundly violent and evil. They have been properly horrified by so much poor dominion that they have overreacted and rejected the notion altogether. Their goal is ultimately not to be connected with the animal creation but actually divested from it.[79] The proper analogy for need is one based on intimacy and love. Evil notions of intimacy exhibit themselves in promiscuity and other sorts of sexual sin. Virtuous intimacy is one expressed in the bonds of marriage. CAR activists, in their hatred of harvesting wildlife, are like the radical feminists who believe that all sexual relations are actually reducible to forms of domination.[80] While not every individual needs to hunt or trap to obtain nourishment,[81] it is apparent that humans do have a need to express lethal rule over animals as expressed in hunting. Aldo Leopold, a founding member of the Wildlife Society,[82] said there are various kinds of recreational hunters. He observed that the well fed duck hunter, rare fern plant hunter, beech tree graffiti artist, and the naturalist speaker are each in their own way hunters. They are hunters because each seeks his/her own pleasure from nature as demonstrated by the acquisition of a trophy, an object that proves "I was there."[83] Leopold, an avid hunter himself, argued emphatically for society to develop a wilderness aesthetic. He did not believe that the two

78. Linzey and Regan, *Animals and Christianity*, 171. We have not even dealt with the role the consumptive use of wildlife plays in Native American culture, an activity which Linzey disparages.

79. Cartmill, *A View to a Death in the Morning*, 220.

80. Webb, *On God and Dogs*, 69–84. Webb is one exception in that he believes that humans can have mutually beneficial relationship with animals in certain limited circumstances, such as pets.

81. This is not to deny that some hunt and/or trap to help reduce their grocery bill and/or derive additional income.

82. The Wildlife Society is an association of professional wildlife biologists dedicated to sustainable use of our wildlife resources. http://www.wildlife.org.

83. Leopold, *A Sand County Almanac with Essays on Conservation from Round River*, 280–84

values, hunting and a love of ecosystems, were contradictory. He avoided defending the role of hunting as a purely economic value, although he recognized that money was made from it, because he questioned whether an economic benefit was strong enough motivation for us to protect the natural world.[84] Leopold thought that hunting was one way for modern humanity to reacquaint itself with the natural world. He understood that hunting could be (and was) reduced to little more than procurement of a big trophy.[85] But he saw that the loss of an environmental consciousness, or as he called it a "land ethic," stemmed from our estrangement from the land.[86] Leopold recognized that when land is converted to agriculture with the result of no more hunting, something important is lost.[87] He explained how children do not show much surprise over seeing a golf ball, but do upon witnessing their first deer. The person who is not impressed with the deer he calls "over civilized."[88] Individuals who destroy land with apartment buildings are destroying something very important to humanity, the need to be connected with the land. He calls us to protect wilderness (areas free of human development) in spite of our need for recreation, science, aesthetics, and economic interests.[89]

Our relationship to animals is also manifested in our choice of food. Michael Pollan, in *Omnivore's Dilemma*, proffers the strange thesis that what we eat plays a big role in what we are. Even the way we prepare and present the food plays a role in defining who we are as humans.[90] He does not believe in dietary determinism, but does suggest that eating both in content and manner connects us with nature in a most profound way. He speaks somewhat sadly that the industrialization of agriculture has distanced us from our connection with the origin of our food.[91] Theologians have thought along the same lines, using the Lord's Supper as a useful

84. Ibid., 200–1, 218, 240ff., 246ff.

85. Ibid., 294.

86. Ibid., 129.

87. Ibid., 160.

88. Ibid., 227.

89. Similar arguments, although expressed more mystically, can be found in Eaton, *The Sacred Hunt*, vii–206.

90. Pollan, *Omnivore's Dilemma*, 6.

91. Ibid., 10, 34–35. He is not alone in his concern. See Cheeke and Davis, "Possible Impacts of Industrialization and Globalization of Animal Agriculture on Cattle Ranching in the American West," 4–5.

metaphor and rubric to understand humanity's relationship to food.[92] The Lord's Supper speaks to our creatureliness in that we have to eat to live, but also to human dominion, as we have extracted resources from the earth to sustain ourselves. Furthermore, it speaks to the structures needed to manipulate the wheat into bread, and so also approves of human industry. Practically speaking, there is strong evidence that those who are connected more closely to the earth in terms of the food chain recognize their need to administer appropriate rule and stewardship. It should not surprise us that sportsmen were the ones who fought for legislation to enact seasons and bag limits as well as protecting land from developers.[93] Although their concern is pejoratively labeled by CAR activists as utilitarian or "enlightened self-interest," the fact remains their connection to animals motivated them to protect them, and do so at financial loss,[94] an activity that animal rights activists rarely do.[95]

Permitting the consumptive use of wildlife also helps protect the environment. It has been shown that people who enjoy hunting or trapping, or know it is available, are more likely to tolerate property damage by animals because they can experience the joy of the chase during the game or fur season.[96] Everyone should be able to agree that without tolerance, the continued viability of wild animal populations (who do not respect property boundaries) is bleak.

Returning to the issue of Christian virtues, CAR activists are correct to note that Scripture is clearly against greed and over consumption. Luke 12:13–48 contains sayings and parables warning Christians about the dangers of greed and the worry over property that leads to greed. Christ's words are especially relevant as He condemns worry about raiment (Lk 12:28). Christians should certainly think twice about purchasing a fur coat, given the price tag. But stating this caution in no way implies that

---

92. Leithart, "The Way Things Really Ought to Be: Eucharist, Eschatology, and Culture," 167–68.

93. Mighetto, *Wild Animals and American Environmental Ethics*, 5.

94. For a history of the controversies in the conservation movement see Jacoby, *Crimes against Nature*, xi–305.

95. Navigator, *Charity Navigator*, Np. This site evaluates administrative efficiency of charities. Animal rights groups are frequently just lobby groups who seek to spend other people's money.

96. Boddicker, *The Issue of Trapping*, 37; Southwick et al., *Potential Costs of Losing Hunting and Trapping as Wildlife Management Methods*, 16–17.

the underlying product is somehow evil. For it just as easily applies to a person's purchase of a Rolls Royce, Renoir or Van Gogh, or mini-mansion in the suburbs. This writer has trapped a number of beaver (*Castor canadensis*) in the course of his activities as a wildlife damage controller. He had several of the beavers' hides tanned, which his wife then made into a hand muff. It certainly was not necessary, as the author's wife could have worn nylon mittens. Yet on the financial side the cost was minimal, as it only cost time, gas, traps, and tanning services. Given that the writer was already contracted to control the beavers, the cost was negligible. In light of what was just presented, was the writer's activity an expression of vanity? Linzey is on very fragile ground here, as many activities by humans are vain. Ultimately, the question that CAR activists have to answer is how far should Christians take this evaluative tool of necessity to heart? For if we are not careful, we can easily deprive ourselves of a number of pleasures simply because they do not meet the basic requirements of sustaining life. That criticism, along with the idea of our freedom in Christ, should make us look to another argument against the fur trade.

After the Catholic Bishops of Canada supported the Inuit people's right to trap for fur, Linzey published a letter which roundly criticized them. Linzey's comments were uncharacteristically harsh (Linzey is normally very charitable of his opponents). But in this letter, he comes dangerously close to *ad hominem* attack when he raises the possibility that the support for aboriginal fur-trapping rights provided by the Catholic Bishops of Canada may stem from the guilt felt for their poor treatment of the Inuit in the past. Linzey plays to old colonial animosities by wondering if support for the Inuit flows from those who are profitably exploiting their trapping expertise.[97] Some have argued that *ad hominem* arguments are simply logical fallacies, and arguments that utilize them can be simply rejected.[98] However, while *ad hominem* arguments need to be viewed with caution, this writer is not convinced that they are always wrong. For it appears that the New Testament uses what could be described as *ad hominem* arguments to show that moral turpitude does impact decision making (Titus 1:10–16; Jude 16). The question then is, do these accusations apply, and if they do, are they sufficient to accept Linzey's claim? Regarding the Catholic Bishops of Canada, the only way we could know

97. Linzey and Regan, *Animals and Christianity*, 173.
98. Hurley, *A Concise Introduction to Logic*, 106–8.

if their motive for supporting the Inuit fur-trade stemmed from guilt over the Church's prior treatment of them would be to ask them directly. Even if we assume that the Bishops were trying to atone for past sins, Linzey must still demonstrate that the fur trade is morally wrong. The fact is, one can do the right thing for the wrong motives.

Linzey charges his opponents with profiteering, that the Inuit were being exploited by the white-man and that the Inuits themselves were exploiting nature for personal profit. Linzey's argument is ingenious because it resonates with the natural disposition people have against profit making. Many people still believe that if A makes a profit from the work of B then A has exploited B. The problem for Linzey, though, is showing how the Inuit have been exploited. They claim to have been trapping animals and using their fur long before the white man came to the continent. Their fur trapping activities may have increased due to demand for fur and the financial demands of the modern world, but this in itself does not constitute exploitation. The Inuit are not held captive and prevented from pursuing other work, or even leaving their tribal lands. Canada is, by all accounts, a free country in all the Western meaning of the word. So the element of employment slavery does not apply to the Inuit, and therefore Linzey must make his case on other grounds.

Linzey's rejection of the economic need argument is also proper. For if fur trapping is morally wrong, then the economic losses incurred by ending the fur trade are simply the cost of discipleship. Scripture clearly references the economic impact of Christianity when Luke tells the story of the Ephesian idol manufacturers who stirred up the city due to their fears that their idol-making business was threatened by Christianity (Acts 19:23–41). However, given that regulated fur trapping utilizes the earth's renewable resources in a responsible way, it could be argued that Linzey's greed argument simply fails. Nowhere in Scripture is one condemned for making a living off exploiting the land's resources, provided it is done so responsibly. Since using a renewable resource is about as close to responsible as humans can get, it is difficult to see how CAR activists can employ a greed argument. To do so would mean that planting crops also suffers from the greed argument.

ARGUMENT FROM STEWARDSHIP

The CAR argument from stewardship is comprised of two smaller arguments relating to the environment, and individual health. In light of contemporary environmental concerns, the environmental argument from stewardship is one of the most interesting. The argument simply claims that the energy and resources required to harvest meat and utilize fur is unsustainable due to the energy inputs involved and resultant pollution. The loss in energy manifests itself in several ways. First, meat production requires vast tracts of land. Father Dear says, "…the intensive production of animals for meat requires about 25 times as much land as the production of the same amount of food from vegetable sources."[99] Statistics vary, but none make meat production look efficient. One says 1 kg of meat requires 6 kg of plant protein from grain and forage. Additionally, that same kilogram of meat requires 100,000 liters of water compared to only 900 kg to produce 1 kg of wheat.[100] Linzey says it takes 7–8 pounds of grains to provide 1 pound of meat. A vegan-based diet requires 0.5 to 0.6 acres of land to feed one human. A mixed diet of meat and plants requires over 1.6 acres with 1.3 of those acres to feed the animals. The impact of this land requirement is often felt in ecologically sensitive areas such as rainforests, which have to be cut down to make room for cattle production.

Second, half of the water in the United States is used to raise animals for food, thereby making meat eaters require 14 times more water to sustain their lives as is needed by non-meat eaters.[101] Finally, cattle production causes extensive pollution due to the animals' excrement. Dear states that livestock produce 130 times as much excrement as the entire U.S. population.[102] The energy argument is even employed against the fur industry. Gregory H. Smith of the Ford Motor Company determined that a fur coat made of animals trapped in the wild required 433,000 BTUs to manufacture, as opposed to 120,300 BTUs to manufacture a fake fur.[103] This argument takes on even greater force given the recent concern over the burning of fossil fuels adds to global warming.

---

99. Dear, "Christianity and Vegetarianism: Pursuing the Nonviolence of Jesus," 11.

100. Francione, "Animals—Property or Persons?" 116.

101. Dear, "Christianity and Vegetarianism: Pursuing the Nonviolence of Jesus," 11.

102. Ibid.

103. Nilsson et al., *Facts About Furs*, 176–78. His conclusions were confirmed by William J. Sauber in 1979.

CAR activist add moral force to this position by saying that if we eliminated meat from our diet, then more food would be available to feed the hungry. So much grain and money is used to create beef that not enough is available to feed the poor, and the cost savings could be donated to the poor.[104] The idea being that if Christians reduce their own consumption of resources, there will automatically be more for those who lack them. This perspective can be observed in the pithy bumper sticker which reads, "Live simply so others may simply live." In their view, eating meat presents an excessive, and therefore unChristian, use of the earth's limited resources.

CAR activists also claim that a carnivorous diet is not only unnecessary to good health, it can actually damage one's health.[105] Meat eating has been linked to diabetes, heart disease, cancer, and obesity. The negative effects of meat eating should come as no surprise since the CAR activists believe that humans were not designed to be carnivores in the first place. The following quote describes the argument succinctly,

> Human anatomy and physiology resemble herbivores in many other ways. Our saliva contains digestive enzymes (unlike carnivores); our dental incisors are broad, flattened, and spade-shaped (not short and pointed); our canine teeth are short and blunted (not long, sharp, and curved); our molars are flattened with nodular cusps (not sharp blades like many carnivores); and our nails are flattened (not sharp claws).[106]

EVALUATION OF THE ARGUMENT FROM STEWARDSHIP

As in so many other instances, CAR activists make some important points.[107] The problem with their argument stems from a confusion between the way meat is produced in the U.S. and all meat in general. There is no doubt that U.S. cattle raising practices have huge environmental impacts, beginning with the high corn diet, itself full of water and fossil

104. Kaufman and Braun, *Vegetarianism as Christian Stewardship*, 17–21.

105. Ibid., 16–17.

106. Ibid., 16; Young, *Is God a Vegetarian?* 23. Though Young acknowledges some debate on the issue.

107. I will not engage the energy argument used against the manufacture of fur coats due to difficulties in such a calculation. Let it be said, however, that one wonders whether the energy metrics took into consideration the energy expended bringing the oil to the U.S.

fuel consumption,[108] and ending with the volume of fecal output which fouls our water supply. But poor production of a product does not mean that the product itself is evil. The anti-meat movement should be making these arguments against the industrialization of meat production, as there is much to argue against it.[109] First, they fail to distinguish between four different types of meat production: grazing, mixed farming, industrial,[110] and consumptive use of nature (i.e. hunting, trapping, and fishing). Aside from the contempt for killing animals no matter how they were raised, CAR activist complaints are really directed toward the negative environmental impacts that result from factory farming and consumptive use of nature. Raising cattle through grazing and mixed farming (which combines ranching with crop production) account for about half of all meat production (not counting consumptive use sources). What is important to note is that these two forms of meat production are considered essentially closed systems. In other words what goes in generally matches what comes out, on an energy or environmental basis. This is not to suggest that ranching in any form does not have negative environmental impact. Attempts to increase production can cause ranchers to exploit water sources to increase forage or grow crops for feed. Cattle produce incredible quantities of methane, which adds to global warming.[111] All human activity has negative environmental impact, depending on one's definition. All parties agree that industrial ranching poses the greatest environmental challenges due to the high concentration of fecal material relative to land area used. But what is interesting is that the negative challenges posed by industrial ranching can be mitigated through proper

108. Pollan, *Omnivore's Dilemma*, 45–46. Pollan says that every bushel of industrial raised corn (industrial raised corn is intensively raised corn typical of production in states like Iowa and Nebraska) requires ¼ to ⅓ of a gallon of oil to raise it. Or to put it more simply, it takes more than one calorie of energy to get one calorie of energy from industrial corn.

109. Lomborg, *The Skeptical Environmentalist*, 102–4. The real environmental effects of intensive agriculture should be more carefully nuanced, according to Lomborg. He rightly points out that environmentalists have frequently overstated (in some cases wildly so) declines in environmental quality. One case in point was Lester Brown's belief that China would face a food shortage as it continues towards increasing its consumption of meat as he expects. Lomberg shows that the crisis Brown predicted was rather flawed.

110. Barrett, "Livestock Farming: Eating up the Environment?" A316.

111. Ibid., A316–17. But for a different perspective see Fairlie, "The Vital Statistics of Meat," 18.

management.[112] The solution, though, is not to stop eating meat but to change the manner in which it is produced.[113]

The anti-meat movement is correct that, all things being equal, more energy would be provided by an acre of plants than would be provided if we fed that acre to cows. But CAR activists overlook the ability of cattle to be net producers of food by taking advantage of environmental conditions. Grass requires less rainfall than trees and therefore can grow in areas where many crops cannot be raised without irrigation. Cattle provide, in a sense, a free lunch, because they can convert inedible grass (inedible to humans anyway) to edible meat. In effect, including cattle into the food chain actually increases food production because it takes advantage of a food supply that would be otherwise unavailable.[114] Linzey's disparagement of this fact by saying that even under those conditions an animal only returns 1/10 of what it eats into food [115] demonstrates a truly remarkable level of ignorance, as the comparison is irrelevant; the land would not be available for agriculture production in the first place. Consider the American bison (*Bison bison*). The fact is, before the arrival of the Europeans, the Great Plains fed hundreds of thousands of bison. If the sod busters did not take over the land, the Great Plains would have continued to produce hundreds of thousands of pounds of bison meat annually with little to no negative environmental impact. Furthermore, scientists have shown that range-fed cattle, under proper management, can actually improve the quality of the rangeland.[116] Mixed farming also has an incredible ability to work in harmony with nature. Polyface farm, a working farm of 100 acres of grassland and 450 acres of woods located in Pennsylvania, actually produces 30,000 eggs, 10,000 broilers, 800 stewing hens, 25,000 pounds of beef, 25,000 pounds of pork, 1,000 turkeys and

112. Ibid., A316.

113. For a more detailed explanation on the benefits of livestock production see Mearns, *When Livestock Are Good for the Environment.*

114. Sedivec et al., *Controlling Leafy Spurge Using Goats and Sheep*, Np. The article actually explains how goats and sheep can be used to control an invasive plant species while gaining weight and reducing the need for herbicide use. Fairlie also says that the 10:1 ratio used to explain livestock inefficiency actually applies to pure range fed cattle. If one is using more nutritional feed, the ratio can be as low as 4:1, Fairlie, "The Vital Statistics of Meat," 17.

115. Linzey, *Animal Rights: A Christian Assessment of Man's Treatment of Animals.* 35–36.

116. Pollan, *Omnivore's Dilemma*, 70.

500 rabbits in one year. The farm is able to accomplish this feat by seeking to treat the farm as a self-contained mini-ecosystem.[117] Free-range chickens provide nitrogen to the soil through their droppings, as well as sanitation work through eating insects and parasites that could encourage disease in the cattle.[118] The chickens then provide food through their meat. Cattle also provide a convenient way to store excess food, and eating meat broadens our pallet and makes us less vulnerable to famine.

Consumptive use of nature, that is obtaining meat through hunting, trapping, or fishing, has perhaps the least environmental footprint when properly utilized. In this situation, humans do not have the obligation of investing energy into the animals. All they have to do is simply harvest the self-producing bounty of the land, provided that the harvesting does not damage the reproductive capability of the species.

It is also important to recognize that plant agriculture as well comes with a steep environmental impact, a fact ignored by the anti-meat movement. For example, knowing that 1 ton of grain requires 1,000 tons of water,[119] helps explain why so many rivers in the Western U.S. were dammed, and why so many farmers have to pump water. Fecal production and its high nitrogen content of cattle production is frequently blamed for fouling watersheds. Yet, research has shown that the distribution of this nitrogen is regionally based. In the Gulf of Mexico, 50% of all the nitrogen causing eutrophication actually comes from fertilizer used in agriculture, compared to 15% from animal farming.[120] Even if the CAR activists succeeded in ending cattle production along with reducing grain production used to feed the cattle, there would still be a need for fertilization to maintain intensive agriculture practices. Otherwise, more land would have to be put under production. Lomberg argued that the reason our forests are doing so well is because intensive agriculture allows us to grow more food on less land.[121] This intensive agriculture allows us to have more forests than cropland worldwide, thereby protecting biodiversity.[122] Agriculture also impacts wildlife, sometimes in a way beneficial to man. McNeill observes

117. Ibid., 222ff.

118. Ibid., 210–11.

119. Lomborg, *The Skeptical Environmentalist*, 154.

120. Ibid., 198–99.

121. Ibid., 64.

122. Ibid., 112–13.

that increased agriculture removed habitat needed by ground squirrels, which in turn reduced Bubonic plague outbreaks.[123]

Vegetarians, at least the high-society versions, must consider how improvements in shipping has enhanced/enabled their lifestyle. Modern vegetarianism is based on the ability to ship a wide variety of plants from areas where food can be grown year round. Cornell ecologist David Pimental says that a one pound box of pre-washed lettuce contains 80 calories. Yet growing, packing, shipping, and chilling the lettuce on its journey from the U.S. West coast to the East coast takes 4,600 calories of fossil fuel. Add 4% more if the lettuce was grown in a conventional and not organic fashion.[124] Without shipping, vegetarians in Northern climes would have to eat a diet of locally produced and canned vegetables such as potatoes and cabbage. This author suspects that vegetarians would tire of their diet very quickly if their vegetables had to be locally produced. Nevertheless, it must be noted that vegetarianism is not without its own environmental cost.

Animal rights activists overstate the facts regarding the anatomical and physiological aspects of the human body. They again force the debate into two camps, as if those were the only available options. The evidence actually supports the classification of humans as an omnivore, meaning humans are designed to eat a whole host of items, both plant and animal. Our teeth and jaws share qualities suitable for grinding, which is needed for grains, and tearing, which is needed for flesh.[125] Michael Pollan points out that the human digestive system contains an enzyme whose only function is to break down elastin, which is a protein only found in meat.[126] The question for animal rights advocates is, "If God did not want us to eat meat, why did He provide the enzyme needed to consume it?" If one argues that God did this until we spiritually and morally matured enough to recognize that we did not need meat, it should be recognized that obtaining vitamin B_{12} through vegan-only means is not easy.[127]

123. McNeill, *Plagues and Peoples*, 251.

124. Pollan, *Omnivore's Dilemma*, 167.

125. Ibid., 6, 289.

126. Ibid., 289.

127. de Jong et al., "Severe Nutritional Vitamin Deficiency in a Breast-Fed Infant of a Vegan Mother," 259–60. One would have thought that the mother, who was a vegan for several years, was sufficiently knowledgeable to avoid this potential tragedy with her child.

Perhaps the strongest anthropological argument against carnivorous activity is health. Vegetarians and vegans constantly crow about the deadly health effects of meat on human health. Two arguments come into play here. First, the question is how dedicated should Christians be about healthy living? The point is not for Christians to abuse their body with unhealthy lifestyles. Stewardship requires us to treat our bodies as God's property. Yet, does God require Christians to become health obsessed? What standard should we apply to determine our relative health? With morals, we have the person of Jesus Christ as our standard. What will be our ideal for health? Jack LaLanne? Achilles? Hercules? Body-Mass Index Score?[128] Should cardio-vascular health take priority over exterior looks, or should it be some ratio of both? How should a Christian who adopts this lifestyle, behave when, on a mission's trip, meat is placed in front of him or her?

The second argument relates to the need to distinguish between corn-fed cattle and non-corn fed cattle. Pollan mentions what is known as the "French Paradox." The French Paradox refers to the finding that French people eat a lot of fat and yet have lower heart disease rates than their American counterparts.[129] There is a growing body of evidence that suggests that the American practice of feeding cattle corn rather than grass is a contributing cause to the detrimental effects attributed to red meat. Range-fed cattle are able to incorporate the vitamins contained in the grass into the meat, thereby making the meat healthier. The grain-based diet of contemporary cattle production distorts the balance between Omega 3 and Omega 6. Omega 3 thins the blood while Omega 6 clots it. Grain-fed cattle has more Omega 6 than range-fed cattle.[130] Couple this production problem with the increasing sedentary nature of Western living, and you have a volatile combination.[131] Additionally, it has been demonstrated that plants can pose dangers to human health. Particularly, plants may pose hazards through their own natural pesticide defenses (versus the artificial ones used by the farmer) and hormones.[132]

---

128. National Institutes of Health, *Body Mass Index Calculation Page.*

129. Pollan, *Omnivore's Dilemma*, 300.

130. Ibid., 266–68.

131. Barrett, "Livestock Farming: Eating up the Environment?" A315.

132. Lomborg, *The Skeptical Environmentalist*, 233–38.

It would appear that living on this planet is dangerous to our health no matter what one does or eats.

Nevertheless, meat can and does play an important role in human health. Meat is an excellent source of iron, zinc, and calcium. While Americans probably eat too much meat, findings are clear that children in the developing world need more in order to grow up to be healthy adults. A study revealed that children with some meat in their diet tested better than those who did not.[133] It appears that the oft-stated maxim, "In all things moderation," is true with meat eating as with other activities.

CONCLUSION

We have evaluated three main moral arguments presented by CAR activists to convince us not to eat meat or participate in consumptive wildlife activities. We have seen that their arguments fail because they neglect to pay dutiful attention to the facts, or neglect to adequately account for the morality of the consequences of their proffered moral ideals. While they correctly call us to consider the effects of our choices, their position would actually force us to make immoral choices or reduce our freedom to enjoy the bounty of the earth. We now turn to see if the CAR activists can demonstrate scientifically that the harvesting of wildlife is damaging to the environment.

133. Barrett, "Livestock Farming: Eating up the Environment?," A314.

6

The CAR Movement's Argument from Science:
The Case Study of Coyote Trapping

INTRODUCTION

IN PREVIOUS CHAPTERS, I evaluated CAR arguments opposing human use of animals. The arguments have been decidedly abstract and theoretical. In this chapter, I focus on a particular type of human-animal interaction, wildlife trapping. CAR activists, unsurprisingly, are opposed to trapping on grounds similar to their opposition to other interactions with animals. But they also oppose trapping on the basis that it is excessively cruel, and poor environmental policy. We will discuss the validity of these additional arguments to determine if they have sufficient merit to convince Christians to adopt their anti-trapping stance. CAR activists share many of the views of the broader animal protectionists[1] concerning the need to protect animals from harm stemming from human behavior.[2] My goal is to determine whether it is morally and environmentally wrong for Christians to trap wildlife, as the CAR activists claim.

---

1. Animal protectionist is a broad term that describes individuals and groups who wish to severely restrict human use of animals, including animal rights activists and strict animal welfarists. Animal rights activists believe that animals deserve rights comparable to those of humans, e.g. life, self-determination, etc. because they too are sentient beings. Animal welfarists believe that humans may kill and eat animals provided they are treated responsibly.

2. The environmental aspect of the animal protectionist movement will be clearly apparent to anyone surfing environmental websites. Many will dedicate an area of their site to animal rights. However, it must be known that for some, animal rights is not strictly an environmental issue. Some would put more emphasis on a justice or ethical view of how fellow beings should be treated, whether or not there was an environmental benefit to such treatment.

The subject of trapping may appear to be too narrow an issue in light of the complexities of Christian environmental theory and human-wildlife relations. However, I contend that as abortion is a bell-weather issue regarding one's views on the sanctity of life, so trapping helps us refine our positions regarding environmental ethics, policy, and broader debates regarding animal-human relations. Trapping is also a relevant issue because it occurred in Biblical times. Residents of the Egypt used clap traps to catch the birds that migrated through the region. These clap traps were activated by the trapper pulling the trap closed when the trap filled with birds (cf. Psa 124:7).[3] Trapping, particularly since the development of the foothold trap,[4] has been the subject of intense controversy.[5] Trapping places questions concerning the extent of human dominion in stark relief. It is arguably the most difficult of all the consumptive wildlife activities (such as hunting and fishing) to defend, due to the widespread perception that trapping is cruel.[6] Finally, trapping has been the subject of political activism[7] by animal protectionist groups seeking to restrict and/or ban trapping altogether.[8] Thus, by discussing trapping, we avoid creating a straw-man of the CAR position,[9] while dealing with a concrete

3. Brewer, "Hunting, Animal Husbandry and Diet in Ancient Egypt," 453–55.

4. The trap is also known as a leg-hold. It is preferable to call it a foot-hold because trappers seek to catch the animal on the pad of the foot rather than on the less muscular leg where the bones may be broken. A quick look at one's own anatomy will quickly demonstrate why this is important. Compare the difference between the toughness of the palm of your hand with the toughness of your forearm. Darwin, "Trapping Agony," Np.

5. Minnis, "Wildlife Policy-Making by the Electorate," 75–83. Minnis provides a review of some of the politics of wildlife management which have occurred in the U.S in recent years.

6. Cf. Fitzwater, "Trapping—the Oldest Profession," 106. Even Plato derided trapping as "slothful." Cartmill, A View to a Death in the Morning, 32. Scripture also uses trapping to illustrate foreseen and unforeseen disaster (Prov 7:23; Eccl 9:12; Jer 43:48).

7. A brief overview of animal protectionist legislation in the United States and around the world see publications by Rowan and Rosen, "Progress in Animal Legislation: Measurement and Assessment," 79–94. and Irwin, "A Strategic Review of International Animal Protection," 1–8.

8. Animal protectionists are not always clear about their ultimate goals, as demonstrated by the inconsistency between what they say and what they do. See Boddicker, The Issue of Trapping, 73 and the present writer's personal experience in the 1996 Massachusetts Ballot Initiative known as Question 1.

9. Linzey, Animal Gospel, 134. Linzey condemns the development of humane trapping standards as a "confidence trick." He also condemns fur trapping in Linzey, Christianity and the Rights of Animals, 125–28.

ethical issue of contemporary significance facing Christians interested in environmental ethics.[10]

Trapping is an activity where a device, called a "trap", is created or adopted for the purpose of capturing an animal. The device may be mechanical, consisting of moving parts such as a foothold, or structural, such as a pit dug into the ground. Trapping, as a technique, is employed by the plant kingdom (Pitcher plant, *Sarracenia spp.*), animal kingdom (web weaving spiders), and humans.[11] Traps provide their users one key advantage; they multiply the trappers' efforts. Trapping differs from hunting$_2$ in that a device allows the trapper to take an animal without having to be present.[12] Hunting$_2$ requires one to increase the amount of time in the field in order to increase the chance of hunting success. Additionally, no amount of time in the field can increase the number of places the hunter can hunt simultaneously. Traps, in contrast, work whether the trapper is physically present or not. Trappers can sleep, farm, and perform other duties knowing that their traps are still "working." Traps also multiply the trapper's presence. For they allow the trapper to work multiple areas simultaneously, thereby increasing the extent of his presence in duration and location.

Before reviewing the evidence, we must distinguish different types of trapping. Trapping is not a monolithic activity, as it occurs for different reasons. "Consumptive trapping" involves the capturing of animals deemed desirable for their fur, meat, or products. This type of trapping normally results in the death of the animal, but live-captures for zoos or pet markets do occur. Fur-trapping is a specific kind of consumptive trapping in that the primary goal is to capture animals considered valuable for their pelt rather than for their meat or to resolve a predation

10. I believe Christian environmental thinking must move beyond simplistic sloganeering or vacuous platitudes and provide concrete answers on the extent of human dominion. See Bouthier, "Religious Leaders Weigh in on Responsibility toward Environment," Np; Campolo, *How to Rescue the Earth without Worshiping Nature*, 70; DeWitt, *Caring for Creation*; Evangelical Environmental Network, *Frequently Asked Questions*.

11. I recognize that many people consider humans part of the animal kingdom. However, this writer rejects the materialist and reductionist views of scientists, arguing that humans are qualitatively different than animals and thus must be placed in their own category.

12. Cf. Cartmill's definition of hunting. Cartmill, *A View to a Death in the Morning*, 29–30.

issue.[13] "Control trapping" designates the capture and removal of animals considered dangerous or causing disturbance to human interests, such as troublesome house mice (*Mus musculus*), other invasive species,[14] or to prevent overpopulation or extinction.[15] As with consumptive trapping, control trapping frequently results in the death of the offending animal.[16] "Research trapping" refers to the capture of animals for study or population surveys. Since CAR activists focus their opposition on consumptive and control trapping, this chapter will do likewise.

Trapping is a complex issue covering a variety of tools, techniques, and species. The sheer breadth of data can overwhelm the non-professional. To reduce the subject to a more manageable size, the debate over consumptive trapping will be discussed in more general terms. However, since control trapping is decidedly more concrete and specific, I have chosen to evaluate CAR's opposition to coyote (*Canis latrans*) trapping for simplicity.[17]

13. Organ et al., *Trapping and Furbearer Management in North American Wildlife Conservation*, 2. Technically, all mammals have hair or fur. Furbearer has a more specific meaning of referring to those mammals specifically valuable for their fur. It should also be noted that trappers have found other uses for these animals, including using them for meat and lure making (see p. 1 and 8).

14. Invasive species is a derogatory term to designate organisms that are not native to a given habitat and whose presence causes a negative impact on the harmony of the habitat. Island habitats are very vulnerable to invasive species, as can be seen in the work done in New Zealand. Various, *Newsletter*.

15. Linzey believes that humans have a duty to protect a species either from itself (as in overpopulation) or from others (when it is threatened with extinction). His overriding mandate is for humans to be required to perform these culling activities as humanely (presumably painlessly and targeted) as possible. Clearly he is uncomfortable with this position, and perhaps fearing potential abuse continues by raising suspicion about the figures presented by the government which would be used to justify a cull. Ironically, Linzey makes this population claim based on his belief that humans have to manage their own population growth. His idea being if we have to do it then it is morally justified for us to require animals to do so. Sometimes we have to treat animals as groups. Linzey, *Animal Rights*, 38–39.

16. Translocation of the problem animal is one such exception. For the potential negative impacts to translocated animals see Van Vuren et al., "Translocation as a Nonlethal Alternative for Managing California Ground Squirrels," 351.

17. By such a limitation, I engage animal protectionist arguments at their strongest point, as land trapping results in greater injury potential than water trapping, where drowning sets can be employed.

As noted above, CAR activists believe that trapping or any killing of animals, except to save human life, is immoral.[18] They ground this belief in their reading of Scripture and their understanding of the environmental evidence. Unfortunately, proving that CAR activists are mistaken on their understanding of human-animal relations does not necessarily translate into support for trapping. CAR activists assert that trapping must be condemned by Christians because of its cruelty and threat to ecosystems.[19] In other words, CAR activists believe that Christians should refrain from trapping or severely limit their trapping activities on the basis that trapping violates God's requirement that humans protect His creation. Humans, even as subordinate lords over creation, cannot use their position and power as unrestricted license (1 Cor 6:12; 10:23). Since CAR activists employ scientific arguments to support their view that trapping constitutes a violation of our requirement to "care for creation," the remainder of this chapter will evaluate the validity of these arguments.

TRAPPING AS UNNECESSARILY CRUEL

CAR activists[20] assert that trapping constitutes an unacceptable level of pain and suffering[21] that, when coupled with other negative aspects of trapping, becomes an unacceptable form of wildlife management. In other words, the cruelty alleged to be inflicted by trapping, particularly the steel foothold trap, is so gratuitous that any of its environmental benefits are outweighed by its deficits.

---

18. The CAR position on using trapping to protect endangered species is unclear.

19. Gerstell, *The Steel Trap in North America*, 303f. Gerstell is quite right that the basic arguments against trapping have not changed. See also HSUS, *Trapping: The inside Story*; Linzey, "A Reply to the Bishops," 170–73.

20. It should be noted that CAR activists simply refer to the arguments against trapping presented by other animal protectionists. Linzey, "A Reply to the Bishops." 170. n. 1. Linzey specifically and approvingly refers to the 1973 edition of *Facts about Furs*.

21. The argument from compassion is presented in two variations, qualitative and quantitative. The qualitative argument states that trapping is unacceptable simply because it causes suffering and pain. In the ethical version of the argument from cruelty, animal activists argue that humans have no more right to inflict suffering or pain on a sentient being, such as a raccoon, than they would have a right to inflict pain on a mentally retarded child. For a detailed discussion of the Argument from Marginal Cases read Pluhar, *Beyond Prejudice*, 1–123. That argument was dealt with in the previous chapter. The quantitative version holds that trapping causes so much pain and suffering that it is unacceptable. We will only be discussing the second version in this chapter.

The evidence for this argument[22] can be found in *Cull of the Wild: A Contemporary Analysis of Wildlife Trapping in the United States*[23] (hereafter *COTW*) and *Facts about Furs*[24] (hereafter, *FAF*). These texts employed several categories to express the comprehensive nature of the suffering inflicted by trapping. First, they condemn the trappers' equipment as barbaric and excessively cruel. Foothold traps[25] are especially hated because animals caught in these traps suffer shoulder dislocations, cuts, bruises, swelling, broken bones,[26] tooth damage, and "wring off" (also known as "chew outs") in their struggle to free themselves before the trapper's return.[27] "Wring offs" occur when the animal's leg breaks at the joint. As the animal struggles and/or gnaws at the broken limb, ligaments are twisted till they sever, allowing the animal to escape. The resultant wound puts the animal at risk for infection and possible death. While the amount of pain involved and the number of animals affected is disputed,[28] these events have occurred and to some extent still occur, but hard data is lacking.[29]

---

22. Animal Welfare Institute, *Aims*, Np. Their mission is ". . . to reduce the sum total of pain and fear inflicted on animals by humans."

23. Fox and Papouchis, *Cull of the Wild*.

24. Nilsson et al. *Facts About Furs*. Although Andrew Linzey cited the 1973 edition, this writer will be using the 1980 edition.

25. The foothold is a steel trap which employs two half moon jaws which close on the appendage which depresses the trigger, thereby holding the animal by that appendage. Nilsson et al. *Facts About Furs*, 128–29 actually explain the physics behind the damage.

26. Nilsson et al. *Facts About Furs*, 86; Papouchis, "A Critical Review of Trap Research," 41.

27. In the United States, most trappers are required to check their traps anywhere from daily to every 48 or 72 hours depending on the situation and the laws of one's state. Fox and Papouchis, *Cull of the Wild*, 76.

28. Nilsson et al. *Facts About Furs*, 89–90. *FAF* mentions that fur trappers claim that traps in the hands of experienced trappers do not cause animals to suffer. The distinction between pain and suffering relates to differences of opinion about the mental and psychological status of animals. Trappers claim that wild animals have a higher tolerance for pain and therefore a properly set and maintained foothold does not cause an animal enduring agony. Boddicker says that wild animals have "evolved an ability to survive serious injury." Boddicker, *The Issue of Trapping*, 61.

29. It is perfectly understandable that solid statistics are essentially unavailable. People tend not to publicize their failures and trappers are no different. See the following publications for some indication as to the scope of the problem. Atkeson, "Incidence of Crippling Loss in Steel Trapping," 324. HSUS, *Trapping*, 1. Their fact sheet says that one study found that 29% of all raccoons chewed or twisted off their limb to escape.

The second part of the argument from cruelty asserts that traps are not selective, thereby injuring/killing many non-target animals.[30] Just as human rights advocates would be outraged by police rounding up people without any real evidence of guilt, so the animal protectionists argue that traps injure many animals that trappers did not seek. Without verifiable data, the *COTW* estimated that 5 million non-target animals may be captured in the U.S. each year.[31] The *FAF* cited an Australian study that found that 95% of all the trapped animals were non-target, and also a U.S. survey that revealed 67% of captures were non-target.[32] Trapping, therefore, is the moral equivalent of using a 1,000 pound bomb to kill a fly. It just doesn't meet the proportionality standard in that too many "innocent" animals become injured in the trappers' quest of their quarry.

EVALUATION OF THE ARGUMENT, TRAPPING AS UNNECESSARILY CRUEL

In light of these remarkable claims, one may wonder how Christians could support trapping with devices that inflict so much pain on target and non-target animals alike. Trapping, so described, appears to be the height of environmental mismanagement and abuse of our stewardship role. Although many of the criticisms of trapping are true,[33] they fail to provide the full context for those facts and thereby present uniformed readers with a distorted picture of trapping.

In regards to the first part of the argument from suffering, it should be said that trappers do not wish for "wring outs," as they represent a lost capture. Furthermore, while not denying that traps can cause pain and injury,[34] trappers are not sadists. The question, however, is, "How much pain may Christians morally inflict in the process of capturing free-range animals?" It is critical to be careful here, as your answer will impact your

30. Fox and Papouchis, *Coyotes in Our Midst*, 16. For a more detailed listing of stats see Fox and Papouchis, "Refuting the Myths," 25.

31. Fox, "Trapping in North America," 2.

32. Nilsson et al. *Facts About Furs*, 90.

33. This comment should not be taken to mean that I necessarily agree with all their statistics (e.g. the non-target capture statistics are highly debatable).

34. Unless one is a follower of Rene Descartes who believed that animals were mere machines, I accept this point as assumed. Rene Descartes, "Animals Are Machines," in *Animals and Christianity: A Book of Readings*, ed. Andrew Linzey and Tom Regan (New York: Crossroad Publishing Co., 1988). 46. Where Descartes likens animals to "automata."

moral evaluation of Christ's miracle of the fishes (Lk 5). Furthermore, should we consider the pain of the individual animal caught in the trap in isolation from, or in light of, the benefits achieved through compensatory culling[35] or controlling invasive species?[36] To assert that a particular capture method is unduly painful, one must have another option against which to compare it.[37] I would caution readers to diligently inquire about the standard employed by animal protectionists. Many of them consider all injuries sustained during an animal's capture, no matter how slight, as providing sufficient grounds to designate the method as cruel.[38] For example, most animal protectionists will argue that the mere death of the animal (unless to end suffering not induced by humans) is by definition cruel, as the animal will have lost its expectation of life.[39] Yet, loss of life is not what is generally understood as constituting cruelty in regards to animals.[40] This radical understanding of suffering caused one fur trapper to remark that animal protectionists would not be happy even if we trapped and killed the animals with "sweet dreams and tender kisses."[41] The animal protectionist argument only has force if it is wrong to trap an animal at all.[42]

If humans can morally trap and kill animals as long as it is performed properly, then what standard should be used to define what is "proper"?

35. Reynolds, "Trade-Offs between Welfare, Conservation, Utility and Economics in Wildlife Management," S134. Specifically, is it morally better or worse for an animal to perish due to starvation or by trapping? See Boddicker, *The Issue of Trapping*, 29f.

36. Clements and Corapi, "Paradise Lost? Setting the Boundaries around Invasive Species," 48–51. Feral pigs cause tremendous environmental damage in Hawaii. These pigs have been controlled with snares. Snares were set to kill but are not always successful. But the article does not say how frequently the snares were checked, nor does it mention that shooting can also cause suffering. It does note that snaring is cost-effective.

37. Other elements of trapping methods must also be considered, such as safety for the trapper and other persons, selectivity, practicality, and cost effectiveness.

38. Linzey, *Animal Gospel.* 62–66, 134, 144, 148.

39. Regan, *The Case for Animal Rights*, 101–2.

40. Otherwise eating the flesh of animals that did not die on their own would constitute animal cruelty by definition.

41. Mike Page, personal phone conversation.

42. Which is why animal protectionists spend so much energy trying to convince readers that so called "non-lethal" techniques work to stop wildlife damage. Cf. Fox and Papouchis, *Coyotes in Our Midst*, 21–29. The point is simply to show that these arguments only have force if one asserts that wildlife can only be regarded as a pest or visual pleasure rather than a resource to be responsibly harvested.

Reynolds[43] explains that the present standard, hypothalamic-pituitary-adrenal (HPA) axis (which is a blood test of hormones levels believed to signify different amounts of stress) has limitations.[44] If we rely on physical injury tests, as is done with Best Management Practices,[45] how much value should we place on the significance of animal's foot swelling, when the animal will be killed upon the trapper's arrival anyway? Using cage traps would not necessarily solve the problem as the *FAF* considers them humane only if the trap is checked twice daily, a requirement that would dramatically reduce trapping's cost-efficiency.[46]

Consider other forms of capturing animals. Dorsett lists a number of different lethal control techniques for coyotes, such as M-44s, shooting with calls, shooting with dogs, shooting from aircraft, denning, and livestock protection collars.[47] How does one compare the suffering caused by trapping to the suffering inflicted by other methods? Shooting, despite the public's greater acceptance, does not always result in a clean kill.[48] What about toxicants, such as sodium cyanide and sodium monoflouroacetate? These toxicants kill coyotes through internal injury and suffering is thereby more difficult to quantify.[49] In the United States, Wildlife Services personnel employ sodium cyanide in devices called M-44s. When a coyote bites and pulls on the M-44, sodium cyanide is injected into its mouth. Death often follows within 30 seconds to 5 minutes.[50] Is this device more or less humane than a foothold from the coyote's perspective? Should we factor

43. Reynolds, "Trade-Offs between Welfare, Conservation, Utility and Economics in Wildlife Management," S134.

44. Reynolds, "Trade-Offs between Welfare, Conservation, Utility and Economics in Wildlife Management." Boddicker contends the goal of suffering is the issue, but notes that for the animal (who being unaware of the goal) the pain is still the same. Boddicker, *The Issue of Trapping*, 50.

45. For details about Best Management Practices see Association of Fish & Wildlife Agencies, *Best Management Practices*; Fox, "The Development of International Trapping Standards," 66–68.

46. Nilsson et al., *Facts about Furs*, 105.

47. Dorsett, "Lethal Options for Controlling Coyotes," 158–61.

48. Alcorn, *Coyote Man*, 126. Even an early developer of the use of calls in hunting coyotes was not a perfect shot.

49. It is ironic how many people hate trapping but will easily employ poison, in a clear example of out of sight-out of mind thinking.

50. Fox and Papouchis, *Coyotes in Our Midst*, 16. For technical data on the M-44, see Blom and Connolly, "Inventing and Reinventing Sodium Cyanide Ejectors," 1–31.

in the potential risk to the person setting the device?[51] The point being made is not to denigrate humane concerns. It is just to explain that the standard one employs in large measure predetermines the conclusion.

Turning to part 2 of the argument, readers should be reminded that trappers have a financial interest in capturing the right animal. Here, again the problem of definition comes into play. If a trap is set for a coyote but catches a red fox, it could be legitimately said that the capture is a non-target. Yet non-target does not necessarily mean unwanted. It may not have been the exact species desired, but that does not necessarily mean that trapper cannot use the species. It is critical that Christians press animal protectionists for greater clarity in their use of terms.

Pets are by far the most emotionally charged non-target animal. Animal protectionists gain a great deal of political capital when pets become trapped, due to the intense media coverage responding to the shock of a pet-idolizing public.[52] One survey found that individuals were motivated to support trap bans because of a pet that was injured or killed in a trap.[53] Yet in all the outrage and finger pointing that occurs when pets are trapped, two questions are rarely asked: "Was the trap legally set?" and "Was the pet on a leash?"[54] These two questions are not asked because owners see their pets as extensions of the family with essentially equal rights and privileges. Many owners bristle against any restrictions on

51. Fox and Papouchis, *Coyotes in Our Midst*, 16. Authors note that 20 people have been injured by the device between 1983–1999.

52. Fox and Papouchis, "Refuting the Myths," 25. Note the image of a house cat caught in a #2 or possibly #3 double longspring foothold to further accentuate the authors' point. The image came from http://www.banlegholdtraps.com/trap_parent.htm and the site does not claim all its images are authentic. This writer suspects that this particular cat-in-trap-photo is staged. On pet statistics see *2002 U.S. Pet Ownership and Demographic Sourcebook*. No one denies that pet ownership brings joy to many people. According to the *2002 U.S. Pet Ownership Resource Book*, American's own 132 million dogs and cats. This number is actually low as it does not include birds, horses or exotic pets. The same source stated that the average veterinary cost per animal amounted to $ 178.50 for dogs and $84.60 per year. Include other financial costs such as feeding and time lost due to care for these animals, and the economic impact of pet ownership reaches into the billions of dollars. Christians should think about the amount of money and attention spent on pets in light of other pressing needs.

53. Cockrell, "Crusader Activists and the 1996 Anti-Trapping Campaign," 70.

54. Hudkins, "Prohibit the Trapping of Wildlife in County Road Rights-of-Way." I also have personal knowledge. Christians should ask a third question, namely whether the rise in the status of pets to family member, as denoted by the term "companion animal," is an appropriate attitude for a Biblical Christian.

their pet's rights and freedoms. Like naïve and doting parents, pet owners rarely even consider the possibility that their pet may have done something considered wrong. According to the Centers for Disease Control, each year more than 4.7 million people sustain dog bites, with 800,000 seeking medical attention. Almost half of those seeking medical attention require treatment in an emergency department, and about a dozen die.[55] We have not even mentioned how free-roaming dogs can attack livestock. House cats pose disease risks to humans and are a significant threat to the environment, a fact frequently overlooked.[56] Granted, pet owner misbehavior does not make trapping morally acceptable, but the point being made here is that free-roaming pets also negatively impact the environment. The public policy question becomes, "If trappers bear responsibility for catching free-roaming pets (all of which are not even injured), what responsibility do owners have for the negative effects of their pets' actions?" It is essentially an issue of distributive justice rather than relying on the tyranny of public opinion polls. I would suggest that the reason legislators ban traps stems from their awareness that trappers comprise such a small minority that such action will carry no negative political consequences.[57]

More to the point, a critical failure of the entire argument from cruelty lay with its excessive preoccupation with the trap.[58] Animal protectionists talk about the foothold as if it had only one design.[59] Their use of the term "foothold" is comparable to one saying that all vehicles pose the same risks of injury to their occupants as all the others. However, just as there are different kinds of cars, with differing safety standards, so there are different kinds of footholds with different injury rates. Footholds not only have different jaw spreads, and spring tension, they also have different versions such as off-set, double jaw, toothed-jaw, laminated, padded,

55. Centers for Disease Control, *National Dog Bite Prevention Week.*

56. For publications about the impact of free-roaming cats both for and against, visit http://www.icwdm.org/wildlife/housecat.asp.

57. According to Fox and Papouchis, *Cull of the Wild*, vii. less than 1/10 of 1% of the U.S. population traps for profit or recreation. Further evidence of the lack of political power of trappers is denoted by the recent government survey that neglected to mention trappers. U.S. Department of the Interior and others, "2006 National Survey of Fishing, Hunting, and Wildlife-Associated Recreation."

58. Fox and Papouchis, "Refuting the Myths," 28. Ms. Fox notes that 81% of trappers surveyed said they had learned their skills through "trial and error."

59. See Cathy Liss's Foreward in Garrett, *Alternative Traps*, 1.

and more. All footholds are not the same, nor do they injure animals in equal measure.[60]

The second problem with the argument against traps is the unstated assumption that technology improvement or an equipment ban holds the answer. In this regard, the animal protectionist perspective echoes that of the anti-gun lobby which directs its anger at an inanimate object rather than the morally responsible operator. Certainly in political terms, it is easier to regulate devices than behavior, so this may be part of the animal protectionist's strategy. Yet, their rhetoric repeatedly ignores that trapping involves the trapper-trap connection. Traps do not set themselves.[61] The trapper's skill in placement, choice, modification, and set construction (i.e. baiting) plays an important role in reducing injuries and non-target captures. For example, coyote trappers can reduce the risk of capturing free-roaming house cats, by simply increasing the tension needed to spring the trap.[62] Trapping injuries can be addressed by reducing trap check times[63] or using different traps noted below. While one suspects that animal protectionist standards are so high as to present insurmountable difficulties for a humane fur trade (on their definition),[64] it is worth noting that progress has been made.[65] It is regrettable that every state does not require trapper education, given that many trappers still learn by "trial

---

60. Padded-jaw footholds have done remarkably well in reducing animal injuries see Shivik et al., "Initial Comparison: Jaws, Cables, and Cage-Traps to Capture Coyotes," 1381.; Papouchis, "A Critical Review of Trap Research."

61. Animal protectionists regularly speak of traps "doing things." See Garrett, *Alternative Traps*, 17. "Interestingly, while the steel trap brought the beaver to near extinction . . ." Clearly readers should know that the trap did not cause beaver populations decline. Trappers, who used the trap, did that, as Garrett says earlier. My point is that this sort of confused speaking has a big impact in the political arena.

62. A fact noted in "Trapping Devices, Methods, and Research," 34.

63. For trap check requirements see Fox, "State Trapping Regulations," 71–111.

64. Boddicker states that, "The perfect trap would catch only the animal sought and would hold it without pain or damage, or kill it instantly and protect it from scavenger." Boddicker, *The Issue of Trapping*, 69. Animal protectionists would not care about protecting the dead animal from scavengers, but the rest of definition is about as good as any for the ideal trap in the perspective of animal protectionists.

65. I concede that improvements in humane trapping has been stimulated by the trapping industry's attempt to blunt the political force of the animal protectionists. Ideally, trappers should have worked to improve their techniques out of respect for God and the animal kingdom.

and error."[66] However, *COTW* painted too bleak a picture. Thankfully, a great deal of trapper education opportunities are available to those willing to seek it out, including field training, periodicals, books, and online bulletin boards.[67] While I strongly recommend trapper education, the fact is there are limits to what can be taught in a classroom setting. Trapping is like legal work, it takes practice. Even experienced trappers regularly admit that the animals teach them new things all the time.

Animal activists, in their political activism against footholds, fail to remind the public that the problems of pain/suffering and injuries to non-targets are not exclusively the domain of footholds. Box and cage traps[68] (mistakenly called live-traps)[69] have the same type of problems which are used to justify opposition to foot-holds. First, box and cage traps are not species-specific and in some cases are more likely to capture non-target animals than other traps.[70] Second, cage trapped animals can and do sustain physical injury.[71] For example, beavers captured in the Bailey Live Trap during the winter can suffer hypothermia because the trap keeps them in the cold water, a fact not mentioned in the *COTW*.[72] One study on river otters (*Lutra canadensis)* concluded that padded-jaw foothold traps were preferable to the Hancock cage trap because foothold trapped

66. For progress on a variety of species see articles published in Proulx, *Mammal Trapping*. Fox and Papouchis, "Refuting the Myths," 28.

67. I am personally aware of the existence of these, and other, educational opportunities for trapper training.

68. Box traps are enclosure devices with solid walls. Cage traps are enclosure devices with wire mesh walls.

69. Cf. "Trapping Devices, Methods, and Research." 34. The animal protectionists have made great headway exploiting the term live-trap as a synonym for cage traps. The persistent use of this highly emotive term has successfully ingrained in the public mind that all other traps by definition kill and are thus inhumane. The fact is footholds, snares, and other restraint devices also capture animals "alive."

70. Munoz-Igualada et al., "Evaluation of Cage-Traps and Cable Restraint Devices to Capture Red Foxes in Spain," 833, 835. Although this study attempted to capture foxes (not coyotes), the point being made is that cage traps caught 17 non-target animals and only 3 target. Furthermore some of the cage-trapped foxes suffered injuries, such as minor muscle degeneration with one even breaking a tooth.

71. See Garrett, *Alternative Traps*, 7.; Boddicker, *The Issue of Trapping*, 45, 51; Howard, *Nature Needs Us*, 126. Even the anti-foothold AVMA recognizes that achieving euthanasia standards in the field pose many practical challenges. American Veterinary Medical Association, *AVMA Guidelines on Euthanasia*, 18–19.

72. "Trapping Devices, Methods, and Research," 39. For information on hypothermia in beavers caught in a Bailey Live Trap see Vantassel, "The Bailey Beaver Trap," 173.

otters were less likely to break their teeth.[73] Readers may be surprised to learn that the much maligned foothold has actually been involved in a wildly successful river otter reintroduction program to much of their native range in the United States.[74] Additional research (using European otters, *Lutra lutra*) has been done using cell phones to notify trappers when an otter has been caught, which reduced injury scores significantly.[75]

As a side note, Linzey mentions consumptive wildlife use as a cause of otter declines. He is probably speaking of European otter (*Lutra lutra*), which experienced incredible decline in the 1950s. Unfortunately for Linzey, he has blamed hunting for the decline when the most likely cause was environmental pollution.[76] If he was referring to sea otter (*Enhydrous lutra*), then he is correct that excessive harvesting did lead to its decline in the early twentieth century.[77]

In regards to coyotes, cage and box traps are not effective.[78] To deny trappers access to traps other than cage or box traps is to essentially deny them the opportunity to trap coyotes.

A more realistic view of trapping is to recognize that the trap and the trapper work in combination. To put it numerically, we could describe the relationship as an equation, trap choice minus trapper skill=suffering (8−4=4). Improved trap design would mean that the suffering associated with the trap would be lower to begin with. Couple the trap with an improved skill of the trapper and the suffering number can be low indeed (7−5=2). Just as automobiles have become safer, the fact remains that driver behavior remains the number one cause of accidents and injuries.

---

73. Blundell et al., "Capturing River Otters," 190. Otters, being predators, rely on their teeth to capture and masticate their prey. Since their teeth do not grow back when damaged, tooth loss would have a major impact on their quality of life. Although some believe that cage trapped otters exhibited less stress. O'Neill et al, "Minimizing Leg-Hold Trapping Trauma for Otters with Mobile Phone Technology," 2776.

74. Organ et al., *Trapping and Furbearer Management in North American Wildlife Conservation*, 34. For a detailed history of the project see also Krause, "Thank You, Mr. Sevin, Sir.," 46–60.

75. O'Neill and others. 2776. "Functioning alarms reduced the injuries suffered from an average cumulative score of 77.7 to just 5.5 on the International Organization for Standardization 10990–5 trauma scale ($Z = -5.074, P \leq 0.001$)."

76. Mason and Macdonald, "Growth in Otter (Lutra Lutra) Populations in the UK as Shown by Long-Term Monitoring," 148.

77. Laidre and Jameson, "Foraging Patterns and Prey Selection in an Increasing and Expanding Sea Otter Population," 800.

78. Way et al., "Box-Trapping Eastern Coyotes in Southeastern Massachusetts," 695.

Fortunately, advances in trap design have been made. Research performed by Shivak, DeLiberto and others demonstrated that newer devices may reduce injury.[79] The Belisle˚ Footsnare[80] has achieved the humane requirements of the Agreement on International Humane Trapping Standards (AIHTS) for lynx, coyote and bobcat. Another cable restraint trap, called The Collarum˚, captures coyotes by throwing a self-loosening cable around the coyote's neck and boasts a 100% target capture rate. In other words, during field studies, the trap never caught anything but a coyote. In further testimony of the trap's humaneness, animal control officers are using it to capture stray dogs.[81] While advances in technology that reduce human error are certainly welcome, the fact is there are limits to where technology will take us.[82] Trapping wildlife is not a "one-size fits all."[83]

Animal protectionists are correct in noting that many trappers are reluctant to adopt less injurious technology.[84] What animal protectionists neglect to say is that trapper resistance stems from three different areas. The first is economic. Traps constitute a major investment, especially in light of lower fur prices, in part due to animal protectionist's efforts to change the social acceptance of wearing fur.[85] In this regard, trappers are no different than people who avoid replacing their gas guzzling cars with more efficient hybrids. Trappers also tend to be culturally conservative. Like farmers, trappers are reluctant to try new things because what they

79. Following information derives primarily from Shivik et al., "Preliminary Evaluation of New Cable Restraints to Capture Coyotes," 606–13; Shivik et al., Initial Comparison: Jaws, Cables, and Cage-Traps to Capture Coyotes." 1375–1383.; Phillips et al., "Leg Injuries to Coyotes Captured in Three Types of Foothold Traps," 262–63.

80. http://www.fur.ca/index-e/trap_research/index.asp?action=trap_research&page=traps_certified_traps.

81. Huot and Bergman, "Suitable and Effective Coyote Control Tools for the Urban/Suburban Setting." 312–22. Readers should be aware that I have maintained a business relationship with Mr. Huot for a number of years.

82. Earle et al., "Evaluating Injury Mitigation and Performance of #3 Victor Soft Catch® Traps to Restrain Bobcats," 625. Authors state, "It is difficult to design a footholding device that captures and holds a high percentage of any target species while maintaining low injury scores." But farther down the authors explain that some traps do perform quite well in terms of performance, selectivity, and low injury scores for raccoon and opossum, such as Egg™ and Duffer™.

83. All of the new trap designs have limitations. None to this point have been as versatile as the foothold.

84. Papouchis, "A Critical Review of Trap Research," 41.

85. Fox, "Trapping in North America. A Historical Overview," 4.

have works. A more sinister problem is the inconsistency between animal protectionist rhetoric and animal protectionist behavior. In particular, animal protectionists have worked to ban more humane capture equipment and have not worked to legalize more humane equipment.[86] Finally, a more intractable problem stems from trapper suspicion that the animal protectionists will never be satisfied with anything less than a total trap ban. Outsiders may dismiss such fears as groundless fear mongering. However, the legal actions taken by animal protectionist groups suggest the trappers' concerns are not without warrant.[87]

TRAPPING AS ENVIRONMENTALLY IRRESPONSIBLE

Trapping's alleged deleterious effect on the environment constitutes the second argument employed by animal protectionists. Recall that animal protectionists by and large adopt a minimalist view of human intervention into the affairs of wildlife. While they recognize that humanity has a role to play in relation to animals, the guiding principle appears to be Albert Schweitzer's "Reverence for Life Ethic."[88] They argue that humans should only kill wildlife with serious justification.[89] For many, serious justification would include protection of human life and species preservation, as in overpopulation, or threatened extinction.[90] They also encourage the employment of habitat restriction and modification as a means of wildlife damage control, as could be done through fencing or other forms of habitat modification.[91]

---

86. To cite only two, the banning of the "Coyote Getter" and the lack of effort to legalize tranquilizer traps. Boddicker, *The Issue of Trapping*, 47, 70. On tranquilizer traps see Sahr and Knowlton, "Evaluation of Tranquilizer Trap Devices (Ttds) for Foothold Traps Used to Capture Gray Wolves," 597–605.

87. For example, study the Question 1 ballot initiative vote which took place in Massachusetts in 1996. I was personally involved in this controversy, including debates on radio and TV (Dan Yorke Show out of Springfield MA. WHYN radio AM 560 and Channel 40 WGGB-ABC television) with one of the first 10 signatories of the ballot initiative, Peter Teraspulsky (Sept–Oct, 1996).

88. Linzey and Cohn-Sherbok, *After Noah*, 104.

89. Ibid., 105.

90. Linzey makes this population claim based on his belief that humans have to manage their own population growth. His idea being if we have to do it then it is morally justified for us to require animals to do so. Sometimes we have to treat animals as groups. Linzey, *Animal Rights*, 38–39.

91. Fox and Papouchis, "Refuting the Myths," 26. It should be noted that the effects on

Animal protectionists assert that the trapping industry and wildlife damage control programs (such as the USDA-APHIS-Wildlife Services[92] agency, hereafter WS, and private wildlife control companies) constitute the worst expression of environmental stewardship.[93] Here they strike at the strongest historic claims of the consumptive wildlife proponents, namely that trapping helps: 1. to keep nature in balance by removing surplus animals, 2. to resolve wildlife damage issues, such as livestock predation, and 3. to reduce the spread of zoonotic diseases.[94]

Animal protectionists claim that nature is completely self-regulating.[95] When animal populations lack balance, nature automatically makes the necessary adjustments. Humans must learn not to interfere because they usually caused the imbalance in the first place. For example, animal protectionists argue that coyote trapping induces coyotes to disperse over greater distances (causing problems elsewhere). Furthermore, trapping increases coyote recruitment rates, as the remaining adults can better feed their young.[96] Second, trapping fails to provide important environmental benefits because it has contributed to the extinction and/or threatened extinction of many species, such as the sea mink (*Neovison macrodon*, extinct) and wolf (*Canis lupus*, threatened).[97]

EVALUATION OF THE ARGUMENT, TRAPPING IS ENVIRONMENTALLY IRRESPONSIBLE

As usual, animal protectionists raise some important issues, but issues separated from context and clear definitions only result in muddled thinking. First, when the wildlife managers speak of surplus animals they mean those animals that will die whether or not they are trapped. It is axiomatic that a habitat will only allow animals to survive that it can feed and house,

---

the ecosystem and the animals have not been properly studied, nor have the potential impacts been considered by animal protectionists. Essentially, they assume these techniques are non-lethal as opposed to less-lethal.

92. For a review of Wildlife Services activities see Jones Jr. and GAO Staff, "Wildlife Services Program: Information on Activities to Manage Wildlife Damage," 1–70.

93. Linzey, *Animal Rights: A Christian Assessment of Man's Treatment of Animals.* 38.

94. For the following arguments see Fox and Papouchis, "Refuting the Myths," 25–27.

95. Fox and Papouchis, "Refuting the Myths," 25.

96. Fox and Papouchis, *Coyotes in Our Midst*, 18–19.

97. Nilsson et al., Facts about Furs, 162ff.

a principle known as "carrying capacity."[98] The issue is whether trapping is additive to animal mortality, in which case reducing trapping pressure will result in higher animal numbers, or whether trapping is compensatory to animal mortality, in which case reducing trapping pressure will have no effect on animal numbers. Different species have different mortality and fecundity rates, and therefore respond to trapping pressure differently.[99] This is why wildlife managers have different rules regarding season length and take limits. At issue is whether or not wildlife is considered a resource available for utilization. Since animal protectionists are disinclined to accept human utilization of wildlife, they would answer that wildlife is not a resource. Therefore, it should not surprise us that, in their view, trapping does not constitute a viable wildlife management practice. However, from a resource perspective, the post-trapping rebound in coyote populations is not a negative event but actually a positive one for it insures coyote survival and opportunity for a good harvest the following season.[100]

Another issue is at stake, however, namely the kind of death surplus animals will experience. Walter Howard raises this question at length and argues that in nature, life exists only with death. He calls this phenomenon the "death ethic." In light of this ethic, the question for humans is what sort of death should excess wildlife experience. We know the additional animals will die. But should we cull them ourselves or should we let starvation, disease, and the damaging effects that result from those activities do the job?[101]

Second, animal protectionists know full well that in the modern United States, Canada, and Western Europe, regulated trapping is not a factor in wildlife extinction.[102] In fact, the reverse is true. Sportsmen's fees have funded reintroduction programs of extirpated species. Agencies have used trappers to remove predators threatening endangered species.[103] The

98. Howard, *Nature Needs Us*, 213.

99. Banci and Proulx, "Resiliency of Furbearers to Trapping in Canada," 175–203.

100. Note that we have not even considered the problem of "cultural carrying capacity" which refers to how much wildlife and its damage the public will tolerate before demanding control measures to be instituted. Cultural carrying capacity is typically a significantly lower population figure as compared to the population the habitat will sustain.

101. Howard, *Nature Needs Us*, 11–47.

102. Organ et al., "Fair Chase and Humane Treatment: Balancing the Ethics of Hunting and Trapping."

103. Direct control (e.g. hunting and trapping) is not always the best method to protect endangered species, but it is an important tool. See Goodrich and Buskirk, "Control

sportsmen's record has not always been perfect, but they have had a positive impact on preserving species.[104]

Animal protectionists cast a great deal of ire on wildlife damage control programs, especially the work performed by WS, which has historically administered predator control programs in the U.S. For example, activists reject the idea that coyote control programs are needed to protect flocks from costly predation. Aside from the political issue of whether or not taxpayer funds should be spent on behalf of private businesses, animal activist criticism of WS has garnered support from advocacy groups strictly on environmental grounds. William Stolzberg,[105] in a recent article on WS' coyote control program, says that the agency simply kills too many non-targets. The idea being, if the problem is coyotes, WS should avoid killing so many other animals. The problem is exacerbated by recent findings which have shown that not all coyotes kill sheep. Therefore, any control program that traps coyotes just for being coyotes rather than targeting problem coyotes seems to run counter to the arguments used to justify the program in the first place. No wonder that Stolzberg says that little has changed since the landmark *Leopold Report of 1964* condemning the WS predator management practices. Stolzberg notes that this blanket war against coyotes has resulted in an explosion of ground predators, such as raccoons and skunks, which are responsible for attacking the nests of migratory birds.[106] So the argument is, if we are to protect the integrity of the environment we have to work towards protecting all species within the habitat. Finally, Stolzenburg rejects the idea that coyote predation has forced shepherds out of business.[107] In place of WS, animal protectionists hold up their work with sheep producers of Marin County, California as a better coyote management model.[108] They claim that their use of various non-lethal control measures (although lethal control by property owners

---

of Abundant Native Vertebrates for Conservation of Endangered Species," 1357–1364.

104. Baron, *The Beast in the Garden*, 32f. Baron notes the acreage set aside by hunting president Theodore Roosevelt and the pioneering work of Aldo Leopold, founder of the Wildlife Society.

105. Stolzenburg, "Us or Them," 14–21.

106. Ibid., 20.

107. Ibid., 16. Fox and Papouchis, *Coyotes in Our Midst*, 12. One study said that cattle losses to coyotes accounted for only 2.2% of all livestock losses. In a follow up study 5 years later the losses dropped to 0.15%. See also Berger, "Carnivore-Livestock Conflicts: Effects of Subsidized Predator Control and Economic Correlates on the Sheep Industry," 751.

108. Fox, "Coyotes and Humans: Can We Coexist?" 290–91.

was not banned), such as prohibition of feeding coyotes, changes in husbandry practices, hazing of coyotes, guard animals, and fencing, resulted in a reduction in sheep losses.

At first glance, the claim that coyote trapping does not diminish livestock predation appears significant. Christian ethics would not support a policy that simply does not achieve the desired results. However, after a closer look at the data a different picture emerges.[109] First, the trouble with averages is that not all ranchers suffer predation equally.[110] Nevertheless, assuming that all U.S. ranchers suffered only 0.15% losses to predation, why would this small amount require the conclusion that predator trapping is unnecessary?

Second, what about the problem of self-interest? It is easy for unaffected parties to diminish the significance of another's loss. What if we turned the question around and asked how one would react to a shoplifter who stole over the course of a year 0.15% of your assets? Should you give the shoplifter a pass simply because it is such a small amount? It is true that weather killed more cattle than coyotes. However, ranchers cannot control weather. So should they not work to diminish the losses that are within their control? What if we broaden the question to cover damage other than simply livestock predation? Conover[111] says that in a survey about the extent of wildlife damage sustained in the previous year by 2 million agricultural producers, 24% said they had suffered damage from coyotes, 25% suffered raccoon damage, and 9% suffered skunk damage. One can see that non-target captures are not always a true loss when considering that a landowner can suffer damage from multiple species.[112]

Also, the Marin County experiment was not the glowing success the animal protectionists would like us to believe. Larson, in a review on

---

109. Even a negative article on the Federal coyote control program states that definitive evidence against the positive effects of coyote control in regards to increasing sheep production is unavailable. Berger. 758.

110. Larson, "The Marin County Predator Management Program: Will It Save the Sheep Industry?" 295. For detailed discussion of the economics of predation see Jones, "Economic Impact of Sheep Predation in the United States," 6–12.

111. Conover, *Resolving Human-Wildlife Conflicts*, 104.

112. Although our focus has been on the agricultural damage caused by coyotes, wildlife in the U.S. have caused crop and livestock losses of $944 million in 2001. Southwick et al., *Potential Costs of Losing Hunting and Trapping as Wildife Management Methods*, 2. This figure does not account for the costs wildlife bring when damaging infrastructure (flooding), deer strikes to automobiles and households.

the program, provided several reasons why the data should be held in suspicion.[113] She explained that the county program instituted a compensation program to encourage ranchers to adopt the new (less-lethal) practices. Ranchers would receive $500 for each of the four suggested practices adopted, up to a total of $2,000 annually. Those who adopted at least two of the recommended practices would be compensated for any sheep losses. In her review of the reporting data, Larson observed that around the program's third year, the county had to limit the compensation provided to no more than 5% of the total flock. Such a limitation suggested to her that the program was not limiting the number of sheep losses. Second, Larson suspected that sheep losses were under-reported because only ranchers enrolled in the county program would be motivated to report. She noted that one herder (not involved in the program) claimed to have lost 150 lambs annually in fiscal years 2003/04 and 2004/05, which was more than all the reported losses in the county program. Third, Larson said it was very likely that during the program's lifespan, ranchers may have been killing more coyotes on their own than were taken when WS field agents operated. Finally, she cautioned that any comparisons regarding control effectiveness between the programs is partly hindered by differences in data collection and the fact that WS at its height was responsible for controlling predation on 73,000 acres of land, which dwarfs the County program, which never exceeded 10,275 acres in the past 5 years. In light of Larson's findings, it would seem clear that animal protectionists have not proven that trapping is an unnecessary component for effective predator management.[114]

What about animal protectionist assertion that trapping is not necessary to mitigate wildlife disease epidemics, such as rabies?[115] If by rabies control, animal protectionists mean eliminate or drastically reduce the incidence of rabies in wildlife populations, then they are correct. Trapping, by itself, will not achieve that level of disease management. Ironically, to achieve that reduction in disease levels, trapping would have to reduce

---

113. Larson, "The Marin County Predator Management Program: Will It Save the Sheep Industry?"296–97.

114. After attending a presentation where Ms. Fox highlighted the success of the Marin County Program, I inquired if she was going to respond to Ms. Larson's criticisms. She responded that she was planning to but did not know when. Personal Communication, Estes Park, CO, September 30, 2008. I found it interesting that she did not mention or respond to Larson's criticism of the Marin County Program during her presentation.

115. Nilsson et al., *Facts about Furs*, 157–60.

an animal population to threatened or endangered status. That would be similar to killing 5 of the 6 billion earth's human population to control the spread of the flu. This is why the Centers for Disease Control do not recommend wholesale, nationwide trapping to control rabies; it is not cost effective. But as before, animal protectionists do not provide the entire picture. While broad-scale trapping is not recommended for disease control, writers of the *Compendium of Animal Rabies Prevention and Control* recommended it for use in targeted locations as explained in the following quote:

> However, limited control in high-contact areas (e.g., picnic grounds, camps, or suburban areas) may be indicated for the removal of selected high-risk species of wildlife.(9) The state wildlife agency and state health department should be consulted for coordination of any proposed vaccination or population-reduction programs.[116]

The effectiveness of high intensity trapping in designated areas is also supported by others.[117] Rabies, being population density dependent, is vulnerable to population declines. The reason for this is due to the virus' terminal nature. In order for the virus to continue living, it must find another host before it kills its present one. The longer it takes to find another host, the less likely it will find a new one before it kills its present one. In light of this reality, it is indeed strange to claim that trapping actually spreads the disease. Here again, the animal protectionists play with the meanings of words. In blaming the sportsmen for transporting infected raccoons and causing the Mid-Atlantic rabies epidemic, the *COTW* insinuated that hunting and trapping caused the epidemic. The fact is, the hunters' desire to increase game numbers motivated them to relocate raccoons. But to suggest that hunting and trapping caused the epidemic carelessly confuses the motivation for an action with the action itself. The other claim, that trapping removes immune adult animals causing a reproductive spike of weaker and less immune animals,[118] also flies in the face of their complaint that trapping is indiscriminate. Either trapping is discriminate or indiscriminate. It takes a special and rare situation for a

116. National Association of State Public Health Veterinarians Inc., "Compendium of Animal Rabies Prevention and Control, 2000," 19–30.

117. Cf. Broadfoot et al., "Raccoon and Skunk Population Models for Urban Disease Control Planning in Ontario, Canada," 301–2.

118. Fox and Papouchis, "Refuting the Myths," 27.

trapper to be able to set a trap that will only capture animals of a certain age. Finally, it should be noted that trapping by private individuals costs states nothing. In fact, trapping is a revenue generator, as trappers pay the state for the privilege to trap animals. Therefore, the actions of private trappers can be reasonably claimed to reduce the incidence of rabies because trapping can reduce the overall population of a species in a given locale. Furthermore, these trappers do their work in a cost-effective manner.[119]

CONCLUSION

As noted above, how one understands humanity's relationship to the planet will in large degree determine one's decision and evaluation of the evidence and goals regarding environmental policy. Few topics bring this fact into sharper review than the issue of wildlife management, of which trapping plays a controversial part. But trapping cannot be ignored. Humans and animals compete over natural resources.[120] The fact is, humans must kill to live, be it directly on one's own or through the use of surrogates. Becoming a vegan or vegetarian does not isolate one morally, because clearing land and protecting crops causes harm to animals.

Christians must recognize that the claims of animal protectionist groups concerning the effects of trapping need to be carefully evaluated. Whether or not readers find these explanations about the value of trapping convincing, I hope that it encourages environmentally cognizant Christians to think carefully about the complexities involved in wildlife management before backing any particular plan of action. I suspect that most Christians, while not explicitly adopting animal protectionist ideology, have failed to properly evaluate animal protectionists' criticism of trapping and the consequences entailed by adopting their hands-off approach to creation care. Perhaps, in their desire to correct past failings, these Christians do not realize that they risk jettisoning not only an important Christian doctrine, namely, that God made the earth for humanity, not vice-versa,[121] but also unduly restricting humanity's ability to extract renewable resources that wildlife provide. For example, one

119. This point cannot be over stated. Animal protectionists seem to prefer state-run wildlife programs. Christians must consider whether it is better to have tax dollars spent on wildlife control or on social programs for the poor.

120. Franklin, *Animal Rights and Moral Philosophy*, 89.

121. Christian animal rights activists repeatedly assert that humans are to serve the earth. See Linzey and Cohn-Sherbok, *After Noah*, 21.

major Evangelical environmental group says that humans should avoid acting violently with the non-human creation.[122] Regrettably, since they do not define what is meant by violence, uneducated Christians may think that trapping of animals under ecologically sustainable conditions is included.

---

122. Cf. Evangelical Environmental Network, *Frequently Asked Questions*, Np. While the site does not condemn trapping it does use the language of violence in an undefined way.

7

Summary Assessment
of the CAR Movement's Position

THE CAR MOVEMENT HAS provided Christians with an important opportunity to reflect upon and refine its historic understanding of human-animal relations. Just as the Christological debates helped Christians
refine their Christology, so the CAR movement has helped us develop a
more precise statement on the role and place of animals in God's creation.
Evangelicals should take to heart several positive aspects of CAR theology.

First, many CAR proponents have presented their case without excessive rancor or preoccupation with the righteousness of their cause.[1]
Although their tone can be rather strident at times, it is fair to say that
CAR activists have forcefully presented their case within the parameters
of Christian behavior. They have rejected violence[2] and instead have chosen to the path of persuasion, backed by a committed lifestyle, to convince
people to adopt their point of view. Linzey is quite correct to note that we
are all sinners, and need to maintain a humble attitude in conversations
with those who disagree. Having received plenty of hate-mail,[3] I can as-
sure readers of his hope that more people would follow Linzey's example.
Second, in a time of rampant moral relativism, Christians should be
thankful when people stand for objective moral truth. Additionally, CAR
activists correctly understand that belief and action, intellectual commit-
ment and lifestyle are intimately connected. If for nothing else, Christians

1. Linzey, *Christianity and the Rights of Animals*, 101f; Linzey, *Animal Gospel*, 125.

2. Linzey, *Animal Gospel*, 86ff.

3. During the late 1990s I received hate-mail from those claiming to be supporters of
the animal rights. Unlike my critics, I included my full name and contact information in
all correspondence.

should commend CAR activists for their belief that integrity, namely what is on the outside matches the inside, still means something.

Third, Christians must be grateful that CAR activists call upon the name of Christ (Lk 9:49). Their stated desire to follow Christ and participate in His redemptive mission is a worthy activity that all Christians should, in principle, agree with. We should be pleased for their desire to follow Christ, even though their views differ from historic Christian teaching and practice (Mk 9:40). Fourth, CAR activists correctly call upon Christians to think about the consequences of their lifestyle choices, and consider if those choices result from vices rather than virtue. CAR activism does flow from a proper concern, too frequently ignored, namely that everything, including animals, belongs to God and as such ought to be treated with the respect appropriate of God's property. Specifically, they are correct to remind Christians that animals, like all creation, have worth beyond their instrumental value for human purposes because they ultimately belong to God.[4] Christians, as noted in chapter 1, have not taken their creation-care responsibilities seriously enough. Christians must recognize that creation belongs to God, and it must be treated with the care appropriate to that recognition.

Despite these positive aspects, there are important reasons why Christians should not accept CAR views. First, Christians should be cautious about any belief system that utilizes vague language and uses verbal confusion to advance its cause. CAR activists are surprisingly careless with their wording. Their employment of highly emotionally laden terms such as abuse, animal cruelty, and violence when referring to the simple acts of killing animals, sport hunting, and meat eating,[5] allows them to mischaracterize the opposing position. This "Straw-Man Argument" is then used to exploit the ignorance of their followers and sympathizers. For example, CAR activists label various actions, such as hunting, fishing, and trapping as "cruel". However, upon investigating a specific behavior, such as using a cage-trap to capture furbearing animals, one discovers that they understand the term cruel as synonymous with death. Unfortunately, when the public

---

4. Linzey and Cohn-Sherbok, *After Noah*, 6, 11–13.

5. Linzey, *Animal Theology*. Sometimes Linzey just uses the terms without defining them at all pp.16–17. Other times cruelty is understood as sport hunting, which is defined as "wanton killing," 123. Killing animals is called violence p. 129. See p. 38 in Linzey, *Christianity and the Rights of Animals,* where Linzey seems incapable or unwilling to accept that mankind can kill animals and still value them.

hears the word "cruel", it imagines a creature experiencing intense agony over extended periods of time. Thus by expanding the definition of "cruel", CAR activists can employ a powerfully emotive word to gain support of those who would not necessarily be in support of their cause. I trust that this book has shown that CAR activists have not demonstrated the immorality of animal death initiated by humans. Additionally, I have demonstrated that any statement suggesting that killing of animals is by definition wrong would have the unfortunate side effect of besmirching Christ's character. For if killing of animals is by definition cruel, as CAR activists suggest, then we have in effect made Jesus Christ a participant in cruelty.

Second, the CAR position is fundamentally impossible to implement. As has been highlighted in the previous chapters, a lifestyle free of killing animals is impossible for any human to obey. The impossibility is not due to human moral inability or perversity, as a CAR activist may counter, but due to physical impossibility. All human activity negatively impacts some animals, while positively impacting others. For example, when a house is built, animals that lived or used that space now become displaced and most likely to suffer an earlier death. Simultaneously, the house becomes fertile territory for commensal pests, such as house mice, to invade and thrive in. The question CAR activists fail to ask is, "Does God ever command His people to do that which is physically impossible to do?" I believe the answer is a resounding "No!" God does not command us to jump tall buildings in a single bound, nor does He require us to live in a way that does not utilize wildlife resources. CAR activists have also failed to acknowledge that vegetarianism also negatively impacts animals. They have not proven that vegetarianism results in "less" animal suffering, as they claim. I suggest that vegetarianism does not reduce animal suffering at all but simply makes animal suffering become more distant.[6]

Third, their cavalier handling of Scripture flows from their Liberation theology interpretive model, which assumes that power over something automatically implies abuse of the subordinate creature.[7] Like a scientist

6. Even some so called "non-consumptive uses" of wildlife may harm wildlife. For some species, wildlife viewing can be harmful as the tourism can lead to increased habitat destruction. See Organ et al., "Fair Chase and Humane Treatment: Balancing the Ethics of Hunting and Trapping." Additionally, one could ask whether even the desire to photograph wildlife or to engage in wildlife viewing exhibits an instrumentalist attitude of wildlife.

7. Cf. Meeks, *God the Economist*, 131–33. He argues that good work is: distinctively personal, cooperative, equalitarian, and self-giving.

who forces the data to fit the preconceived model, CAR activists have taken their understanding of what creation should be and either ignored or massaged Biblical data to fit that model. In their desire to correct the negative consequences of pure instrumental behavior and treatment of the environment, they have over-corrected. They have disparaged and/ or overlooked the vast amount of research that shows humans are completely capable of harvesting wildlife in ways that protect the underlying habitat/ecosystem and viability of the species. In all their writings, they do not explain what the purpose of animals was besides communing with God (cf. Job 40:15ff). In other words, what "work" do animals perform?[8] Following their beliefs would require humans to distance themselves from the animal kingdom and let "nature" take its course. In this regard, their call for seeing humans as fellow creatures in the environment contradicts their stated goals. If the instrumental view over-emphasized humanity's dominion role, then the CAR view under-emphasized humanity's place in the environment.

This confusion over humanity's relationship to animals, and ultimately nature, is understandable. William Cronon, editor and participant in the book *Uncommon Ground*,[9] discusses how controversies over humanity's use of the environment turn on the issue of what kind of environment people want. Cronon identifies a number of different views of nature, including nature as naïve reality, nature as Eden, nature as commodity, nature as enemy, and nature as contested terrain.[10] So any talk of nature has to define what concept of nature is meant.

The problem is that our understanding of what is "natural" is very much a construct of our own values, as our view of nature involves our thoughts on power, property, work, and our place in it.[11] If our understanding of nature is a construct of our own values, then it begs the question where we should look to find those values. For example, when moderns speak of "nature" or "natural," they frequently mean that portion of the planet that is free from human presence. In contrast, the ancients considered "wilderness" areas to be out of balance, where one element

8. Cf. Meeks, *God the Economist*, 131–33, 151. Meeks says that work helps one be included as part of community.

9. Cronon, "Beginnings Introduction: In Search of Nature," 23–56.

10. He also discusses nature as virtual reality, but that is an issue beyond the scope of our project, 43ff.

11. Cronon, "Beginnings Introduction: In Search of Nature," 26.

dominated another, whether it be dryness or wetness or something else.[12] Wilderness was associated with demons and evil. Wilderness meant land devoid of life.[13] Pre-modern views of nature saw humans as part of nature and in harmony with it. Nature was a place for humans to experience and live, not to dominate or avoid.[14]

I suggest that the CAR movement has a decidedly modern and industrialized view of nature because it sees virtually any human-animal interaction as exploitive.[15] Not only is this view emphatically modern, it is also unsupported by Scriptural testimony. Scripture does not separate humanity from nature.[16] God made both entities to be together. Scripture also connects Israel's physical environment with the state of her moral behavior. If she obeyed God's commands, then harmony would be kept or restored (Isa 51:3–4; 41:18–19; Jer 25:38–39). Physical nature reflected the moral standing of the community.[17] There were environments where humans could stray from the path and become lost both physically and spiritually. Olwig argues that in the Bible, if people are good, then they live in a good place (Eden). But they do not become good because they live in a good place. He says, "It would be diabolic, and contrary to the word of the Bible, to confuse the biblical ideal of a natural state of human affairs with the physical nature that symbolizes that state."[18]

In a similar vein, Jeanne Kay contends that the nature of human dominion, as expressed in the Hebrew Bible, was granted to the righteous who obey God's commands.[19] She claims that environmentalists, while employing the same moralistic structure presented by the Old Testament,

12. Olwig, "Reinventing Common Nature: Yosemite and Mount Rushmore—a Meandering Tale of Double Nature," 386.

13. Ibid., 384.

14. Ibid., 380.

15. Webb, *On God and Dogs*, Webb is one exception, as he believes that humans can have mutually beneficial and non-exploitive relationships with animals, such as can occur with households pets.

16. As chapter 2 and 3 show, the evidence for this claim can be found in all strata and genre of Scripture.

17. Olwig, "Reinventing Common Nature: Yosemite and Mount Rushmore—a Meandering Tale of Double Nature," 384–85.

18. Ibid., 399.

19. Kay, "Human Dominion over Nature in the Hebrew Bible," 214–15. She says that debates over whether dominion means domination or stewardship, in her view, exhibit a simplistic assessment of Biblical testimony.

actually find environmental damage through natural causes, whereas Scripture blames human disobedience to God's commands for ecological disaster. "In rejecting the Bible's explicit texts on nature, secular environmentalism has paradoxically enshrined most of its underlying values."[20] Ironically, she says that modern environmentalism's rejection of environmental destruction as a sign of God's judgment came from the enlightenment plus Darwinian biology.[21]

Kay says that in the Biblical world, the environment acts as a barometer by which one can evaluate one's obedience to God's commands.[22] She adds that we should avoid single glance readings of Genesis 1:28, as the Bible does limit humanity's dominion in all three covenant contexts: the Garden, Noah, and Israel, noting that the Bible expresses horror over greed, lust, and oppression.[23] Although not arriving at definitive conclusions, her tone expresses much sympathy with the shepherd model of dominion that I will explain more fully in the next chapter. She observes that the Pentateuch exhibits harmony broken by human activity. The prophets present nature as beyond human control when God is angry at sin (Ez 26:4–5,14; Jer 14; Hab 3:17). Obedience to God is presented in the context of a positive environmental response (Isa 11:5–9; 60:13; Hos 14:6–9).[24] In fact, she notes that the images are so pastorally and agriculturally based it is difficult to read them in simply terms of human domination. However, Godly people are presented with dominion over the animals (Dan 6:17–23; 1 Kgs 17:6; 2 Kgs 2:24). The writings portray a more complex view, showing that humanity's lack of control over the beasts is not always due to sin (Job 39:26–7), or, put another way, due to God's desire for humans not to have dominion. The CAR activists are correct in seeing human use of animals, and by extension the environment, as an important ethical issue. Unfortunately, the problem with the world is not that we kill and eat animals as they contend. The problem is that we are in rebellion against God, and that rebellion brings forth human death (Rom 3:23) and environmental imbalance.

20. Kay, "Human Dominion over Nature in the Hebrew Bible," 230.

21. Ibid., 223–27. It is interesting to note Harrison's observation that our destructive domination of the environment stems from our fear of death. Presumably, Harrison is not a Christian. Harrison, "Toward a Philosophy of Nature," 436.

22. Ibid., 217.

23. Ibid., 221–22.

24. This concept of balance is fully developed in Murray, *The Cosmic Covenant.*

One suspects that the radical nature of their claim results from an over-correction of humanity's failure to properly steward the earth. They believe that if humans can see animals, and by extension the planet, as having intrinsic value, then humans would be motivated to change their behavior. While certainly agreeing with the goal of proper stewardship, I do not think that a bio-centric ethic[25] is Biblical, or needed to correct the problem of humanity's misuse of wildlife. Some have suggested that we adopt a theo-centric ethic. They argued that we must see the world from God's point of view. While agreeing with the notion in principle, I do not find it particularly enlightening because the debate at its core is over exactly what God wants us to do. Both sides agree that God owns the earth and that we are just managers of His property. The issue is, what sort of managers does God want us to be? We must now establish what ought to be a Christian view of human-wildlife interactions.

25. See Taylor, *Respect for Nature.*

8

Shepherdism: A Biblically Grounded Ethic for Human-Wildlife Relations[1]

WITH THE WEAKNESSES OF the CAR view made plain, I now present a model for human-wildlife relations, designated with the neologism 'Shepherdism', that more accurately reflects Biblical teaching and scientific knowledge. Shepherdism is fundamentally related with Dominionism except that Shepherdism avoids the negative stereotypes held against Dominionism, while upholding God's decree that humans maintain their superintendence over animals.

METHODOLOGICAL ISSUES

Every theologian must make Christian teaching relevant to his generation by integrating both Scripture (book of the Word) and human knowledge (book of Nature) into a coherent belief system. The reason we utilize both books stems from the belief that God, as the ultimate author of both, does not contradict Himself. What is true in one book will be true in the other. To anyone who has studied the controversy between creationism versus evolution, it becomes clear that in many ways the two books do not always reconcile easily. CAR theologians avoid this dilemma by simply ignoring those Scriptures they disagree with, as flowing from the human vessel that God encountered. I have attempted to be fair with their position during my critique. However, in putting forth my vision of a truly Biblical theology on wildlife, I believe that such a theology must account for the entire witness of Scripture. Regrettably, Evangelicals[2] also face challenges in harmonizing the book of the Word and the book of Nature.

1. Many thanks to Calvin L. Smith for suggesting the need for this chapter. Smith, "Dissertation Review."

2. I turn my attention more narrowly to Evangelical Christians as I share their

Historically, Evangelicalism has been involved in two main controversies regarding Scripture. The first concerns Scripture's accuracy and the second its sufficiency. Accuracy relates to the Bible's truthfulness in what it records, both doctrinally and historically. Sufficiency, on the other hand, deals with the notion of the Bible's relevance to provide appropriate insight to guide Christians in their daily lives. For the most part, the inerrancy debate has been decided in favor of the view that the Bible is accurate in everything it intends to teach. In lay terms, what the Bible says is what God says. Yet, Evangelicalism has not come to terms regarding the question of Scripture's sufficiency.[3] While Evangelicals believe both books cannot ultimately contradict, they disagree not only how to interpret the two books but also on how much weight to accord them when making a doctrinal decision. Some contend that the Bible only provides spiritual guidance regarding how we can get to heaven, and it is wrong to use appeal to a book for concepts that modern science has shown to be outdated. To illustrate, some believe that evidence from science raises serious doubts as to the traditional understanding of the creation narratives. Similarly, to ask Scripture to provide answers regarding the contemporary environmental crisis is equivalent to asking for the chapter and verse on how to make penicillin. Others believe that while Scripture does not speak to everything, all the topics it does address carry the weight of divine authority. Thus when Scripture says for us to be fruitful and multiply (Gen 1:28), that blessing/command remains true despite environmentalist arguments that the world is overpopulated.[4]

It is the debate concerning how we should understand and weigh the two books that funds the controversy about environmental issues, and more narrowly our treatment of animals within the Evangelical community. I believe the failure of Evangelicals, on both sides of the argument; is to recognize this difference in perspective. This is not to suggest that we are just prisoners of our presuppositions or biases. Rather it is to acknowledge that the debate would be substantially improved if speakers would

---

theological perspective and commitments. Certainly, Christians from other traditions may find this information helpful. But unless they accept fundamental aspects of an Evangelical view of Scripture, I doubt they will find these arguments very compelling.

3. Cf. Hindson and Eyrich, *Totally Sufficient*.

4. Ehrlich and Ehrlich, *The Population Explosion*.

be more transparent about their views and thereby more concrete about what it is they are debating.[5]

To avoid participating in this error, I will layout my own hermeneutical and theological biases. I am a committed Evangelical Christian who believes that the Bible (66 books of the Protestant Canon) alone is sufficient for guiding faith and practice.[6] Church Tradition is valuable, but holds only a subordinate role in guiding Christian belief and practice.[7] If Scripture contradicts Tradition then it is Tradition that must be modified. It is this belief that is behind the notion that the Church should always be reforming. I believe that the Bible must be interpreted according to the intent of its authors (both divine and human), with due regard to the analogy of faith and progressive revelation, a revelation that reached its zenith with the Incarnation (Heb 1:1–3). When Scripture conflicts with Science (the book of Nature), the conflict is only apparent and not real. God, being the author of both, cannot be inconsistent. Conflicts will ultimately be resolved by either revising our understanding of Scripture, Science, or both. However, in those situations where the conflict seems intractable, I tend to put my confidence in the church's understanding of Scripture rather than in the scientific theories of the present age.

Some may find it odd that I begin with Scripture, since it could be asserted that Scripture provides no theology of the environment. They may argue that the topic is more properly informed by scientific research. We must go to the scientist first and then determine how Scriptural testimony fits, assuming it speaks at all to the subject.

In one sense, I agree that the Bible does not provide a comprehensive theology of the human use of animals, let alone the environment. The reason why Scripture provides so few principles to guide us in our environmental stewardship[8] is because God desires to grant us freedom to develop our own expression of the cultural mandate. Proverbs 25:2 says, "It is the glory

5. I suggest that the furor over the statements by Beisner are an example of Evangelicals not coming to grips with a proper understanding of his hermeneutical perspective, or the pro-environmental effect of his economic views.

6. The author holds that the Bible is infallible and inerrant in the autographs, and in a Trinitarian understanding of God.

7. Mathison, *The Shape of Sola Scriptura*. Using Mathison's rubric, the present writer would place himself within the Tradition I camp as opposed to the Tradition II. Tradition I holds that Scripture is the final source and is properly interpreted according to the *regula fidei*.

8. Hall, "Toward a Theology of Sustainable Agriculture," 2–5.

of God to conceal a matter, But the glory of kings is to search out a matter (NASB)." God wants us to learn and explore. Thankfully, He has created a planet that, despite the Fall, is still sturdy and vibrant enough to handle our mistakes and recover.[9] I also think that the Bible's neglect of the animal rights issues actually argues against the CAR position, as it demonstrates how the CAR view is really another form of legalism threatening our "freedom" in Christ. Nevertheless, I do believe that Scripture does provide some broad parameters to guide and direct our approach.

First, we must acknowledge that all of creation, including animals, belongs to God. Scripture repeatedly and in various genres and contexts asserts that He is the creator, owner, and sustainer of the earth (Gen 1–2; Ex 9:29; Psa 24:1; Jn 1:1–3; 1 Cor 10:26; Col 1:16). If we accept that statement, then we must likewise accept that God has the right to deal with His property as He sees fit. One of the more key Christian doctrines presently under attack is the notion that God's sovereignty means that God has the right and authority to do with His creation as He wills. I suggest that the Western values of independence and equality has encouraged resistance to the notion of human submission to God's decrees and appropriate acknowledgement of His sovereignty. We, therefore, do not believe that humanity has authority of an animal because we do not accept that God has this authority over our destiny. Instead we offer arguments stemming from a mistaken notion of "fairness", as if we may appeal to a moral code of behavior that co-eternally exists outside of God's nature.

The second principle from Scripture is that humans are special, both in our ontology and our position. In fact it is our ontology, our being created in the image of God (Gen 1:26–27; Jms 3:9), that provides us with our positional authority over the animal kingdom (Psa 8) because God never gives a task without giving the ability to accomplish that task. Privilege

---

9. Christians should be cautious about simply adopting the present environmental dogma that the earth is going to collapse in a heap of sewage and degradation. The fact that so-called environmentalists have overstated and hyped the problems we face does not mean all is well. It just means that Christians should be careful in their analysis of the rhetoric used. Certainly the rhetoric used by CAR activists that consumptive use of furbearing wildlife, at least as Canada and the U.S. are concerned, is somehow environmentally destructive, is patently false. Lomborg calls the hyperbolic claims of the environmental movement "the litany." Lomborg, *The Skeptical Environmentalist*, 3–4. This is not to say that Lomborg's version is completely correct; see Berry, *When Enough Is Enough*, 24–25. Rather, environmentalists should be careful about globalizing what are in fact local problems.

brings responsibility. One need only read Deuteronomy to see how God demanded obedience from the Israelites in response to His gracious gift of freedom from Egypt and of land in Canaan. For our purposes, God has given us the task of tending (i.e. using) and keeping (i.e. protecting) the Garden (Gen 2:15).

I have already explained how many Christians have sought to diminish humanity's rule by de-emphasizing and/or reinterpreting God's call for humanity to be in charge. To the contrary, Scripture will not allow us to redefine our rightful role to express rule over creation. As made clear throughout this book, humanity's right to kill animals falls within God's command of doing everything for the glory of God (1 Cor 10:31). CAR activists have overemphasized the protection of the environment in their desire to protect God's property. I suspect that this reaction came about due to humanity's failure to rule justly and soberly. But in so doing they have committed the opposite error of treating animals in a way that exceeds their station, and thereby run the risk of making animals an idol.[10] We are only caretakers of the earth under God's authority. I like the principle that we should view the image of God as primarily having to do with appropriate relationships with power, mankind with God and mankind and humanity, as stated by Moo.[11]

The problem, of course, centers on how to help us achieve balance in our rule over, and care of, God's creation. Beisner answers this problem by separating Genesis 1 (to rule) from Genesis 2 (to care). He says that God wants us to impose our rule in those areas where our rule does not exist. However, once we have achieved that rule, then we must transition our behavior to one of protection and care. Beisner's view also takes into account contemporary human power. I asked him whether, given modern man's ability to project power at a distance, it would still be possible to consider a 20-square-mile tract of wildland as part of the Garden and thus free from the need to be further subdued. He answered in the affirmative.[12]

It is at this stage that some may point out that humanity is Fallen. We have difficulty in fulfilling God's obligations, as sin taints everything we do and think. I agree. The Fall and resultant depravity have severely limited our ability and willingness to serve God (Rom 3:23). Our sinful pride

10. Haas, "Creational Ethics Is Public Ethics," 10.

11. Moo, "Nature in the New Creation," 481.

12. Beisner, "Wilderness and Garden," Stephen Vantassel (Lincoln: Telephone, 2008).

(1 Jn 2:16), greed (1 Tim 6:10), and erroneous worship (Mt 22:37; Rom 1:21f), brings further environmental problems, both directly through our misuse of the land (such as over-harvesting wildlife), and as God changes the environment to punish our sinful behavior (e.g. drought due to support for abortion).[13] Additionally, the curse makes it more difficult for us to gain a return on our work (Gen 3:17–19). But it is still possible (Psa 104:14ff) for two key reasons.

The first reason relates to God's concern for environmental justice. Environmental justice is the view that recognizes that the poor disproportionately live in environmentally hazardous areas and therefore works to alleviate that inequity.[14] I would believe environmental justice also extends the poor's use of animals. Scripture clearly teaches that our obligations to animals and the environment is a second-order obligation to what we owe to our human neighbors. No matter how one wishes to twist Biblical testimony, it continues to be human-centric in its focus regarding ethics. If we treat our neighbor with appropriate Christian principles, we will likewise treat the animal kingdom as God wants. Readers should note that stating the principle in this matter reverses the common animal rights claim that how we treat animals implicates how we will treat humans. I contend the Biblical claim is that how we treat humans will determine how we treat animals. Permit me to provide some further explanation. Dever argues that the use of land plays a central role in Biblical ethics. He says,

> "I would contend that almost everywhere in the Biblical tradition the demand for social justice revolves around land and its uses—entrusted to Israel as Yahweh's steward, governed by divine law, inalienable, and an inheritance forever."[15]

13. The writer believes that some environmental problems stem directly from our behavior. But he also believes that some environmental problems are caused not through our direct abuse of the land but through our disobedience, which God then punishes through sending environmental catastrophes (cf. Amos 4:6f). This idea was gleaned from listening to John MacArthur's, founder of Masters Seminary in Sun Valley, CA, sermon on Matthew. For the Biblical background that disobedience to covenant laws results in devastation of the land see Weinfield, *The Promise of the Land*, 189–93. Interestingly, new research has shown that divorce can harm the environment because it requires former spouses to consume more resources by having to go to separate homes. The number of homes more than the number of people led to environmental degradation. See Lehrer, "Ecological Freakonomics," 27 which summarized the findings of Yu and Liu, "Environmental Impacts of Divorce," 20629–34.

14. Grizzle et al., "Evangelicals and Environmentalism: Past, Present, and Future," 11–14.

15. Dever, *Who Were the Early Israelites and Where Did They Come From?* 186.

If Dever's assessment is true, as I believe it is, then adoption of CAR policies will result in oppression of the poor. Limiting human dominion over the animals would harm not only the environment but also the poor, who frequently live in areas that are in desperate need of animal control.[16] Wildlife also provides the poor with the opportunity obtain "free" meat through hunting. I suggest that the command to let the land rest in Exodus 23 was not simply for the benefit of the wild beasts (Ex 23:11) but so that the poor could have game to hunt during the sabbatical year.[17] As a side note, animal rights activists express the cultural values not of those tied to the land but actually those freed from the land and its brutal realities. Statistical surveys reveal that two-thirds of animal rights activists come from urban areas and have incomes above the national average.[18] In effect, those who have a better financial condition and live in the artificial and ravaged environments known as cities, are telling rural residents how to handle their land, which has not been so damaged as to remove wildlife.[19] Adoption of the animal rights position would force the poor to live in even more squalid conditions because it would remove their ability to remove nuisance animals (e.g. mice, rats,) from their property with less expensive methods.[20] The regulatory effect on rural residents, now deprived of their right to hunt, would diminish their income due to crop and livestock damage. Such regulation would essentially be a hidden tax. Ironically, implementation of a hands-off approach to wildlife would result in greater animosity towards wildlife. Farmers are more likely to tolerate crop damage if they know they can enjoy the autumn deer hunt.[21]

The second reason is that the Holy Spirit plays a vital role in the sanctification process of the believer. If sin has made it difficult for us to

16. For one example, see Tenthani, "Malawi Curbs Crocodile Menace," Np.

17. For a good discussion of social concern in Deuteronomy which stimulated my thinking in this area. Vogt, "Social Justice and the Vision of Deuteronomy," 37.

18. Guither, *Animal Rights*, 66, 64.; Organ et al., "Fair Chase and Humane Treatment: Balancing the Ethics of Hunting and Trapping," Np.

19. The class nature of this debate cannot be overemphasized. See Boddicker, "Profiles of American Trappers and Trapping," 119–1949; Organ et al., "Fair Chase and Humane Treatment: Balancing the Ethics of Hunting and Trapping."

20. Isaiah 5:8f speaks of large landholders who take away the inheritance lands of those in debt. Modern urbanites through restrictive regulations have other ways to remove land from the use of rural owners. Cf. Widyapranawa, *The Lord Is Savior*, 22–23. Contra Hall, "Toward a Theology of Sustainable Agriculture," 3.

21. Boddicker, *The Issue of Trapping*, 19.

perceive and do the will of God, the Holy Spirit must help us to do the opposite. If He does not, then vast sections of Scripture are irrelevant, as we would be commanded to be like Christ when God knows full well that such behavior isn't even a remote possibility (Rom 12:1ff; Gal 5:17ff).

The third principle Scripture provides is through the person and work of Jesus Christ. Scripture teaches that Christ is the image of the invisible God (2 Cor 4:4; Col 1:15). In short, when we see Christ, we understand God in concrete terms because He is the perfect translation of God to the human mind (John 1:1–14). But Christ is more than simply an expression of who God is to us; He is a model for our behavior. It is Christ's role as leader that calls us "to follow" Him rather than to simply be intellectually informed (Mk 8:34; Jn 21:22). In other words, Christ is not only the revelation of God, He is also the ideal and goal to which we should conform our behavior. Such is the mystery of his being both God and man. Paul develops the theme of Christ being the source and goal by discussing the practical implications of our identification with Christ (Col 3).

It is Christ's behavior toward animals and the broader environment that I believe has not been adequately reflected upon. Christ clearly paid attention to the natural world, as it provided Him with illustrations for His teaching. He emphasized humanity's position by employing *a fortiori* arguments in Matthew 6:25ff and 10:31. He spoke of the good shepherd who cares for His flock (John 10). So far these points are positive, and demonstrate a positive concern for animals. However, Christ also spoke and behaved in ways that suggest that an animal rights belief or excessive concern for animal welfare is inappropriate, or at least highly doubtful. Christ made statements that all foods have become clean (Mt 15:11; Mk 7:19). Rather than diminishing humanity's rule over the animal kingdom by affirming the Kosher laws, or by expanding them to include additional animals, Christ expanded the extent of what constitutes a moral diet. Since Christ would have to have been aware of the variety of foods eaten in the pagan cultures surrounding Palestine, it stands to reason that allowing His followers to eat those foods, He likewise baptized the methods employed to garner those foods. I do not want to push that argument too far, other than to say that in light of Christ's oversight of the treatment of harvested fish (Lk 5:6) and drowning pigs (Mk 5:13), it is reasonable to conclude that humans may inflict and/or ignore a fair amount of animal suffering.

Now it is important at this point to state that while Christians have freedom to eat meat, we are in now way commanded to do so. Aside from one's own conscience,[22] eating or refraining from meat does not impart moral superiority. Like celibacy and marriage, it is just an option to be done to the glory of God.[23] Meat eaters should refrain from compelling vegetarians to eat meat.[24] In other words, the consumption of meat is not a spiritually significant issue, other than to say that believing that meat consumption is wrong amounts to a denial of our freedom in Christ and promulgates an evil doctrine (1 Tim 4:1f).

There remains one final general principle to explain before we move on to more specific questions regarding animal and wildlife use. The principle is that the Bible appears to distinguish between the way we treat domesticated and wild animals. A key reason for the confusion in the CAR activist's argument stems from their blurring of this distinction. Scripture affirms that the basic needs of animals should be met when they are in our control.[25] Note, however, that our obligation to meet their basic needs does not deny our fundamental privilege to kill and eat them in our call to serve God's Kingdom.[26] In contrast, humans do not have the same obligations in regards to wildlife (those not under our control) because they in a sense belong to no one other than to God. The fact that these animals

22. Scripture teaches that we should never do anything that violates our conscience (Rom 14:22–23).

23. Vantassel, "Celibacy: The Forgotten Gift of the Holy Spirit," 20–23.

24. Reinders, "Blessed Are the Meat Eaters," 509–37. Reinders describes Christians who fought the vegetarian beliefs of Buddhist converts by exhorting them to eat meat as a testimony for their conversion to Christ. While the present writer understands this view, he would advise against ever following this example. Paul's condemnation of Peter was because of the hypocrisy inherent in his change of behavior (Gal 2:12ff).

25. See humanitarian concern for animal's needs in Mt 12:11; Lk 13:15; 14:5.

26. Mk 2:22 refers to animal hides used in wineskins. Nevertheless, Christians should remember that even animals under their care are still subordinate in worth and importance. This is especially important to remember in light of the growing number and costs accruing to pet ownership. No one denies that pet ownership brings joy to many people. But Christians need to carefully consider whether their pets are becoming "companions." The issue at hand is not whether or not Christians should own pets. The issue is the spiritual implications of such a huge expenditure of material, temporal, and emotional treasure. 2002 U.S. Pet Ownership and Demographic Sourcebook, which says that American's own 132 million dogs and cats. This number is actually low as it does not include birds, horses or exotic pets. The same source stated that the average veterinary cost per animal amounted to $178.50 for dogs and $84.60 per year. Include other financial costs such as feeding and time lost due to care for these animals, and the economic impact of pet ownership reaches into the billions of dollars. On other troubling implications see McClure, *Pet Owner or Guardian?*

are wild means that they are more difficult to capture in a pain-free manner. Thus the Bible frequently speaks of traps, snares, and nets, echoing, I believe, a strong trapping tradition.

SPECIFIC ETHICAL NORMS

With Scripture's broad parameters being set forth, we can now turn to the specific question of "What constitutes legitimate treatment and use of wildlife?" What specific guidelines can we establish regarding animal care?

First, I believe it is imperative to recognize that our responsibility to a species should be distinguished from its responsibility to individual members of that species. The story of Noah exemplifies a key principle in sustainable ecology, namely that species matter more than individuals. God simply saved a representative portion of the various kinds and destroyed the rest. Clearly God treats animals as groups, but people as individuals and groups.[27] The implication is that humans may kill animals but they should not exterminate species (see Dt 22:6).[28] Scripture also clearly supports removal of wildlife which threaten human interests and to obtain food (1 Sam 17:34-6; Lev 17:13).[29] Individual animals do not have a sacrosanct right to life, but species have the right to exist. Thus humans are to practice proper management of animal populations in their encounters with wildlife (cf. Ex 23:11). Therefore, I believe that if a dam threatens to make a species extinct, then we must not build the dam.[30]

27. The "you are more valuable than the sparrow" story of Mt. 10:29f//Lk 12:6ff underscores the point. God cares about the individual but in no way the same way as he cares about the individual human. Rather God takes a shepherding role. He cares about all the sheep individually but this does not stop the shepherd from eating one of them.

28. I disagree with the view that says jobs should trump preserving a threatened or endangered species. The position stated in the following article is too simplistic. "A Comprehensive Torah-Based Approach to the Environment," 25. I recognize that the data supporting the protectionist views regarding the Spotted Owl are hotly debated. However, in complex systems, bias should be toward caution because there is no reset button when a species goes extinct. I also believe that human creativity, so amply praised by the authors (18–19), should tell us that there are other ways to make money from forests besides cutting down trees. The issue, therefore, is not jobs versus species, but which jobs. Only if we believe that God granted humans the right to keep a job in perpetuity should one say that the job trumps species protection. And that latter statement is one I believe most people would reject. People have a *prima facie* case to preserve their jobs, not a fundamental right.

29. van Selms, "Hunting," 78–83.

30. A famous real-world case concerns a fish known as the snail darter. "Snail Darter

Happily these sorts of occurrences are rare, at least in North America and Western Europe. Instead, God has created a world that, despite the curse, exhibits remarkable fecundity. Biologists tell us that species typically produce more young, and some species exceedingly more, than will likely survive. Nature, and by that I mean non-humans, will be responsible for killing off the excess. Humans can participate in that process by culling that portion of the population of that species. This fact leads us to our next point. When populations of wildlife become so abundant that they degrade the environment or significantly impede or threaten human-health and safety, animal rights activists oppose active culling of the animal population. Instead they argue that we should work towards contraception[31] of wildlife or other so-called non-lethal forms of control to handle the problem. They contend the burden is on humans, because ultimately "humans are the problem", not the animals, which are natural.[32] Aside for the illogic of that argument, I contend that animal rights activist attitudes turn the blessing of animal abundance into a curse. Let me explain. When a forester walks into a forest should he complain, "There are too many trees here, this is a huge problem?" or should he think, "It is a good thing we have lots of trees as we can now harvest the abundance efficiently and without fearing we will exterminate the trees?" Note how the CAR perspective transforms the fact of species abundance into a problem rather considering it to be a blessing. In effect, we have an interesting view of the curse. Rather than it being an interference with human interests (i.e. inedible thorns taking up nutrients instead of edible plants), the curse becomes an abundance of edible products that are immoral for us to kill and eat. The result is that deer and other abundant species lose their value as precious resources and devolve into "rats." The irony is rather than

---

Halts Dam: For Now," 403.

31. For discussion of the controversy on deer contraception see Kirkpatrick and Turner Jr., "Urban Deer Contraception: The Seven Stages of Grief," 515–19.

32. These countries have shown that sustainable harvest of furbearing species can be done, and the evidence for its success is overwhelming. It could be reasonably argued that the animal rights opposition to these responsible harvests is actually harmful to the environment, as it threatens habitats and endangered species, and removes our connection to the land that is so critical to our continued protection of it. Lehrer, "Ecological Freakonomics," 27. Lehrer cites research by John Marzluff of the University of Washington that showed bird diversity was greatest "when 50–60% of the land is forested." Beyond the 50% threshold, bird diversity was reduced. The finding was that human use of the land could benefit species.

respect for nature, the resulting damage causes people to hate the deer rather than enjoy them for their beauty and meat.

Furthermore, the ugly issue of our treatment of the poor comes up again. Wildlife contraception is expensive. For example, in free-range deer the costs exceed $1,000 per deer over a two-year period.[33] It is important to understand what is at stake here. Rather than having hunters pay the state, through the purchase of hunting licenses, to work for free, animal activists want public money spent on contraception. I have long been amazed at why social advocates have not been decrying the injustice of this sort of wasteful spending.[34] Monies that could have been used for the poor are now squandered on birth control for deer to find a solution to a problem that we already have a viable and efficient cure for, namely regulated sport hunting. Even if the money would not be spent on the poor, it could be used to buy land to safeguard it against the ravages of urban sprawl. Lest readers think employment of expensive wildlife solutions is an historical aberration, I would assure them the trend will continue given the steady reduction in traditional consumptive uses of wildlife.

To answer the question "Can Christians hunt, trap, or fish?" I believe we must observe Christ's behavior in regards to fishing. Since He presented no objections to harvesting of free-ranging animals, neither should we. But how should we answer the question regarding the suffering that hunted, trapped, and fished animals endure? Again, I say that Christ should be our model. I contend that Christ's acceptance of fishing with nets provides a useful standard by which to guide our behavior. Netted fish sustain injuries through being crushed, suffocated, or both. Despite the pain fish underwent, Christ never condemned fishing.[35] The principle that can be derived from that is that God has granted humanity the right

33. Walter et al., "Evaluation of Immunocontraception in a Free-Ranging Suburban White-Tailed Deer Herd," 190.

34 The BLM's Wild Horse and Burro Management Program is a classic example of misguided expenditure. These horses used to be hunted but are now on the public dole at the cost of $21.9 million in Fiscal Year 2007. This money only accounts for the direct cost of holding wild horses and burros in short and long-term facilities. In 2008 the money spent was even higher. Gorey, *Wild Horse and Burro Quick Facts.*

35. Luke 15:27 "fatted calf" also provides some insight. If we look at Prov. 15:17 as the stall-fed calf, isn't it possible that the fatted calf was a stall-fed calf? While the calf certainly didn't suffer the degradations of the alleged actions of modern veal manufacturing, certainly the calf was treated a certain way to develop tender meat. See Stewart, "Cattle," 255.

to use those means to capture animals for food, etc., that are economically efficient while considering animal pain. In other words, if there was another economically feasible way to capture fish that caused less suffering for fish, Christ would have taken it. Therefore, Christians are permitted to not only eat animals, they may employ means to capture them that will cause pain and injury during the capture and death process.[36] It is noteworthy that other than the "clean animal" dietary restrictions, there is precious little regarding the treatment of wild game, especially in light of the fact that Israelites hunted before the Exile.[37]

I do believe, however, that God's prohibition against eating blood does provide a key principle for the treatment of animals. God required the Israelites to avoid eating the blood of the animal because the "life was in the blood" (Gen 9:4; Lev 17:11). Although scholars debate God's exact reasoning behind the commands, it did require that Israelites eat only dead animals. They could not eat an animal while it was alive. This observation may seem to be an odd one to make, but it is an important one, as I believe it provides a principle of killing the animal quickly. I recall watching a segment on TV which discussed a Far East tradition of eating live fish. The program explained how the chef would scale the fish, then fry it quickly enough so that it would still be alive by the time it reached the dinner table. I was horrified at what I witnessed and hoped it was some sort of camera trickery. Whether it was or was not, my point is that Christians should not do that to one of God's creatures. The life belongs to God and should be returned to Him. Respect for God's creation involves capturing and killing an animal in a manner that is responsible and economically viable, as I argued from Christ's fishing work. This sort of sliding scale concept of humane treatment means that as technology improves, so will our standard of humanness improve. But that does not

36. It is critical that readers distinguish between capture methods and euthanasia. Hunting with a gun is a way to capture free-range animals. It is inappropriate to require a hunter to meet the same humane standards as a veterinarian in his/her office.

37. Rakow, *Hunting & the Bible*. Essentially, there are two rules, namely, the blood must be drained (Lev. 17:13–14), and you cannot take the mother bird with her eggs (Dt.22:6). There is some debate over the exact reason why God required the blood to be drained. Here are a couple of ideas. (Please note that the author does not suggest that these options are necessarily exclusive). Hyland, *The Slaughter of the Terrified Beasts*, 31, suggests that the reason for the blood restriction was to ensure that the animal was truly dead. Keil and Delitzsch, *The Pentateuch*, 1:410 see a cultic reason, namely that God didn't want the blood that was used for expiation of sin to be eaten.

mean that God will require us to avoid animal flesh, at least on this side of Eternity.

But what about questions concerning "canned hunts", circuses, zoos, and other controversial uses of wildlife? I believe the answers to these sorts of ethical problems can be answered by asking two questions. First, "Does this use align with the structure and direction found in God's created order for both the animal and the human?" This question comes from Haas's distinction between the structure and direction in God's creation.[38] By "structure," he means the enduring aspects of creation that God has upheld against the effects of sin. Animals being subordinate to humans would be an example of this enduring structure. By "direction," he refers to the purpose and role that an aspect of creation is to play.[39] This view would be applied to trapping in the following manner. Question, "Where does the raccoon (*Procyon lotor*) fit in God's created order?" Answer, "It is an animal that thrives in human-impacted environments." Question, "What role does this animal play in the direction of creation?" Answer, "In North America, the raccoon is an abundant species with an excellent pelt. The animal is suitable for food, clothing, and recreational opportunities through hunting and trapping."

The second question relates to economic value. The trouble with calling for stewardship as a guide in environmental stewardship is that it fails to provide concrete guidance for behavior. Preservationists call for the non-use of God's resources because of a belief that human activity is by, definition, damaging. We have seen that this view is unbiblical in that it separates nature from humanity in a way that God never intended. As Anderson and Terrell have amply demonstrated, even those who condemn utilitarian and/or anthropocentric views of nature ultimately exhibit utilitarianism/anthropocentric views. For humans are still the only ones doing the valuing, and they are "valuing" of the earth's resources is in a manner different than that of others.[40] The problem is, how should we find God's value for creation? Ultimately, I believe Anderson and Terrell are on the right track when they say that an economic model accords with Scripture (Lk 14:28) provided that it follows God's concerns for the poor,

---

38. Haas, "Creational Ethics Is Public Ethics," 3.

39. Ibid., 11.

40. Anderson and Terrell, "Stewardship without Prices and Private Property? Modern Evangelicalism's Struggle to Value Nature," 572, 577–79.

the environment, and for justice.[41] While the article did not address how economics would help us perform cost-benefit analysis of activities that may lead to the extinction of a particular species, they are quite right to suggest that economics can factor in long-term environmental impacts in ways that statist-environmentalism cannot.[42] I hold that, at least as far as wildlife is concerned, scientific-based management provides an excellent model that state governments in the U.S. have been implementing successfully for decades. It is imperative that Christians work to stop those who seek to hijack these wildlife management practices in the name of Christianity or compassion.

In short, Christians need to evaluate the intent of the animal's use. God put them on earth to be used, but this does not mean that every use is morally valid. Infliction of pain just for the "fun of it" is morally evil. But that does not mean that the pain suffered by a hunted, fished, or trapped animal is morally evil, as the infliction of pain is not the goal. The goal is to harvest the animal, and this can only be done by causing pain. I am sure many will not be satisfied by this statement. But the answer must remain fuzzy, because what is responsible harvest in this generation would be considered cruel and barbaric in another as improvements to harvest methods continue.

Turning to the topics specifically mentioned, I can now say the following. "Canned hunts" are not so much a problem for the animal as it is for the notion of fair chase. Furthermore, canned hunts[43] imply the animals are directly under a human's care, which, as I have argued earlier, places greater moral responsibilities on the human. Likewise circuses are legitimate, provided the animals are properly cared for. To those who say the wild animals should remain wild, I would simply note that all our domestic species were at one time wild. Since Scripture has no condemnation of that, then it follows that our "taming" the wild beast in the circus is not a problem, provided the species is not endangered of extinction. Zoos play an important role not only for public education but also for research,

---

41. See also Beisner, *Prosperity and Poverty*.

42. Anderson and Terrell, "Stewardship without Prices and Private Property? Modern Evangelicalism's Struggle to Value Nature," 587.

43. It should be mentioned that canned hunts is a notoriously vague term. There is a big difference between hunters who stand ready to shoot an animal being released from a cage and those who enter game preserves encompassing thousands of acres, a distinction not always mentioned by animal rights activists.

so that we can learn more about a wide variety of animals. The Henry Doorly zoo in Omaha, NE, is a world leader in the area of captive breeding. Its research is vital in the protection of a wide variety of threatened and endangered species.

Hearkening back to our earlier diagrammatic model, we would like to place the environmental issue into this larger context.[44] This diagram is useful in that it affirms the hierarchal role of humanity over the creation but properly places that role in subordination to God, with due consideration for His Church and other obligations facing believers.[45] I believe the preponderance of evidence shows that humanity has been given dominion in a manner closer to the traditional understanding. Creation was to serve humanity as humanity served God. The hierarchal nature of the relationship is critical, because without humanity's superior standing and power, our actions would be immoral[46] or ineffective. God created the world to be in dynamic equilibrium.[47] God wanted humans to play the role of environmental stabilizer and even enhancer, for human and perhaps even wildlife interests.[48] For only we have the God-like ability to see beyond ourselves, to plan, to restrain ourselves, and to radically alter environments. Even in the Garden, lethal control probably had to be initiated in order to protect and keep the Garden from the predation of free-roaming wildlife. It is too simplistic to believe that just because Adam and Eve may not have eaten animals, they did not have to kill them. Keeping the Garden meant more than just telling the animals to behave. An added bonus to this perspective is that it avoids the problem of adding to the difficulties of the problem of evil, as it removes the issue of animal suffering from the debate.

44. Diagram adapted from Hall, "Toward a Theology of Sustainable Agriculture," 3.

45. Further explanation of my perspective on the proper view of human-wildlife relations that avoids the pagan notions of biocentrism and the self-exaltation of the extreme industrialist can be found in Stephen Vantassel, "The Ethics of Wildlife Control in Humanized Landscapes—a Response," Pending.

46. For an illustrative discussion of the problem of conflicting values see Paul W. Taylor, *Respect for Nature*, 20f.

47. Cf. Todd, "Ecological Arguments for Fur Trapping in Boreal Wilderness Regions," 116–17.

48. Todd, "Ecological Arguments for Fur-Trapping in Boreal Wilderness Regions," 122. Todd argues even undisturbed, purportedly self-sustaining and balanced habitats can benefit from well managed fur harvests.

Figure 4. An improved model of humanity's relationship to creation.

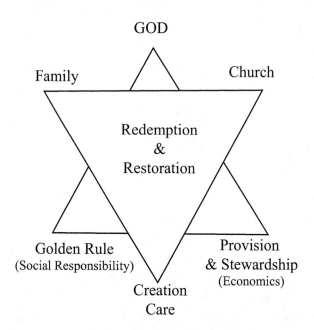

WHAT OF THE FUTURE?

One key aspect still missing from a theology of human-animal relations concerns the place of animals in the *eschaton* (end times). Many, not just animal rights activists, believe that Isaiah predicts a time when animal-on-animal violence will end (11:6; 65:25). Perhaps this interpretation is proffered because it accords with the view that the predation which emerged as a result of the Fall would be rolled back in the next age.

I suggest that this interpretation of Isaiah misses the point. I believe Isaiah's prophecy must be understood against the agricultural expectations of his day. Since Isaiah was certainly predicting a period of ideal living conditions, I contend that his point was to show his audience that God would usher in a time when they would no longer be plagued by concern over predator attacks on their livestock or themselves and their loved ones. That the lion would lay down the lamb is not written for the lamb's benefit but for the shepherd who would be obligated to protect the lamb. Even if we assume that the lamb should be "happy" over the future prospect of his species being delivered from the threat of predators, there is nothing in the passage to lead one to believe that the lamb is freed from the threat of being part of shepherd's dinner. So whatever way Christians want to interpret the environmental significance of these Isaiah passages, I think they should be sure not to overstate their content.

Furthermore, even if we concede the point that animals and humans alike will live in non-violent, vegetarian harmony, we still have to live now. While eschatology can guide and inform our behavior, we must not over-realize that eschatology because we remain between the ages.[49] The next age has certainly broken into this one, and we have the down payment of the Holy Spirit as proof (Eph 1:13), but we are still waiting for the Messiah's return (1 Cor 11:25–6). Lest anyone think my diminishment of the Isaiah passages was self-serving, I would ask how should the fact that there will be no marriage in heaven impacted his/her present day behavior (Mk 12:21ff). I find it interesting that as much as CAR activists believe our non-violent future should inform our present environmental behavior, they do not use the same logic for arguing for our celibate nature in heaven.[50] Not that I think they should. I just point out this inconsistency to reveal how selective Christians can be in their employment of Scripture. The second question is whether animals, particularly our pets, will accompany us in heaven. With all due respect to C.S. Lewis[51], I think Christians should avoid such idle speculation about that which Scripture has nothing to say.

CONCLUSION

"What is humanity's role in relationship to the animal kingdom and more specifically, wildlife?" I have argued the Biblical response does not reside in utilitarianism (do what you want with animals) or Linzey's "Animal rights view of animals." Rather it lies in accepting our "dominion responsibilities"[52] under a rubric I have designated with the neologism

49. Ladd, *A Theology of the New Testament*, 66–67.

50. While various environmentalists and CARs have a dim view of human reproduction (as they contend there are too many people anyway), they do not seem to have problems with sex, just sex that lead to procreation.

51. Lewis, *The Problem of Pain*, 138–42.

52. The position espoused here is remarkably similar to the concept of stewardship that Linzey assails in *Christianity and the Rights of Animals*, 86ff, with the exception that God does care about animal suffering but that the suffering is not a paramount concern.

"Shepherdism." Shepherdism accepts the reality of human power but seeks to integrate that power into a comprehensive view of human-nature relations. Shepherdism believes that humans ought to use their power to responsibly care for the earth and mitigate the imbalances that inevitably occur due to human activity. Shepherdism rejects the idea that use equals abuse. What is good for animals is conceived as applying first to the continuation of the species rather than to the future of any individual animal. Shepherdists understand that death and predation are a normal part of the natural order in this present age. Humans, as rulers of the biosphere, may utilize animals (e.g. hunting) provided that God's property (the entire ecosystem and its human inhabitants) and species diversity are protected. Humans are considered to be just as much a part of nature as animals, and demands for humans to distance themselves from the realities of nature is not only impossible but improper, as it will lead to our neglect of nature and the environment that sustains all life. Shepherdism recognizes that humans have caused great harm to the environment, but also knows that the environment has caused great harm to humans. The key is to balance interests, knowing that God sustains both humans and animals (Jn 1:1–3; Col 1:17; Heb 1:3). Shepherdism recognizes that God created animals to fill the world, to beautify it, to demonstrate wisdom, and ultimately to please God. Yet, God in his beneficence placed animals in our care to enjoy and derive substance from. It is to define that freedom and responsibility that this book was written. It is for freedom that Christ set us free, and I will end by noting that fishing, hunting, and trapping are proper activities for the Christian.

Perhaps creation groans because it realizes that its suffering does not glorify God where in the sinless Garden it did.

Appendix

Other Unanswered Questions Regarding Wildlife Use

WHILE SCRIPTURE PROVIDES INSIGHT on human use of wildlife, it does not answer all the questions. In particular, Christians need to investigate issues surrounding the ethics of vivisection, cloning, and trans-species organ donation. Clearly humans have been granted more dominion authority than the CAR activists claim. However, Christians should always remember that "can does not imply ought," especially in light of our Fallenness.

DeWitte, whose ideas this writer appreciates, believes that we must protect all species.[1] The question that must be asked is whether the protection of every species is Biblically mandated.[2] The issue is further complicated by the way species are now identified. Traditionally, a species consisted of animals that could mate with each other and spawn fertile offspring. Today, the definition is far less obvious because taxonomists now rely not only on phenotypic (visual and structural clues) evidence but genetic (DNA) evidence as well. While DNA evidence sometimes reduces the number of species as in the case of birds,[3] it can also increase them. One recent example was the decision to treat exemplars in the genus *Geomys* as distinct species rather than just variants or subspecies based on DNA analysis.[4] The result is that Nebraska now has three pocket gophers in the *Geomys* genus rather than just one (*Thomomys* was not discussed in the article). The problem is that the distinctions between these species

1. DeWitt, *Caring for Creation*, 21–24.

2. Regrettably, I do not remember where I came across this idea.

3. Powell, September 4, 2008.

4. Genoways et al., "Hybrid Zones, Genetic Isolation, and Systematics of Pocket Gophers (Genus *Geomys*) in Nebraska," 826–27.

are so subtle that it is unlikely that Scripture would have defined them as anything different.[5] The Bible speaks more of kinds of animals rather than a more technical sense of species as we speak of today. The importance of this question comes down to land use, as the Endangered Species Act can prevent landowners from using their land due to the identification of a new, and therefore endangered, species on their property. Of course, we should not forget the more important issue of following God's commands. Fortunately, pocket gophers, (no matter the species) are not, nor do they need to be at the present time, on the endangered species list. But such is not the case for other animals, and the legal ramifications can be far reaching.

Although the article by Van Houtan and Pimm provided some useful categories to understand the diversity of views on environmental policy held by Christians, I was disappointed by the simplistic employment of the "genetic fallacy" to dismiss the ideas proffered by the scholars in the Acton Institute.[6] The authors' neglect in balancing Beisner's economic views with his environmental writing[7] was unfortunate, and presented a caricature of his true opinion.[8] Furthermore, they avoided dealing with Beisner's exegesis even though they claimed that Scripture should be allowed to speak. Whether Beisner's views are right or wrong, the important topic of species conservation would have been better served by specific discussion of issues. Additionally, Van Houtan and Pimm should have remembered that science is not immune to the manipulation by ideological commitments, as amply proved by Feyerabend.[9]

5. Kaiser, "Myn," 503–4.

6. Van Houtan and Pimm, "The Various Christian Ethics of Species Conservation," 134ff.

7. The authors not only neglected to engage Beisner's Biblical views but they also did not discuss his scientific views. Furthermore the authors should have availed themselves of Beisner's more detailed environmental views found in his other publications. See the bibliography.

8. Van Houtan and Pimm, "The Various Christian Ethics of Species Conservation," 129–30.

9. Feyerabend, *Against Method*.

Bibliography

Achtemeier, Paul J. *Romans:* Interpretation: A Bible Commentary for Teaching and Preaching, ed. James L. Mays. Atlanta: John Knox Press, 1985.

Adams, Clark E., et al. *Urban Wildlife Management*. Boca Raton, FL: Taylor & Francis Group, 2006.

Adler, Mortimer J. *Aristotle for Everybody: Difficult Thought Made Easy.* New York: Bantam Books, 1980.

Agencies, Association of Fish & Wildlife. *Best Management Practices* Washington, DC: Association of Fish & Wildlife Agencies, 2007, accessed August 5, 2007; Available from http://www.fishwildlife.org/furbearer_bmp.html.

Albright, William Foxwell. *Archeology and the Religion of Israel*. Baltimore: Johns Hopkins Press, 1946.

Alcorn, Ray. *Coyote Man: My Life with the Coyote*, ed. Major L. Boddicker. Brainerd, MN: Major Boddicker, 2007.

Alexander, David. "Feeding the Hungry and Protecting the Environment." In *All Creation Is Groaning: An Interdisciplinary Vision for Life in a Sacred Universe*, ed. Carol J. Dempsey and Russell A. Butkus, 77–98. Collegeville, MN: The Liturgical Press, 1999.

Alexanian, Moorad. "Are Dangerous Animals a Consequence of the Fall of Lucifer?" *Perspectives on Science and Christian Faith* 56, no. 3 (2004): 237.

Anderson, Bernard W. *From Creation to New Creation: Old Testament Perspectives* Overtures to Biblical Theology, ed. Walter Brueggemann, John R. Donahue, Sharyn Dowd and Christopher R. Seitz. Minneapolis: Fortress Press, 1994.

Anderson, William L., and Timothy D. Terrell. "Stewardship without Prices and Private Property? Modern Evangelicalism's Struggle to Value Nature." *Journal of Markets and Morality* 6, no. 2 (2003): 565–95.

Aquinas, Thomas. *St. Thomas Aquinas and the Summa Theologica on Cd-Rom*, trans. English Dominican Friars, CD-ROM ed. (Salem, OR: Harmony Media Inc., 1998).

Assembly, Westminster. *The Westminster Shorter Catechism* [Web site]. Grand Rapids, MI: Calvin College, July 13, 2005 1647, accessed November 11, 2007; Available from http://www.ccel.org/ccel/schaff/creeds3.iv.xviii.html.

Association, American Veterinary Medical. *AVMA Guidelines on Euthanasia (Formerly Report of the AVMA Panel on Euthanasia)*. Schaumburg, IL: American Veterinary Medical Association, 2007.

Association, Christian Vegetarian. *Honoring God's Creation: Christianity and Vegetarianism*. Revised 11/03 ed. Cleveland, OH: Christian Vegetarian Association, 2003.

Atkeson, Thomas Z. "Incidence of Crippling Loss in Steel Trapping." *The Journal of Wildlife Management* 20, no. 3 (1956): 323–24.

Augustine, Saint. *Concerning the City of God against the Pagans*, trans. Henry Bettenson. London: Penguin Books, 1467, 1972, 1984.

Aulen, Gustaf. *Christus Victor: An Historical Study of the Three Main Types of the Idea of Atonement.* Translated by A.G. Hebert. Eugene, OR: Wipf & Stock, 1931, 2003.

Baker, William H. *In the Image of God: A Biblical View of Humanity.* Chicago: Moody Press, 1991.

Ball, Jim. "The Use of Ecology in the Evangelical Protestant Response to the Ecological Crisis." *Perspectives on Science and Christian Faith* 50, no. 1 (1998): 32–40. http://www.asa3.org/ASA/PSCF/1998/PSCF3-98Ball.html

Balz, Horst, and Gerhard Schneider, eds. *Agkistron "Fish-Hook".* Vol. 1, Exegetical Dictionary of the New Testament. Edinburgh: T & T Clark LTD, 1978–80, 1990.

———. *Polis "City".* Vol. 3, Exegetical Dictionary of the New Testament. Edinburgh: T & T Clark LTD, 1978–80, 1990.

Banci, Vivian, and Gilbert Proulx. "Resiliency of Furbearers to Trapping in Canada." In *Mammal Trapping,* ed. Gilbert Proulx, 175–203. Sherwood Park, Alberta: Alpha Wildlife Research & Management Ltd., 1999.

Baron, David. *The Beast in the Garden: A Modern Parable of Man and Nature.* New York: W.W. Norton & Company, 2004.

Barrett, Julia R. "Livestock Farming: Eating up the Environment?" *Environmental Health Perspectives* 109, no. 7 (2001): A312–17.

Barth, Karl. *Church Dogmatics: The Doctrine of Creation.* Translated by G.W. Bromily. Vol. III.4. Edinburgh: T. & T. Clark, 1961.

Bath, Alistair J. "Ursus: The Role of Human Dimensions in Wildlife Resource Research in Wildlife Management." In *Tenth International Conference on Bear Research and Management,* 10, 349–55. Fairbanks, Alaska and Mora Sweden International Association of Bear Research and Management, 1995, 1998.

Bauckham, Richard J. *2 Peter, Jude.* Vol. 50 Word Biblical Commentary. Dallas: Word, Inc., 2002.

Beckwith, R. T. "Sacrifice and Offering." In *New Bible Dictionary,* ed. J.D. Douglas, 1035–44. Downers Grove, IL: InterVarsity Press, 1996, 2004.

Beirne, Piers. "From Animal Abuse to Interhuman Violence? A Critical Review of the Progression Thesis." *Society & Animals* 12, no. 1 (2004): 39–65.

Beisner, E. Calvin. *Prosperity and Poverty: The Compassionate Use of Resources in a World of Scarcity.* Eugene, OR: Wipf and Stock Publishers, 2001.

———. "Radical Environmentalism's Assault on Humanity." In *The Summit Lectures on Economics and Environment,* 11: Summit Ministries, 1992.

———. *Where Garden Meets Wilderness: Evangelical Entry into the Environmental Debate.* Grand Rapids, MI: Acton Institute for the Study of Religion and Liberty and William B. Eerdmans Publishing Company, 1997.

———. "Wilderness and Garden." ed. Stephen Vantassel. Lincoln: Telephone, 2008.

Belben, H. A. G. . "Fasting." In *New Bible Dictionary,* ed. J.D. Douglas, 364. Downers Grove, IL: InterVarsity Press, 1996, 2004.

Berger, Kim Murray. "Carnivore-Livestock Conflicts: Effects of Subsidized Predator Control and Economic Correlates on the Sheep Industry." *Conservation Biology* 20, no. 3 (2006): 751–61.

Berkhoff, Hendrikus. *Christian Faith: An Introduction to the Study of the Faith.* Translated by Sierd Woudstra. Grand Rapids, MI: William B. Eerdmans Publishing Co., 1979.

Berry, R. J., ed. *When Enough Is Enough: A Christian Framework for Environmental Sustainability.* Nottingham, England: APOLLOS, 2007.

Bible, The Holy. The King James Version of 1611 ed. Nashville: Hendrickson Publishers, 2003.

Bietenhard, H., and Colin Brown. "Paradise." In *The New International Dictionary of New Testament Theology*, ed. Colin Brown, 2, 760–64. Grand Rapids, MI: Zondervan Publishing House, 1986.

Bishop, Steve. "Green Theology and Deep Ecology: New Age or New Creation?" *Themelios* 16, no. 3 (1991): 8–14.

Blom, F. Sherman, and Guy Connolly. "Inventing and Reinventing Sodium Cyanide Ejectors: A Technical History of Coyote Getters Adn M-44s in Predator Damage Control." ed. APHIS, 1–35 with appendix.: United States Department of Agriculture, 2003.

Blundell, Gail M., John W. Kern, R. Terry Bowyer, and Lawrence K. Duffy. "Capturing River Otters: A Comparison of Hancock and Leg-Hold Traps." *Wildlife Society Bulletin* 27, no. 1 (1999): 184–192.

Boddicker, Major L. *The Issue of Trapping: A Review and Perspective of Contemporary Analysis of Traps and Trapping by Martha Scott-Garrett and the Humane Society of the United States*. Fort Collins, CO: Colorado State University, 1978.

———. "Profiles of American Trappers and Trapping." In *Proceedings of the Worldwide Furbearer Conference*, ed. J. A. Chapman and D Pursley, 2, 1919–1949. Frostburg, MD: University of Maryland, 1980.

"Book Review: Matthew Scully's *Dominion: The Power of Man, the Suffering of Animals, and the Call to Mercy*. New York: St. Martin's Griffin, 2002." *Christianity Today*, July 1, 2003. http://www.ctlibrary.com/10602.

Booth, Wayne C., et al., *The Craft of Research*. Chicago: University of Chicago Press, 1995.

Borowski, Oded. "Animals in the Literatures of Syria-Palestine." In *A History of the Animal World in the Ancient near East*, ed. Billie Jean Collins, 289–306. Leiden: Brill, 2002.

Bouthier, Kirsten. "Religious Leaders Weigh in on Responsibility toward Environment," *The Associated Press State & Local Wire*, June 18, 2005.

Brewer, Douglas. "Hunting, Animal Husbandry and Diet in Ancient Egypt." In *A History of the Animal World in the Ancient near East*, ed. Billie Jean Collins, 427–56. Leiden: Brill, 2002.

Bright, John. *Jeremiah*. Vol. 21 The Anchor Bible, ed. William Foxwell Albright and David Noel Freedman. Garden City, NY: Doubleday & Company, Inc., 1965.

———. *The Kingdom of God*. Nashville: Abingdon Press, 1953, 1983.

Broadfoot, Jim D., et al. "Raccoon and Skunk Population Models for Urban Disease Control Planning in Ontario, Canada." *Ecological Applications* 11, no. 1 (2001): 295–303.

Brotzman, Ellis R. "Man and the Meaning of Nephesh." *Bibliotheca Sacra* 145, no. 580 (1988): 400–9.

Brown, Francis, et al. *The New Brown-Driver-Briggs Gesenius Hebrew and English Lexicon with an Appendix Containing Biblical Aramaic*. Peabody, MA: Hendrickson Publishers, 1979.

Bruce, F. F. *The Book of the Acts*. Rev. ed. The New International Commentary on the New Testament. Grand Rapids, MI: William B. Eerdmans Publishing Company, 1988.

———. *The Epistles to the Colossians to Philemon and to the Ephesians* The New International Commentary on the New Testament, ed. F.F. Bruce. Grand Rapids, Michigan: William B. Eerdmans Publishing Company, 1984.

Brown, William P. *The Ethos of the Cosmos: The Genesis of Moral Imagination in the Bible*. Grand Rapids, Michigan: William B. Eerdmans Publishing Co., 1999.

Brueggemann, Walter. *Genesis, Interpretation, a Bible Commentary for Teaching and Preaching* Atlanta: John Knox Press, 1982.

Brumley, Albert E. *This World Is Not My Home* [Web page]. NA: Albert E. Brumley & Sons, 1965, accessed November 4, 2007; Available from http://www.my.homewithgod .com/heavenlymidis2/nothome.html.

Bube, Richard H. "Do Biblical Models Need to Be Replaced in Order to Deal Effectively with Environmental Issues?" *Perspectives on Science and Christian Faith* 46 (1994): 90.

Busell, James Oliver. *A Systematic Theology of the Christian Religion*. Grand Rapids: Zondervan, 1962, 1978.

Callaway, Joseph, and J. Miller (reviser) Maxwell. "Settlement in Canaan: The Period of the Judges." In *Bas Ancient Israel Rev.*, ed. Herschel Shanks: Biblical Archeology Society, 2002.

Calvin, John. *Commentaries on the First Book of Moses Called Genesis*, trans. John King, 2 vols., Hull: Cambridge, 1554, 1847. Christian Classics Ethereal Library, Grand Rapids, MI, accessed 11/22/2008. http://www.ccel.org/ccel/calvin/calcom01.i.html.

Campolo, Tony. *How to Rescue the Earth without Worshiping Nature*. Nashville, TN: Thomas Nelson Inc., 1992.

Cansdale, George S. *All the Animals of the Bible Lands*. Grand Rapids, MI: Zondervan Publishing House, 1970.

Carruthers, S. P. "Farming in Crisis and the Voice of Silence—a Response to David Atkinson." *Ethics in Science and Environmental Politics* (2002): 59–64.

Carson, D.A. *Exegetical Fallacies*. Grand Rapids, Michigan: Baker Book House, 1984.

———. *The Gagging of God: Christianity Confronts Pluralism*. Grand Rapid, Michigan: Zondervan 1996.

———. ed. *New Bible Commentary: 21st Century Edition*. Downers Grove, IL: Inter-Varsity Press, 1994.

Cartledge, Paul. *Thermopylae: The Battle That Changed the World*. New York: The Overlook Press, 2006.

Cartmill, Matt. *A View to a Death in the Morning: Hunting and Nature through History*. Cambridge, MA: Harvard University Press, 1993, 1996.

Carons, Rachel. *Silent Spring*. Greenwich, CT: Fawcett Publications, 1962, 1968.

Chafer, Lewis Sperry. "Soteriology." *Bibliotheca Sacra* 104, no. 413 (1947): 3–24.

Chancey, Mark Alan, and Adam Lowry Porter. "The Archeology of Roman Palestine." *Near Eastern Archeology* 64, no. 4 (2001): 164–203.

Cheeke, P. R., and S. L. Davis. "Possible Impacts of Industrialization and Globalization of Animal Agriculture on Cattle Ranching in the American West (Can Environmentalists Save the Ranch?)." *Rangelands* 19, no. 2 (1997): 4–5.

Chilton, Bruce. "Should Palm Sunday Be Celebrated in the Fall?" *Biblical Archeological Review*, March/April 2008, 28, 86.

Clements, David R., and Wayne V. Corapi. "Paradise Lost? Setting the Boundaries around Invasive Species." *Perspectives on Science and Christian Faith* 57, no. 1 (2005): 44–54.

Clifford, Richard J. "Proverbs Ix: A Suggested Ugaritic Parallel." *Vetus Testamentum* 25, no. 2 no. 2a Jubilee Number (1975): 298–306.

Cockrell, Susan. "Crusader Activists and the 1996 Anti-Trapping Campaign." *Wildlife Society Bulletin* 27, no. 1 (1999): 65–74.

Collins, G. N. M. "Federal Theology." In *Evangelical Dictionary of Theology*, ed. Walter A. Elwell, 413–14. Grand Rapids, MI: Baker Book House Co., 1984.

Collins, John J. *Daniel: A Commentary on the Book of Daniel* Hermeneia—a Critical and Historical Commentary on the Bible, ed. Frank Moore Cross. Minneapolis: Fortress Press, 1993.

"A Comprehensive Torah-Based Approach to the Environment." In *Environmental Stewardship in the Judeo-Christian Tradition: Jewish, Catholic, and Protestant Wisdom on the Environment*, ed. Kenneth B. Fradkin, Daniel Lapin, Clifford E. Librach, David Patterson and Garry Perras, 13–32. Grand Rapids, MI: Acton Institute, 2007.

Cone, James H. "Whose Earth Is It Anyway?" *Cross Currents* 50, no. 1/2 (2000): 36–46.

Conover, Michael. *Resolving Human-Wildlife Conflicts: The Science of Wildlife Damage Management*. New York: Lewis Publishers, 2002.

Control, Centers for Disease. *National Dog Bite Prevention Week* Atlanta: Department of Health and Human Services, circa 1999, accessed August 4, 2007; Available from http://www.cdc.gov/ncipc/duip/biteprevention.htm.

Cronon, William. "Beginnings Introduction: In Search of Nature." In *Uncommon Ground: Rethinking the Human Place in Nature* ed. William Cronon, 23–56. New York: W.W. Norton & Co., 1996.

Culver, Robert D. "Mashal Iii." In *Theological Wordbook of the Old Testament*, ed. R. Laird Harris and et al., 1, 534–35. Chicago: Moody Bible Institute, 1980.

Darwin, Charles. "Trapping Agony." *Gardeners' Chronicle and Agricultural Gazette*, August 1863, 1980.

Davies, W. D. *The Gospel and the Land: Early Christianity and Jewish Territorial Doctrine*. Berkely: University of California Press, 1974.

Davis, John Jefferson. "Ecological "Blind Spots" In the Structure and Content of Recent Evangelical Systematic Theologies." *Journal of the Evangelical Theological Society* 43, no. 2 (2000): 273–86.

Davis, Steven L. "The Least Harm Principle May Require That Humans Consume a Diet Containing Large Herbivores, Not a Vegan Diet." *Journal of Agricultural and Environmental Ethics* 16 (2003): 387–94.

de Jong, Rianne Baatenburg, Jolita Bekhof, Ruurdjan Roorda, and Pieter Zwart. "Severe Nutritional Vitamin Deficiency in a Breast-Fed Infant of a Vegan Mother." *European Journal of Pediatrics* 164 (2005): 259–60.

Dear S.J., Father John "Christianity and Vegetarianism: Pursuing the Nonviolence of Jesus." 1–18: People for the Ethical Treatment of Animals, N.D.

Dennett, Daniel C. *Darwin's Dangerous Idea: Evolution and the Meanings of Life*. NY: Simon & Schuster, 1995.

Descartes, Rene. "Animals Are Machines." In *Animals and Christianity: A Book of Readings*, ed. Andrew Linzey and Tom Regan, 45–52. New York: Crossroad Publishing Co., 1988.

———. "Discourse on the Method of Rightly Conducting the Reason and Seeking Truth in the Sciences," *The Rationalists*. 39–98. Garden City, NY: Anchor Books, 1637, 1974.

DeVaux, Roland. *Ancient Israel: Religious Institutions*. Vol. 2. 2 vols. NY: McGraw-Hill Paperbacks, 1965.

Dever, William G. *Who Were the Early Israelites and Where Did They Come From?* Grand Rapids, MI: William B. Eerdmans Publishing Co., 2003.

DeWitt, Calvin B. *Caring for Creation: Responsible Stewardship of God's Handiwork*. Grand Rapids, MI: Baker Books, 1988.

Diamond, Jared. *Collapse: How Societies Choose to Fail or Succeed*. New York: Penguin Books, 2005, 2006.

Dorsett, John W. "Lethal Options for Controlling Coyotes." In *Coyotes in the Southwest: A Compendium of Our Knowledge*, ed. Dale Rollins, Calvin Richardson, Terry Blankenship, Kem Canon and Scott Henke, 158–61. San Angelo, TX: Texas Parks and Wildlife Department, 1995.

Earle, Ralph. "1 Timothy." In *The Expositors Bible Commentary with the NIV*, ed. Frank E. Gaebelein and et al., 11, 341–90. Grand Rapids: Zondervan, 1978.

Earle, Richard D., et al. "Evaluating Injury Mitigation and Performance of #3 Victor Soft Catch ® Traps to Restrain Bobcats." *Wildlife Society Bulletin* 31, no. 3 (2003): 617–29.

Eaton, John. *The Circle of Creation: Animals in the Light of the Bible*. London: SCM Press Ltd, 1995.

Eaton, Randall L., ed. *The Sacred Hunt: Hunting as a Sacred Path-an Anthology*. Ashland, OR: Sacred Press, 1998.

Ehrlich, Paul R., and Anne H. Ehrlich. *The Population Explosion: From Global Warming to Rain Forest Destruction, Famine, and Air and Water Pollution—Why Overpopulation Is Our #1 Environmental Problem*. New York: Simon and Schuster, 1990.

Equine Research Publications, Research Staff of the. "Rupture of the Achilles Tendon." In *The Illustrated Veterinary Encyclopedia For Horsemen*, ed. M. M. Vale and Don M. Wagoner, 223. Grapevine, TX: Equine Research, 1975, 1977.

———. "Rupture of the Gastrocnemius Tendon." In *The Illustrated Veterinary Encyclopedia For Horsemen*, ed. M.M. Vale and Don M. Wagoner, 222–23. Grapevine, TX: Equine Research, 1975, 1977.

Esser, H. H. "Creation." In New International Dictionary of New Testament Theology, ed. Colin Brown, 1, 378–87. Grand Rapids: Zondervan, 1975.

Evangelical Environmental Network. *Frequently Asked Questions* Suwanee, GA 30024: EEN, 2007, accessed August 15 2007; Available from http://www.creationcare.org/responses/faq.php

Fairlie, Simon. "The Vital Statistics of Meat." *Ecologist*, October 2008, 16–20.

Fee, Gordon D. *The First Epistle to the Corinthians* The New International Commentary on the New Testament, ed. F.F. Bruce. Grand Rapids, Michigan: William B. Eerdmans Publishing Company, 1987.

"Feral/Wild Pigs: Potential Problems for Farmers and Hunters." ed. USDA-APHIS, 1–4: United States Federal Government, 2005.

Feyerabend, Paul. *Against Method*. Revised ed. New York: Verso, 1988.

Fields, Helen. "What Comes Next?" *U.S. News & World Report*, January 23, 2006, 56–58.

Fitzmeyer, Joseph A. *The Gospel According to Luke I-Ix: A New Translation with Introduction and Commentary*. Vol. 28 The Anchor Bible, ed. William Foxwell Albright and David Noel Freedman. New York: Doubleday, 1970.

Fitzwater, William D. "Trapping—the Oldest Profession." In *Vertebrate Pest Conference* ed. Richard H. Dana, 101–8. West Sacramento, CA: California Vertebrate Pest Committee, 1970.

———. *Romans: A New Translation with Introduction and Commentary*. Vol. 33 The Anchor Bible, ed. William Foxwell Albright and David Noel Freedman. New York: Doubleday, 1993.

Fox, Camilla H. "The Development of International Trapping Standards." In *Cull of the Wild: A Contemporary Analysis of Trapping in the United States*, ed. Camilla H. Fox and Christopher M. Papouchis, 61–69. Sacramento, CA: Animal Protection Institute, 2004.

———. "State Trapping Regulations." In *Cull of the Wild: A Contemporary Analysis of Wildlife Trapping in the United States*, ed. Camilla H. Fox and Christopher M. Papouchis, 71–111. Sacramento, CA: Animal Protection Institute, 2004.

———. "Trapping in North America. A Historical Overview." In *Cull of the Wild: A Contemporary Analysis of Wildlife Trapping in the United States*, ed. Camilla H. Fox and Christopher M. Papouchis, 1–22. Sacramento, CA: Animal Protection Institute, 2004.

———. "Coyotes and Humans: Can We Coexist?" In *Proceedings of the 22nd Vertebrate Pest Conference*, ed. Robert M. Timm and J. M. O'Brien, 287–93. Davis, CA: University of California-Davis, 2006.

Fox, Camilla H., and Christopher M. Papouchis. "Refuting the Myths." In *Cull of the Wild: A Contemporary Analysis of Wildlife Trapping in the United States*, ed. Camilla H. Fox and Christopher M. Papouchis, 23–29. Sacramento, CA: Animal Protection Institute, 2004.

———. *Coyotes in Our Midst: Coexsting with an Adaptable and Resilient Carnivore*, ed. Karen Hirsch and Gil Lamont. Sacramento, CA: Animal Protection Institute, 2005.

———. eds. *Cull of the Wild: A Contemporary Analysis of Wildlife Trapping in the United States*. Sacramento, CA: Animal Protection Institute, 2004.

Fox, Warwick. *Toward a Transpersonal Ecology: Developing Foundations for Environmentalism*. Boston: Shambhala Publications, 1990.

Francione, Gary L. "Animals—Property or Persons?" In *Animal Rights: Current Debates and New Directions*, ed. Cass R. Sunstein and Martha C. Nussbaum, 108–42. Oxford: Oxford University Press, 2004.

Franklin, Julien H. *Animal Rights and Moral Philosophy*. NY: Columbia University Press, 2005.

Fur Institute of Canada. *Trap Standards* [Website]. Ottowa, Ontario: Fur Institute of Canada, 2007, accessed September 15 2007; Available from http://www.fur.ca/index -e/index.asp.

Furnish, Victor Paul. *2 Corinthians: A New Translation with Introduction and Commentary*. Vol. 32A The Anchor Bible, ed. William Foxwell Albright and David Noel Freedman. Garden City, NY: Doubleday & Company, Inc., 1984.

Gadamer, Hans-Georg. *Philosophical Hermeneutics*. Translated by David E. Linge. Berkeley: University of California Press, 1977.

Gane, Roy E. "Privative Preposition Min in Purification Offering Pericopes and the Changing Face Of "Dorian Gray"." *Journal of Biblical Literature* 127, no. 2 (2008): 209–22.

Garrett, Duane A. *Proverbs, Ecclesiastes, Song of Songs*. Vol. 14 The New American Commentary. Nashville: Broadman & Holman Publishers; Logos Library System, Electronic Edition, 1993, 2001.

Garrett, Tom. *Alternative Traps: The Role of Cage and Box Traps in Modern Trapping, the Role of Spring-Powered Killing Traps in Modern Trapping, and the Role of Legsnares in Modern Trapping*. Revised edition ed. Washington, DC: Animal Welfare Institute, 1999.

Genoways, Hugh H., et al. "Hybrid Zones, Genetic Isolation, and Systematics of Pocket Gophers (Genus *Geomys*) in Nebraska." *Journal of Mammalogy* 89, no. 4 (2008): 826–36.

Gerstell, Richard. *The Steel Trap in North America*. Harrisburg, PA: Stackpole Books, 1985.

Goddard, Jerome. "I Think, Therefore I Am: One Author Tackles the Philosophical and Ethical Considerations of Pest Control." *Pest Control Technology*, March 2008, 120–21, 124, 126.

Goodrich, J. M., and S. W. Buskirk. "Control of Abundant Native Vertebrates for Conservation of Endangered Species." *Conservation Biology* 9, no. 6 (1995): 1357–64.

"Google Search Engine," (Google Inc., 2007). http://www.google.com.

Gordon, Anita, and David Suzuki, *It's a Matter of Survival.* Cambridge: Harvard University Press, 1991.

Gorey, Tom. *Wild Horse and Burro Quick Facts* [Website]. Bureau of Land Management, November 11, 2008 2008, accessed November 18, 2008; Available from http://www .blm.gov/wo/st/en/prog/wild_horse_and_burro/Fact_Sheet.html.

Grimshaw, Jim. "Luke's Market Exchange District: Decentering Luke's Rich Urban Center." In *Food and Drink in the Biblical World*, ed. Athalya Brenner and Jan Willem van Heuter, 86, 33–54. Atlanta, GA: Society of Biblical Literature, 1999, 2001.

Grizzle, Raymond E., et al. "Evangelicals and Environmentalism: Past, Present, and Future." *Trinity Journal* 19, no. 1 (1998): 3–27.

Guither, Harold D. *Animal Rights: History and Scope of a Radical Social Movement.* Carbondale and Edwardsville: Southern Illinois University Press, 1998.

Guthrie, Donald. *New Testament Introduction.* Third ed. Downers Grove, IL: InterVarsity Press, 1970.

Haas, Guenther "Gene". "Creational Ethics Is Public Ethics." *Journal for Christian Theological Research* 12 (2007): 1–36.

Hahne, Harry A. *The Birth Pangs of Creation: The Eschatological Transformation of the Natural World in Romans 8:19–22* [PDF]. Toronto: Tyndale Seminary, 1999, accessed November 4, 2007; Available from http://www.balboa-software.com/hahne /BirthPangs.pdf.

Hall, Steven. "Toward a Theology of Sustainable Agriculture." *Perspectives on Science and Christian Faith* 54, no. 2 (2002): 1–5.

Hamilton, Malcolm. "Eating Ethically: 'Spiritual' and 'Quasi-Religious' Aspects of Vegetarianism." *Journal of Contemporary Religion* 15, no. 1 (2000): 65–83.

Hansen, James, et al. *Evangelicals and Scientists on Global Climate Change* Cambridge, MA: Forum for Religion and Ecology, 2007, accessed July 23, 2007; Available from http: //environment.harvard.edu/religion/religion/christianity/statements/index.html.

Har-El, Menashe. "Jerusalem & Judea: Roads and Fortifications." *The Biblical Archeologist* 44, no. 1 (1981): 8–19.

Harrison, R. K. "Hunting, Hunter." In *New Bible Dictionary*, ed. D. R. W. Wood, 491. Downers Grove, IL: InterVarsity Press, 1996.

Harrison, Robert P. "Toward a Philosophy of Nature." In *Uncommon Ground: Rethinking the Human Place in Nature*, ed. William Cronon, 426–37. New York: W.W. Norton & Co. Ltd., 1996.

Hauret, Charles. "Sacrifice." In *Dictionary of Biblical Theology*, ed. Xavier Leon-Dufour, 452–55. New York: Desclee Company, 1962.

Hawthorne, Gerald F., et al., eds. *Dictionary of Paul and His Letters.* Downers Grove: InterVarsity Press, 1993.

Health, National Institutes of *Body Mass Index Calculation Page* Bethesda, MD: U.S. Government, 2007, accessed May 6 2007; Available from http://www.nhlbisupport .com/bmi/.

Heidel, Alexander. *The Babylonian Genesis: The Story of Creation.* 2nd ed. Chicago: The University of Chicago Press, 1942, 1951.

Heil, John Paul. "Jesus with the Wild Animals in Mark 1:13." *Catholic Biblical Quarterly* 68, no. 1 (2006): 63–78.

Henry, Carl Ferdinand Howard. *God, Revelation, and Authority.* Vol. 4. 4 vols. Wheaton, IL: Crossway Books, 1976–1983, 1999.

Hensley, Christopher, and Suzanne E. Tallichet. "Learning to Be Cruel?: Exploring the Onset and Frequency of Animal Cruelty." *International Journal of Offender Therapy and Comparative Criminology* 49, no. 1 (2005): 37–47.

Hensley, Christopher, et al. "Exploring the Possible Link between Childhood and Adolescent Bestiality and Interpersonal Violence." *Journal of Interpersonal Violence* 21 (2006): 910–23.

Hindson, Ed, and Howard Eyrich, eds. *Totally Sufficient: The Bible and Christian Counseling.* Eugene, OR: Harvest House Publishers, 1997.

Hodge, Charles. *Commentary on the Epistle to the Romans.* New edition & Revised ed. Edinburgh: Andrew Elliot, 1864.

Holladay, William Lee. *Jeremiah 2: A Commentary on the Book of the Prophet Jeremiah, Chapters 26–52* Hermeneia—a Critical and Historical Commentary on the Bible, ed. Paul D. Hanson. Minneapolis: Fortress Press, 1989.

Hope, Edward R. *All Creatures Great and Small: Living Things in the Bible* Helps for Translators. New York: United Bible Societies, 2005.

House, H. Wayne. "The Doctrine of Salvation in Colossians." *BSac* 151, no. 603 (1994): 325–38.

Howard, Walter E. *Nature Needs Us.* Philadelphia: Exlibris Corp., 2006.

HSUS. *Trapping: The inside Story* [PDF]. Washington D.C.: The Humane Society of the United States, 1998, accessed July 23, 2007; Available from http://www.hsus.org /furfree/cruel_reality/trapping/.

Hudkins, State Senator Carol "Prohibit the Trapping of Wildlife in County Road Rights-of-Way." ed. Nebraska State Legislature, LB 299: Nebraska State Legislature, 2007.

Huey, F. B. *Jeremiah, Lamentations.* Vol. 16. Electronic Ed. Logos Library System ed. The New Bible Commentary. Nashville: Broadman & Holman Publishers, 2001, c1993.

"Human Conflicts with Wildlife: Economic Considerations." In *Proceedings of the Third NWRC Special Symposium*, ed. Larry Clark, i–180. Fort Collins, CO: National Wildlife Research Center, 2002.

Huot, Alan A. and David L. Bergman. "Suitable and Effective Coyote Control Tools for the Urban/Suburban Setting" In *Proceedings of the Twelfth Wildlife Damage Management Conference*, ed. Robert Timm, 12:312–22. Corpus Christi, TX: Wildlife Damage Management Working Group, 2007.

Hurley, Patrick J. *A Concise Introduction to Logic.* Second ed. Belmont, CA: Wasworth Publishing Co., 1985.

Hygnstrom, Scott E., et al. eds. *Prevention and Control of Wildlife Damage.* Lincoln: University of Nebraska-Lincoln, 1994.

Hyland, J. R. *The Slaughter of the Terrified Beasts.* Sarasota, FL: Viatioris Ministries, 1988.

———. *God's Covenant with Animals: A Biblical Basis for the Humane Treatment of All Creatures.* NY: Lantern Books, 2000.

Institute, Animal Welfare. *Aims* Washington, D.C.: Animal Welfare Institute, 2007, accessed April 14 2007; Available from http://www.awionline.org/aims.htm.

Interior, U.S. Department of the, U.S. Fish and Wildlife Service, U.S. Department of Commerce, and U.S. Census Bureau. "2006 National Survey of Fishing, Hunting, and Wildlife-Associated Recreation." ed. U.S. Department of Interior: United States Federal Government, 2006.

Irwin, Paul G. "A Strategic Review of International Animal Protection." In *The State of Animals Ii: 2003*, ed. Deborah J. Salem and Andrew N. Rowan, 1–8. Washington D.C.: Humane Society Press, 2003.

Jacoby, Karl. *Crimes against Nature: Squatters, Poachers, Thieves, and the Hidden History of American Conservation*. Berkeley: University of California Press, 2001.

Jeremias, Joachim. *Jerusalem in the Time of Jesus: An Investigation into Economic and Social Conditions During the New Testament Period*. Translated by F. H. Cave and C. H. Cave. Philadelphia: Fortress Press, 1962, 1969.

———. "Paradise." In *Theological Dictionary of the New Testament*, ed. Gerhard Friedrich, 5, 765–73. Grand Rapids, MI: Wm. B. Eerdmans Publishing Co., 1967, 1999.

Jewett, Robert, et al. *Romans: A Commentary* Hermeneia: A Critical and Historical Commentary on the Bible, ed. Frank Moore Cross. Minneapolis: Fortress Press, 2006.

Jobes, Karen H. "The Function of Paronomasia in Hebrews 10:5–7." *The Trinity Journal* 13, no. 2 (1992): 181–91.

Jones Jr., James R., and GAO Staff. "Wildlife Services Program: Information on Activities to Manage Wildlife Damage." ed. Report to Congressional Committees, 1–70: United States General Accounting Office, 2001.

Jones, Keithly. "Economic Impact of Sheep Predation in the United States." *Sheep & Goat Research Journal* 19, no. Special Issue: Predation (2004): 6–12.

Joy, Melanie. "Humanistic Psychology and Animal Rights: Reconsidering the Boundaries of the Humanistic Ethic." *Journal of Humanistic Psychology* 46 (2005): 106–30.

Kaiser, Walter C. "Myn." In *Theological Wordbook of the Old Testament*, ed. R. Laird Harris, Gleason L. Archer Jr. and Bruce K. Waltke, 1, 503–4. Chicago: Moody Bible Institute, 1980.

Kaufman, Stephen R., and Nathan Braun. *Vegetarianism as Christian Stewardship*. Cleveland, OH: Vegetarian Advocates Press, 2002.

Kay, Jeanne. "Human Dominion over Nature in the Hebrew Bible." *Annals of the Association of American Geographers* 79, no. 2 (1989): 214–32.

Kearns, Laurel. "Saving the Creation: Christian Environmentalism in the United States." *Sociology of Religion* 57, no. 1 (1996): 55–70.

Keener, Craig S., and InterVarsity Press. *The IVP Bible Background Commentary: New Testament*. Downers Grove: IL: InterVarsity Press, 1993.

Keil, C.F., and F. Delitzsch. *The Pentateuch: Three Volumes in One*. Translated by James Martin. Vol. 1. 1–10 vols. Commentary on the Old Testament. Grand Rapids, MI: William B. Eerdmans Publishing Co., 1985 reprint.

———. *Proverbs*. Vol. 6. 10 vols. Commentary on the Old Testament. Peabody, MA: Hendrickson, 2002.

Kidner, Derek. *Genesis: An Introduction & Commentary*. Vol. 1 Tyndale Old Testament Commentaries, ed. D. J. Wiseman. Downers Grove, IL: Inter-Varsity Press, 1967.

———. *Proverbs: An Introduction and Commentary*. Vol. 15 Tyndale Old Testament Commentaries, ed. D. J. Wiseman. Chicago: Inter-Varsity Press, 1964.

King, Paul G., and David O. Woodyard. *Liberating Nature: Theology and Economics in a New Order*. Cleveland, OH: The Pilgrim Press, 1999.

Kirkpatrick, Jay F., and John W. Turner Jr. "Urban Deer Contraception: The Seven Stages of Grief." *Wildlife Society Bulletin* 25, no. 2 (1997): 515–19.

Kline, Meredith G. *Kingdom Prologue*. 1–3 vols. S. Hamilton, MA: Meredeth G. Kline, 1985–1986.

Knight, George W., III. *The Pastoral Epistles: A Commentary on the Greek Text*. Grand Rapids, Michigan: William B. Eerdmans Publishing Company, 1992.

Koehler, Ludwig, et.al. *The Hebrew and Aramaic Lexicon of the Old Testament* Translated by M.E.J. Richardson, ed. M.E.J. Richardson. Leiden, The Netherlands: Koninklijke Brill NV, 1994–2000.

Krause, Tom. "Thank You, Mr. Sevin, Sir." *American Trapper*, May-June 2001, 46–60.

Kremer, Craig S., and InterVarsity Press. *The IVP Bible Background Commentary: New Testament*. Downers Grove, IL: InterVarsity Press, 1993.

Kuhn, Thomas. *The Structure of Scientific Revolutions*. Third ed. Chicago, IL: University of Chicago Press, 1996.

Ladd, George Eldon. *A Theology of the New Testament*. Revised ed. Grand Rapids, MI: Eerdmans, 1993.

Laidre, Kristin, and Ronald J. Jameson. "Foraging Patterns and Prey Selection in an Increasing and Expanding Sea Otter Population." *Journal of Mammalogy* 87, no. 4 (2006): 799–807.

Lambdin, Thomas O. "Egyptian Loan Words in the Old Testament." *Journal of the American Oriental Society* 73, no. 3 (1953): 145–55.

Lampe, G. W. H. "The New Testament Doctrine of Ktisis." *Scottish Journal of Theology* 17 (1964): 449–62.

Larson, Stephanie. "The Marin County Predator Management Program: Will It Save the Sheep Industry?" In *Proceedings of the 22nd Vertebrate Pest Conference*, ed. Robert M. Timm and J. M. O'Brien, 294–97. Davis, California: University of California-Davis, 2007.

Lea, Thomas D., and Hayne P. Griffin. *1, 2, Timothy, Titus*. Vol. 34. Electronic Ed. Logos Library System ed. The New American Commentary. Nashville: Broadman & Holman Publishers, 1992, 2001.

Lehrer, Jonah. "Ecological Freakonomics." *Conservation Magazine*, July-September 2008, 22–27.

Leithart, Peter J. "The Way Things Really Ought to Be: Eucharist, Eschatology, and Culture." *Westminster Theological Journal* 59, no. 2 (1997): 159–76.

Leopold, Aldo. *A Sand County Almanac with Essays on Conservation from Round River*. Ballantine Books ed. NY: Oxford University Press, Inc., 1949, 1966, 1970.

Lewis, C. S. *The Problem of Pain: How Human Suffering Raises Almost Intolerable Intellectual Problems*. NY: MacMillan Publishing Co., Inc., 1962.

Lightfoot, John. *Acts-1 Corinthians*. Vol. 4. 4 vols. A Commentary on the New Testament from the Talmud and Hebraica. Grand Rapids, MI: Baker Books, 1979.

Linzey, Andrew. "A Reply to the Bishops." In *Animals and Christianity: A Book of Readings*, ed. Andrew Linzey and Tom Regan, 170–73. New York: Crossroad, 1988.

———. *Animal Gospel*. Louisville, KY: Westminster John Knox Press, 1998/2000.

———. *Animal Rights: A Christian Assessment of Man's Treatment of Animals*. London: SCM Press, LTD, 1976.

———. *Animal Theology*. Chicago: Univ. of Illinois Press, 1994, 1995.

———. *Christianity and the Rights of Animals*. New York: Crossroad Publishing Co, 1987.

———. "The Place of Animals in Creation: A Christian View." In *Animal Sacrifices*, ed. Tom Regan, 115–148. Philadelphia: Temple University Press, 1986.

———. "Unfinished Creation: The Moral and Theological Significance of the Fall." *Ecotheology* 4 (1998): 20–26.

———. and Dan Cohn-Sherbok. *After Noah: Animals and the Liberation of Theology*. London: Mowbray, 1997.

———. and Tom Regan, eds. *Animals and Christianity: A Book of Readings*. New York: Crossroad Publishing Co., 1988.

Lioy, Dan. *The Book of Revelation in Christological Focus*. Vol. 58 Studies in Biblical Literature, ed. Hemchand Gossai. New York: Peter Lang, 2003.

———. *The Search for Ultimate Reality: Intertextuality between Genesis and Johannine Prologues*. Vol. 93 Studies in Biblical Literature, ed. Hemchand Gossai. New York: Peter Lang, 2005.

Lipkind, M., et al. "Review of the Three-Year Studies on the Ecology of Avian Influenza Viruses in Israel." *Avian Diseases* 47 (2003): 69–78.

Livingston, David. "Creation Stories of the Ancient near East." *Bible and Spade* 5, no. 3 (1992): 77–89.

Logos Bible Software 3.0b. Logos Bible Software, Bellingham, WA.

Lohse, Eduard. *Colossians and Philemon: A Commentary on the Epistles to the Colossians and to Philemon* Hermeneia, ed. Frank Moore Cross. Philadelphia: Fortress Press, 1971.

Lomborg, Bjorn. *The Skeptical Environmentalist: Measuring the Real State of the World*. Cambridge: Cambridge University Press, 2001.

Luce, Stephen B., et al. "Archeological News and Discussion." *American Journal of Archeology* 46, no. 3 (1942): 410–40.

Magisterium,The. "Catechism of the Catholic Church." ed. Pope John Paul II: Vatican, 1992, 1995.

Manahan, Ronald E. "A Re-Examination of the Cultural Mandate: An Analysis and Evaluation of the Dominion Materials." Dissertation, Grace Theological Seminary, 1982.

Manning, Richard. "The Threat to Montana." *Men's Journal*. 2007, 50, 52.

Marshall, I. Howard. *Acts*. Vol. 5. Reprint 1986 ed. Tyndale New Testament Commentaries. Grand Rapids, MI: William B. Eerdmans Publishing Company, 1980.

———. *Commentary on Luke*. The New International Greek Testament Commentary, ed. I. Howard Marshall and W. Ward Gasque. Grand Rapids, MI: William B. Eerdmans Publishing Company, 1978, 1995.

Martin, Norah. "New Ways of Knowing and Being Known," in *All Creation Is Groaning: An Interdisciplinary Vision for Life in a Sacred Universe*, ed. Carol J. Dempsey and Russell A. Butkus. Collegeville, MN: The Liturgical Press, 1999.

Mason, Christopher F., and Sheila M. Macdonald. "Growth in Otter (*Lutra Lutra*) Populations in the Uk as Shown by Long-Term Monitoring." *AMBIO: A Journal of the Human Environment* 33, no. 3 (2004): 148–52.

Mason, Jim. *An Unnatural Order: Uncovering the Roots of Our Domination of Nature and Each Other*. NY: Simon & Schuster, 1993.

Mathewson, Mark D. "Dissertation Review." ed. Stephen Vantassel. Lincoln: Christian Leadership College, 2007.

Mathison, Keith A. *The Shape of Sola Scriptura*. Moscow, ID: Canon Press, 2001.

McCartney, Dan, and Charles Clayton. *Let the Reader Understand: A Guide to Interpreting and Applying the Bible.* Wheaton, Ill: Victor Books, 1994.

M'Caw, Leslie S., and J.A. Motyer. "The Psalms." In *The New Bible Commentary: Revised,* ed. D. Guthrie and J.A. Motyer, 446–547. Grand Rapids, MI: Wm. B. Eerdmans Publishing Co., 1970.

McClure, Kent. *Pet Owner or Guardian?* [Web page]. Schaumburg, IL: Animal Health Institute, 2007 2005, accessed 03/13 2007; Available from http://www.avma.org /advocacy/state/issues/owner_guardian_ahi.asp.

McGlasson, Paul. *Jesus and Judas: Biblical Exegesis in Barth.* Vol. 72 American Academy of Religion Academy Series, ed. Susan Thistlethwaite. Atlanta, GA: Scholars Press, 1991.

McKane, William. *Proverbs: A New Approach.* Philadelphia: Westminster Press, 1970.

McNeill, William H. *Plagues and Peoples.* NY: Anchor Books, 1976, 1978, 1998.

Mearns, Robin. *When Livestock Are Good for the Environment: Benefit Sharing of Environmental Goods and Services.* Washington, DC: World Bank/FAO Workshop, 1996, 2005.

Meeks, M. Douglas. *God the Economist: The Doctrine of God and Political Economy.* Minneapolis: Fortress Press, 1989.

Merz-Perez, Linda, et al. "Childhood Cruelty to Animals and Subsequent Violence against Humans." *International Journal of Offender Therapy and Comparative Criminology* 45, no. 5 (2001): 556–73.

Michaelis, Wilhelm. "Skenopoios." In *Theological Dictionary of the New Testament,* ed. Gerhard Kittel and Gerhard Friedrich, 7, 393–94. Grand Rapids, MI: William B. Eerdmans Publishing Company, 1971.

Middleton, J. Richard. "A New Heaven and a New Earth: The Case for a Holistic Reading of the Biblical Story of Redemption." *Journal for Christian Theological Research* 11 (2006): 73–98.

Mighetto, Lisa. *Wild Animals and American Environmental Ethics.* Tucson: The University of Arizona Press, 1991.

Minnis, Donna L. "Wildlife Policy-Making by the Electorate: An Overview of Citizen-Sponsored Ballot Measures on Hunting and Trapping." *Wildlife Society Bulletin* 26, no. 1 (1998): 75–83.

Mobley, Gregory. "The Wild Man in the Bible and the Ancient near East." *Journal of Biblical Literature* 116, no. 2 (1997): 217–233.

Moltmann, Jurgen. *God in Creation: A New Theology of Creation and the Spirit of God.* San Francisco: Harper & Row Publishers, 1985.

Moo, Douglas J. "Nature in the New Creation: New Testament Eschatology and the Environment." *Journal of the Evangelical Theological Society* 49, no. 3 (2006): 449–88.

Moreland, J.P., and William Lane Craig. *Philosophical Foundations for a Christian Worldview.* Downers Grove, Illinois: InterVarsity Press, 2003.

Morris, Michael C., and Richard H. Thornhill. "Animal Liberationist Responses to Non-Anthropogenic Animal Suffering." *Worldviews: Environment Culture Religion* 10, no. 3 (2006): 355–79.

Munoz-Igualada, Jamie, et al. "Evaluation of Cage-Traps and Cable Restraint Devices to Capture Red Foxes in Spain." *The Journal of Wildlife Management* 72, no. 3 (2007): 830–36.

Murray, Robert. *The Cosmic Covenant: Biblical Themes of Justice, Peace and the Integrity of Creation.* London: Sheed & Ward, 1992.

Museum of Paleontology, University of California, support provided by the National Science Foundation (grant no. 0096613), and the Howard Hughes Medical Institute (grant no. 51003439). *Using the Tree for Classification* Berkeley: University of California-Berkeley, 2006, accessed May 9 2007; Available from http://evolution.berkeley.edu/evosite/evo101/IIDClassification.shtml and http://evolution.berkeley.edu/evosite/history/nested2.shtml.

National Association of State Public Health Veterinarians Inc. "Compendium of Animal Rabies Prevention and Control, 2000." *Morbidity and Mortality Weekly Report* 49, no. RR08 (2000): 19–30.

National Institute on Alcohol Abuse and Alcoholism, (NIAAA). "Health Risks and Benefits of Alcohol Consumption." *Alcohol Research & Health* 24, no. 1 (2000): 5–11.

Navigator, Charity. *Charity Navigator* [web site]. Mahwah, NJ: Charity Navigator, 2007, accessed November 18 2007; Available from http://www.charitynavigator.org.

Nelson, Richard D. *Deuteronomy: A Commentary* The Old Testament Library, ed. James L. Mays, Carol A. Newsom and David L. Petersen. Louisville: Westminster John Knox Press, 2002.

Neuhaus, Richard John. *The Best of the Public Square, Book 3.* Grand Rapids, MI: William B. Eerdmans Publishing Co., 2007.

New American Standard Bible. updated ed. La Habra, CA: Lockman Foundation, 1977, 1995.

Newmyer, Stephen T., *Animals, Rights and Reason in Plutarch and Modern Ethics* (NY: Routledge: Taylor and Francis Group, 2006).

Nicole, Roger. "C.H. Dodd and the Doctrine of Propitiation." *Westminster Theological Journal* 17, no. 2 (1955): 117–57.

Nilsson, Gretta, and & Others. *Facts About Furs.* Third ed. Washington D.C.: Animal Welfare Institute, 1980.

Oesterley, W.O.E. *The Book of Proverbs.* London: Methuen and Co. LTD, 1929.

Olwig, Kenneth R. "Reinventing Common Nature: Yosemite and Mount Rushmore—a Meandering Tale of Double Nature." In *Uncommon Ground: Rethinking the Human Place in Nature*, ed. William Cronon, 379–408. New York: W.W. Norton & Co. Ltd., 1996.

O'Neill, Lughaidh, et al. "Minimizing Leg-Hold Trapping Trauma for Otters with Mobile Phone Technology." *Journal of Wildlife Management* 71, no. 8 (2007): 2776–80.

Organ, John F., et al. "Fair Chase and Humane Treatment: Balancing the Ethics of Hunting and Trapping." In *Transactions of the 63rd North American Wildlife and Natural Resources Conference*, ed. K. G. Wadsworth, 63, 528–43. Washington, DC: Wildlife Management Institute, 1998.

——. et al. *Trapping and Furbearer Management in North American Wildlife Conservation.* No city given: The Northeast Furbearer Resources Technical Committee, 2001.

Oswalt, John N. "'Akzari." In *Theological Wordbook of the Old Testament*, ed. R. Laird Harris, Gleason L. Archer Jr. and Bruce K. Waltke, 1, 436. Chicago: Moody Press, 1980.

——. "Kabash." In *Theological Wordbook of the Old Testament*, ed. R. Laird Harris, Gleason L. Archer Jr. and Bruce K. Waltke, 1, 430. Chicago: Moody Press, 1980.

Packer, James I. "The Adequacy of Human Language." In *Inerrancy*, ed. Norman L. Geisler, 195–226. Grand Rapids, MI: Zondervan Publishing House, 1980.

Page, Mike. "Personal Phone Conversation." ed. Stephen Vantassel. Springfield, MA: Phone, 1998.

Papouchis, Christopher M. "A Critical Review of Trap Research." In *Cull of the Wild: A Contemporary Analysis of Wildlife Trapping in the United States*, ed. Camilla H. Fox and Christopher M. Papouchis, 41–55. Sacramento, CA: Animal Protection Institute, 2004.

Patterson, J. H. "Galilee." In *The Illustrated Bible Dictionary*, ed. J.D. Douglas and et al., 1, 537. Wheaton, ILL: Tyndale House, 1980.

Patton, Kimberley C. ""He Who Sits in the Heavens Laughs": Recovering Animal Theology in the Abrahamic Traditions." *The Harvard Theological Review* 93, no. 4 (2000): 401–34.

Phelps, Norm. *The Dominion of Love*. NY: Lantern Books, 2002.

Phillips, Perry G. "Did Animals Die before the Fall?" *Perspectives on Science and Christian Faith* 58, no. 2 (2006): 146–47.

Phillips, Robert L., et al."Leg Injuries to Coyotes Captured in Three Types of Foothold Traps." *Wildlife Society Bulletin* 24, no. 2 (1996): 260–63.

Plaut, W.Gunther. *Book of Proverbs*. N.Y.: Union of American Hebrew Congregations, 1961.

Pluhar, Evelyn B. *Beyond Prejudice: The Moral Significance of Human and Nonhuman Animals*. Durham: Duke University Press, 1995.

Poletti, Arthur. *God Does Not Eat Meat*. Online ed. Athens, NY: The Mary T. and Frank L. Hoffman Family Foundation. http://www.all-creatures.org, 2004.

Pollan, Michael. *Omnivore's Dilemma: A Natural History of Four Meals*. NY: The Penguin Press, 2006.

Powell, Larkin A. "An Ecologist Struggles with the Problem of Evil: Why Aldo Leopold and Baby Meadowlarks Argue against an All-Powerful God." *Theology* 16 (2008): 96–108.

———."Personal Communication." September 4, 2008. Lincoln, NE.

Preece, Rod. "Darwinism, Christianity, and the Great Vivisection Debate," *Journal of the History of Ideas* 64, no. 3 (2003): 399–419.

Prevention, Centers for Disease Control and. *Impaired Driving* [Web page]. Atlanta: Centers for Disease Control and Prevention, 2006, accessed November 17 2007; Available from http://www.cdc.gov/ncipc/factsheets/drving.htm.

Proulx, Gilbert, ed. *Mammal Trapping*. Sherwood Park, Alberta: Alpha Wildlife Research & Management Ltd., 1999.

Rakow, Tom C. *Hunting & the Bible: A Scripture Safari*. Vol. 1 The Biblical Art of Hunting 1 Series. Silver Lake, MN: Rock Dove Publisher, 1997.

Reicke, Bo. "Positive and Negative Aspects of the World in the NT." *Westminster Theological Journal* 49, no. 2 (1987): 351–69.

Regan, Tom. *The Case for Animal Rights*. Berkeley: University of California Press, 1983.

Reinders, Eric. "Blessed Are the Meat Eaters: Christian Antivegetarianism and the Missionary Encounter with Chinese Buddhism." *Positions* 12, no. 2 (2004): 509–36.

Reynolds, JC. "Trade-Offs between Welfare, Conservation, Utility and Economics in Wildlife Management—a Review of Conflicts, Compromises and Regulation." *Animal Welfare* 13 (2004): S133–38.

Rimbach, James A. "Bears or Bees? Sefire I a 31 and Daniel 7." *Journal of Biblical Literature* 97, no. 4 (1978): 565–66.

Robinson, Paschal. "St. Francis of Assisi," in *The Catholic Encyclopedia* (NY: Robert Appleton Co., 1909). Retrieved November 22, 2008 from New Advent: http://www.newadvent.org/cathen/06221a.htm.

Ross, Allen P. *Creation & Blessing: A Guide to the Study and Exposition of Genesis*. Grand Rapids, MI: Baker Books, 1998.

Ross, Hugh. *The Creator and the Cosmos.* Colorado Springs, CO: NavPress Publishing Group, 1993.

Rowan, Andrew N., and Beth Rosen. "Progress in Animal Legislation: Measurement and Assessment." In *State of the Animals Iii: 2005,* ed. Deborah J. Salem and Andrew N. Rowan, 79–94. Washington D.C.: Humane Society Press, 2005.

Rudrum, Alan. "Ethical Vegetarianism in Seventeenth-Century Britain: Its Roots in Sixteenth-Century European Theological Debate." *Seventeenth Century* 18, no. 1 (2003): 76–92.

Russell, Bertrand. *A History of Western Philosophy.* NY: Simon & Schuster, Inc., 1945.

Ryken, Leland, et al., eds. *Dictionary of Biblical Imagery.* Downers Grove: InterVarsity Press, 1988.

Sahr, Duane P., and Frederick F. Knowlton. "Evaluation of Tranquilizer Trap Devices (Ttds) for Foothold Traps Used to Capture Gray Wolves." *Wildlife Society Bulletin* 28, no. 3 (2000): 597–605.

Santmire, H. Paul. *The Travail of Nature: The Ambiguous Ecological Promise of Christian Theology* Theology and the Sciences, ed. Kevin Sharpe. Minneapolis: Fortress Press, 1985.

Schaff, Philip. *Nicene and Post-Nicene Christianity: From Constantine the Great to Gregory the Great.* Vol. 3. 8 vols. History of the Christian Church. Grand Rapids, MI: Wm. B. Eerdmans Publishing Co., 1950.

Schaeffer, Francis A. *Book One: Pollution and the Death of Man.* Vol. 5. 5 vols. 2nd ed. The Complete Works of Francis A. Schaeffer: A Christian Worldview. 3–82. Wheaton, Ill: Crossway Books, 1982, 1985.

Schafran, Philip. "Is Mankind the Measure?: Old Testament Perspectives on Mankind's Place in the Natural World." *Perspectives on Science and Christian Faith* 47 (June, 1995): 92–102. http://www.asa3.org/ASA/PSCF/1995/PSCF6-95Schafran.html

Schmutzer, Andrew J. "A Theology of Sexual Abuse: A Reflection on Creation and Devastation." *Journal of the Evangelical Theological Society* 51, no. 4 (2008): 785–812.

Scully, Matthew. *Dominion: The Power of Man, the Suffering of Animals, and the Call to Mercy.* New York: St. Martin's Griffin, 2002.

Sedivec, Kevin, et al. *Controlling Leafy Spurge Using Goats and Sheep.* Fargo, ND: North Dakota State University, 1995.

Sheldon, Joseph K. "Twenty-One Years After "Historical Roots of Our Ecologic Crisis" How Has the Church Responded?" *Perspectives on Science and Christian Faith* 41 (1989): 152–58.

Shivik, John A., "Preliminary Evaluation of New Cable Restraints to Capture Coyotes." *Wildlife Society Bulletin* 28, no. 3 (2000): 606–13.

———. et al. "Initial Comparison: Jaws, Cables, and Cage–Traps to Capture Coyotes." *Wildlife Society Bulletin* 33, no. 4 (2005): 1375–83.

Silva, Moises. *Biblical Words & Their Meaning: An Introduction to Lexical Semantics.* Grand Rapids, Mich: Zondervan Publishing House, 1983.

———. *Explorations in Exegetical Method: Galatians as a Test Case.* Grand Rapids, MI: Baker Books, 1996.

———. "God, Language and Scripture: Reading the Bible in the Light of General Linguistics." In *Foundations of Contemporary Interpretation: Six Volumes in One* ed. Moises Silva, 197–286 Grand Rapids, MI: Zondervan Publishing House, 1996.

Simmons, Catherine A., and Peter Lehmann. "Exploring the Link between Pet Abuse and Controlling Behaviors in Violent Relationships." *Journal of Interpersonal Violence* 22, no. 9 (2007): 1211–22.

Singer, Peter. *Animal Liberation: A New Ethics for Our Treatment of Animals*. New York: Avon Publishers, 1975, 1977.

Smith, Calvin L. "Dissertation Review." ed. Stephen Vantassel. Broadstairs, England: Midlands Bible College and Divinity School, 2008.

"Snail Darter Halts Dam: For Now." *Science News*, June 24 1978, 403.

Snoke, David. "Why Were Dangerous Animals Created?" *Perspectives on Science and Christian Faith* 56, no. 2 (2004): 117–25.

Sourcebook, 2002 U.S. Pet Ownership and Demographic. *U.S. Pet Ownership* [Web page]. Schaumburg, IL: AVMA, 2007 2002, accessed 03/13 2007; Available from http://www .avma.org/reference/marketstats/ownership.asp.

Southwick, Rob, et al. *Potential Costs of Losing Hunting and Trapping as Wildlife Management Methods*. Washington, DC: Animal Use Issues Committee of the International Association of Fish and Wildlife Agencies, 2005.

Sprinkle, Joe M. "The Rationale of the Laws of Clean and Unclean in the Old Testament." *Journal of the Evangelical Theological Society* 43, no. 4 (2000): 637–57.

Stallard, Mike. "The Tendency to Softness in Postmodern Attitudes About God, War, and Man." *Journal of Ministry and Theology* 10 (2006): 92–114.

Stanton, Mark, and Dennis Guernsey. "Christians Ecological Responsibility: A Theological Introduction and Challenge." *Perspectives on Science and Christian Faith* 45, no. 1 (1993): 2–7.

Stewart, R.A. "Cattle." In *Illustrated Bible Dictionary*, ed. J.D. Douglas and et.al., 1, 254–55. Wheaton, ILL: Tyndale House, 1980.

Stolzenburg, William. "Us or Them." *Conservation in Practice* 7, no. 4 (2006): 14–21.

Strong, John T. "Shattering the Image of God: A Response to Theodore Hiebert's Interpretation of the Story of the Tower of Babel." *Journal of Biblical Literature* 127, no. 4 (2008): 625–34.

Stuart, Tristram. *The Bloodless Revolution: A Cultural History of Vegetarianism from 1600 to Modern Times*. NY: W.W. Norton & Company, 2006.

Taylor, Paul W. *Respect for Nature: A Theory of Environmental Ethics* Studies in Moral, Political, and Legal Philosophy, ed. Marshall Cohen. Princeton, NJ: Princeton University Press, 1986.

Tenthani, Raphael. "Malawi Curbs Crocodile Menace." *BBC News*, February 7 2001.

Terian, Abraham. "The Hunting Imagery in Isaiah 51:20a." *Vetus Testamentum* 41, no. 4 (1991): 462–71.

Thompson, J. A. *Deuteronomy: An Introduction & Commentary*. Vol. 5 Tyndale Old Testament Commentaries, ed. D. J. Wiseman. Downers Grove, ILL: Inter-Varsity Press, 1974.

Thompson, James W. "Hebrews 9 and Hellenistic Concepts of Sacrifice." *Journal of Biblical Literature* 98, no. 4 (1979): 567–78.

Todd, Arlen W. "Ecological Arguments for Fur-Trapping in Boreal Wilderness Regions." *Wildlife Society Bulletin* 9, no. 2 (1981): 116–24.

"Trapping Devices, Methods, and Research." In *Cull of the Wild: A Contemporary Analysis of Wildlife Trapping in the United States*, ed. Camilla H. Fox and Christopher M. Papouchis, 31–41. Sacramento, CA: Animal Protection Institute, 2004.

Truesdale, Al. "Last Things First: The Impact of Eschatology on Ecology." *Perspectives on Science and Christian Faith* 46 (1994): 116–22.

Tucker, Gene M. "Creation and the Limits of the World: Nature and History in the Old Testament." *HBT* 15 (1993): 105–18.

———. "Rain on a Land Where No One Lives: The Hebrew Bible on the Environment." *Journal of Biblical Literature* 116, no. 1 (1997): 3–17.

Van Houtan, Kyle S., and Stuart L. Pimm. "The Various Christian Ethics of Species Conservation." In *Religion and the New Ecology: Environmental Prudence in a World in Flux*, ed. D. M. Lodge and C. Hamlin, 116–47. South Bend, IN: University of Notre Dame Press, 2006.

van Selms, A. "Hunting." In *The International Standard Bible Encyclopedia*, ed. Geoffrey W. Bromiley, 2, 782–84. Grand Rapids, MI: William B. Eerdmans Publishing Co., 1982.

Van Til, Cornelius. *Christian Apologetics* The Cornelius Van Til Collection. Phillipsburg, NJ: Presbyterian and Reformed Publishing Co., 1976.

Van Vuren, Dirk, Amy J. Kuenzi, Ivette Loredo, and Michael L. Morrison. "Translocation as a Nonlethal Alternative for Managing California Ground Squirrels." *Journal of Wildlife Management* 61, no. 2 (1997): 351–59.

Vantassel, Stephen M. "The Bailey Beaver Trap: Modifications and Sets to Improve Capture Rate." In *Proceedings of the 22nd Vertebrate Pest Conference*, ed. Robert M. Timm and J. M. O'Brien, 171–73. Davis, CA: University of California, 2006.

———. "Celibacy: The Forgotten Gift of the Holy Spirit." *The Journal of Biblical Counseling* 12, no. 3 (1994): 20–23.

———. "The Ethics of Wildlife Control in Humanized Landscapes—a Response." In *Proceedings of the Twenty-Third Vertebrate Pest Conference*, ed. R. M. Timm and M. B. Madon, 23, 294–300. San Diego, CA: University of California, Davis, 2008.

———. *House Cats* Lincoln, NE: University of Nebraska-Lincoln, 2007, accessed December 12, 2007; Available from http://icwdm.org.

———. "An Overview of the Hermeneutics of Vander Goot." In *Church Divinity 1988*, ed. John H. Morgan, 58–67. Bristol, IN: Wyndham Hall Press, 1988.

———. "Should Wildlife Trapping Have a Place in a Christian Environmental Ethic?" *Evangelical Review of Society and Politics* 1, no. 2 (2007): 20–41.

Various. *Newsletter* [web page]. Lincoln, New Zealand: Landcare Research New Zealand Ltd., 2007, accessed June 2007; Available from http://www.landcareresearch.co.nz /publications/newsletters/index.asp

Varner, Garner E. "The Prospects for Consensus and Convergence in the Animal Rights Debate." *The Hastings Center Report* 24, no. 1 (1994): 24–28.

Verbruggen, Jan L. "Of Muzzles and Oxen: Deuteronomy 25:4 and 1 Corinthians 9:9." *Journal of the Evangelical Theological Society* 49, no. 4 (2006): 699–712.

Vogt, Peter T. "Social Justice and the Vision of Deuteronomy." *Journal of the Evangelical Theological Society* 51, no. 1 (2008): 35–44.

Von Rad, Gerhard. *Genesis*. Translated by John H. Marks. Rev. ed. ed. Old Testament Library, ed. Peter Ackroyd et. al. Philadelphia: The Westminster Press, 1972.

———. *Deuteronomy: A Commentary* The Old Testament Library, ed. G. Ernest Wright, John Bright, James Barr and Peter Ackroyd. Philadelphia: The Westminster Press, 1966.

Wallace, Howard N. "Eden, Garden Of " In *The Anchor Bible Dictionary*, ed. David Noel Freedman, 2, 281–83. New York: Doubleday, 1992.

———. "Garden of God." In *The Anchor Bible Dictionary*, ed. David Noel Freedman, 2, 906–7. New York: Doubleday, 1992.

Walter, W. David, et al."Evaluation of Immunocontraception in a Free-Ranging Suburban White-Tailed Deer Herd." *Wildlife Society Bulletin* 30, no. 1 (2002): 186–92.

Walton, John H. *Ancient Near Eastern Thought and the Old Testament*. Grand Rapids, MI: Baker Academic, 2006.

Walvoord, John F., and Roy B. Zuck, eds. *Dallas Theological Seminary: The Bible Knowledge Commentary: An Exposition of the Scriptures*. Vol. 2. Wheaton, IL: Victor Books, 1983–c1985.

Ware, Bruce A. "Male and Female Complimentarity and the Image of God." *Journal for Biblical Manhood and Womanhood* 7, no. 1 (2002): 14–23.

Way, Jonathan G., et al. "Box-Trapping Eastern Coyotes in Southeastern Massachusetts." *Wildlife Society Bulletin* 30, no. 3 (2002): 695–702.

Way, Kenneth C. "Balaam's Hobby-Horse." In *Ugarit-Forschungen: Internationales Jahrbuch Fur Die Altertumskunde Syrien-Palastinas*, ed. Manfried Dietrich and Oswald Loretz, Band 37, 679–693. Munster: Ugarit-Verlag, 2005.

Webb, Stephen H. *On God and Dogs: A Christian Theology of Compassion for Animals*. NY: Oxford University Press, 1998.

Weinfield, Moshe. *The Promise of the Land: The Inheritance of the Land of Canaan by the Israelites* The Taubman Lectures in Jewish Studies. Berkeley: University of California Press, 1993.

Wells, Edward R., and Alan M. Schwartz. "Deep Ecology." In *Historical Dictionary of North American Environmentalism*, 61. Lanham, MD: The Scarecrow Press, Inc., 1997.

Wenham, Gordon J. *Numbers: An Introduction & Commentary* Tyndale Old Testament Commentaries, ed. D. J. Wiseman. Downers Grove, IL: Inter-Varsity Press, 1981.

Wheelwright, Philip, ed., *The Presocratics*. Indianapolis: Bobbs-Merrill Educational Publishing, 1966.

White, Lynn, Jr. "The Historical Roots of Our Ecologic Crisis." *Science* New Series 155, no. 3767 (1967): 1203–7.

Whittingstall, Hugh Fearnley, and Andrew Linzey. "The Debate: Should We All Be Vegetarian?" *The Ecologist* 2004, 23–27.

Widyapranawa, S. H. *The Lord Is Savior: Faith in National Crisis: A Commentary on the Book of Isaiah 1–39* International Theological Commentary, ed. Fredrick Carlson Holmgren and George A. F. Knight. Grand Rapids: Wm. B. Eerdmans Publishing Co., 1990.

Williams, Daniel H. "The Good Life." *Christianity Today* (2007): 50–55.

Williams, D. L. "Rights, Animals," in *New Dictionary of Theology*, ed. Sinclair B. Ferguson and James I. Packer. Downers Grove, IL: InterVarsity Press, 1988, 2000.

Wise, Stephen M. "Animal Rights One Step at a Time." In *Animal Rights: Current Debates and New Directions*, ed. Cass R. Sunstein and Martha C. Nussbaum, 19–50. Oxford: Oxford University Press, 2004.

Wolf, Herbert. "Zebah." In *Theological Wordbook of the Old Testament*, ed. R. Laird Harris and et al., 1, 233–35. Chicago: Moody Press, 1980.

Wood, John, et al. "Christian Environmentalism: Cosmos, Community, and Place." *Perspectives on Science and Christian Faith* 57, no. 1 (2005): 1–5.

Wright, N.T. *The Challenge of Jesus: Rediscovering Who Jesus Was and Is*. Downers Grove, Ill: InterVarsity Press, 1999.

Wright, Richard T. "Responsibility for the Ecological Crisis," *BioScience* 20 (1970). 851–53.

———. "Tearing Down the Green: Environmental Backlash in the Evangelical Sub-Culture." *PSCF* 47, no. June (1995): 80–91. http://www.asa3.org/ASA/PSCF/1995/PSCF6-95Wright.html.

Young, Richard A. *Is God a Vegetarian? Christianity, Vegetarianism, and Animal Rights.* Chicago: Open Court, 1999.

Young, Robert M. "Animal Soul." In *The Encyclopedia of Philosophy*, ed. Paul Edwards, 1, 122–27. New York: Macmillan Publishing Co., 1967, 1972.

Yu, E., and J Liu. "Environmental Impacts of Divorce." *Proceedings of the National Academy of Sciences* 104, no. 51 (2007): 20629–34.

Zohar, Noam. "Repentance and Purification: The Significance and Semantics of *Htat* (Sin Offering) in the Pentatuech " *Journal of Biblical Literature* 107, no. 4 (1988): 609–18.

Scripture Index

2 PETER

2:4ff	107
2:12	97

JAMES

3:9	39, 49, 163

1 JOHN

2:16	165

JUDE

10	97
16	119

REVELATION

2:7	89
19:17	39 Fn 125
21:2	89 Fn 105
21:10	89 Fn 105
21:4	87
21:14	89 Fn 105